June Megennis (also known as June Hall) spent over forty years at the heart
of some of Europe's pre-eminent operatic and musical organisations,
including The London Opera Centre, the Royal Opera House, the London
Symphony Orchestra, the European Community Youth Orchestra, JHS
International Marketing and the Chamber Orchestra Europe, from its
inception, in 1981, to her retirement as its General Manager in 2006.

Her fascinating career crossed the paths of many respected conductors,
musicians, vocalists and other well-known personalities from the world
of Classical Music. June shares many first-hand anecdotes from behind
the scenes. Featured people include: Malvina Major, Kiri te Kanawa,
Gennadi Rozhdestvensky, Leonard Bernstein, Carlos Kleiber, Sir Edward
Heath, Andre Previn, Wilson Strutte, Claudio Abbado, Luciano Pavarotti,
Alexander Schneider, Nikolaus Harnoncourt, Paavo Berglund, Lorin
Maazel, Sir Georg Solti, Sir Colin Davis, Sir Roger Norrington, Michael
Tilson-Thomas, Sir Andras Schiff, Sir Bernard Haitink, Martha Argerich,
Don Alfonso Aijón and Peter and Victoria Readman.

In 2001, she won a European Woman of Achievement Award in the Arts
and Media section. Having retired in 2006, she now resides in Cyprus and
continues to enjoy a life filled with music.

Published in 2023 by

**ΨUPPBOOKS**
UP PUBLICATIONS

U P Publications, St George's House, George St, Hunt-
ingdon, Cambridgeshire, PE29 3GH. UK +44 208 133 0123
manager@uppublications.ltd.uk

ISBN 13: 978-1-912777-78-5 Soft Cover
ISBN 13: 978-1-912777-79-2 eBook

www.uppbooks.com

# Tears and Symphony
## A Musical Journey

June Megennis

**ʯP**

U P Publications
2023

In Memory of Kate
(Kit to her family and friends)
from whom I inherited any musical talent

# Contents

# Prologue

Kate, the second youngest of five siblings, was born in April 1918 into a London East End working class family. They were poor; her father, Richard, drove a horse and cart and delivered coal; her mother, apart from raising a family, took in washing to make ends meet and later became a money lender, for which crime she appeared in a magistrate's court and received a small fine.

Always the life and soul of any party, from a very young age it was evident Kate had a natural musical talent and loved to entertain.

Dressed in her best Sunday clothes, bought for her by her older sister Rose, who was by then working in service, her father would take her with him to the local public house, where she was encouraged to sing and dance on a table. Life was hard and to supplement the family income, just like her siblings, she was forced to leave school early and got a job in a factory which made toothpaste tubes.

One day an uncle purchased an upright piano and taught her harmonic chords in the left hand. Although she never learned to read music, she was able to play popular songs by ear, an ability which stayed with her throughout her life.

Fate did not look kindly upon George. He was born in 1914, just before the First World War, the fourth of nine children, although it was rumoured that, aside from a few miscarriages, there had been four others who either died at birth or were still-born. He was a very bright and clever child, but like so many other children from East End working class families, was forced to leave school at fourteen and get a job. Unfortunately, the only work available was as a labourer at the local Gas Works, totally unsuitable for someone of his stature and intelligence.

He met Kate at a cinema in Stratford and there was an immediate attraction between them. George knew at once he had found his soul mate and the love of his life.

They began dating, fell in love and eventually became engaged but, as Kate was only eighteen, it was necessary to wait until she reached twenty-one before they could marry. This gave them time to save for their future home.

They were married on a beautiful day in June 1939, blissfully happy and looked forward to moving into their new rented apartment, however, their world was soon to be turned upside down.

Within three months war was declared and soon afterwards George received his calling up papers. Although a Regular with the Territorial Army and able to use a gun, he was recruited into the Royal Army Service Corps and after basic training was posted to the north of England and taught how to drive a lorry! He urged Kate to join him and found lodgings for her on a small farm in Chesterfield, Derbyshire.

Whenever he had leave, George would visit and after a while Kate became pregnant. It had been intended for the birth to take place at the farm, but following a bitter argument with the farmer's wife, the Salvation Army came to the rescue and found a place for Kate in Chesterfield General Hospital.

Soon afterwards, George's regiment was sent overseas to join General Montgomery's Eighth Army, firstly in Marseilles in France then North Africa and Italy.

Before he left, George found new lodgings for Kate and her small baby with a friendly mining couple in Doncaster, who, having no children of their own, were invited to be god-parents.

After a few months, a letter arrived for Kate from her mother, who was still in London, informing her that she wished to rent out the two rooms in her house in which the couple had stored their furniture. She delivered an ultimatum, either Kate was to remove them or rent the rooms herself. Kate decided she had little choice but to return to war-torn London's East End and agreed to rent the whole upstairs apartment.

When demobilisation came in 1945, it took some months before many of the troops were able to get back to their old lives and after only nine years George became ill.

*Kate*

*George*

At first diagnosed with arterial sclerosis in his legs, he was treated with analgesics and given a heat lamp but steadily his condition worsened until, unable to walk, he was confined to bed. He died in March 1955 just after his 41st birthday. The doctors said it was due to something, contracted during his time in North Africa, which had affected his kidneys, gradually poisoned his blood and resulted in kidney and heart failure.

Kate was left a widow at the age of 36.

*Wedding, Kate and George, June 3rd 1939*

# 1 Early Life

For the first five years of my life, I did not know my father. Censored blue airmail letters arrived regularly and my mother would tell me Dadda had sent all his love and kisses but I had no idea who she was talking about. Occasionally a tin of rotting lemons and/or walnuts might arrive. Inside one was a present for me, a rag doll dressed in a red layered Spanish dress and a mantilla on its head. Attached to the top of one of its legs was a pair of pearl earrings for my mother. All through her life she wore no other kind.

My grandmother's house was situated in a typical East London Street; a row of terraced houses on either side, each with a small garden at the front with an iron railing and gate. I remember playing outside one day with my skipping rope, when two men came, dismantled the railings and explained to my grandmother that the metal was needed for the War effort.

Regular air raids took place, primarily aimed at the docks, and everyone would hurry to the Anderson shelter at the bottom of the garden which we shared with Mrs. Taylor our next-door neighbour.

We were lucky not get hit by a stray bomb; our local cinema, the Carlton, was razed to the ground. Walking around the streets, after a bombing raid, it was possible to see the devastation; many buildings were badly damaged, or completely destroyed and there were large craters

My Grandmother and Sid, with Becky the dog in our garden

With Mrs Taylor, our neighbour, in her garden

surrounded by huge piles of rubble everywhere. Children were warned never to play anywhere near for fear there might be an unexploded bomb.

During the War, the nearest we ever got to taking a holiday was an annual three weeks trip to the Kent hop fields. At the beginning of September, my mother would pack a few provisions, a kettle and other kitchen utensils and together with our neighbours, who were mostly women and children, we would set off together, travelling either by coach or on the back of an army lorry.

Everyone looked forward to getting away from the grim conditions of the East-End.

After being warmly greeted by the farmer, each family was allocated an unheated shed. I thought it was great fun having to sleep on a straw-stuffed mattress piled on twigs and pillows filled with hops. As there were no facilities in the hut, my mother cooked over a fire outdoors and washed our clothes in a local stream. There were other strategically placed sheds outside which housed the communal Elsan toilets.

While my mother was working in the fields, I was put into the care of an older child, although sometimes I did try to make myself useful by helping to load the hops into a large canvas bag.

After a hard day picking and gathering hops, my mother would quickly prepare a meal and afterwards occasionally allow me to stay up late to join our neighbours around a warm campfire.

Bottles of local beer were provided by the farmer, no doubt made from his own hops, and it would not take long before someone broke into song and encouraged everyone else to join in.

Music was always present in our house. My grandmother possessed a large radiogram, which she had purchased at the 1939 Ideal Home Exhibition. She also had a collection of 78 rpm records, mostly of popular dance music and a few featured tenors John McCormack and Caruso.

The upright piano in the sitting room, usually came into its own at family parties, often after an evening spent at the local public house. My mother was encouraged to play and sing popular songs which everyone could join in. Many thought she should have been on the stage and I inherited from her a reasonably good singing voice and love of dance.

Staying alone for hours I would make up my own little tunes and when not tinkling away on the piano, or playing records, listen to the radio and very quickly learn popular songs of the day.

My grandmother gave me her old used ration books which were full of different coloured pencil lines made by shopkeepers whenever we bought the permitted quantities of food items. I used to go on an imaginary shopping spree to buy from the rabbits and chickens kept in cages at the bottom of the garden.

*Hop picking in Kent*

*Street party celebrating end of World War 2*

The cockerel hated my grandmother. At feeding time, armed with a broom, she would always cautiously venture into the pen because he would try to attack her.

On one occasion I had a terrible fright – she had forgotten to lock the gate and suddenly the cockerel rushed out squawking and headed in my direction. Panicking, I turned and began to run towards the house but tripped, fell on the pathway, and the cockerel ran over me. However, his days were numbered and my grandmother had her revenge.

Within a few weeks, he was dispatched by Sid, destined for the family dinner table.

Most evenings were spent with my grandparents. Sid did not have very much hair, but he patiently allowed me to attack what little he had, wetting it and making waves with some of my grandmother's metal hair grips, no doubt pinching his scalp in the process. He used to sit me on his lap and sing *Cowboy Joe*, pretending to point a gun when we got to the words, 'hifalutin', scootin', shootin' son-of-a-gun from Arizona.'

A variety of dogs came to live with us. The first was a thoroughbred wire-haired terrier called Bessie, considered to be such a good specimen that money was spent on two unsuccessful attempts to get her covered by a male dog. She did not stay very long.

Next came Micky, a Scottish terrier, who ran around on three legs. He had been rescued from a farm, where he had been involved in a fight with another dog which had bitten and badly damaged one of his hind legs. No-one had thought it worthwhile to spend money on a vet. He had quite a character and would roam around the local area, knocking over the pig buckets in search of anything good to eat. He was very loyal and every evening could be seen waiting patiently at the corner of our road, watching for Sid to return from work.

My favourite and constant companion was a fox terrier cross called Becky. She stayed the longest.

After the War ended in September 1945, practically every street like ours organised a party. Long trestle tables, covered in white sheets, were assembled in the middle of the road and each household produced a plate of sandwiches consisting of cheese, SPAM or tinned corned beef, and homemade cakes. The children wore fancy dress, many made from pieces of curtaining, and were treated to lemonade, while the grown-ups enjoyed glasses of beer. A makeshift stage was erected on top of a wall and a man played an accordion for singing and dancing, which continued into the early hours of the following day.

On the day in 1946 when my father finally returned home, there was a great deal of excitement and a big party organised to welcome him. I was put to bed with my hair in rag strips to create curls. Curious and unable to sleep, I crawled out of my cot and went to peer through the bannisters, just as the front door was being opened. Standing there was a stranger, wearing his ill-fitting de-mob suit, and badly in need of a haircut and shave.

Curious to see whether this might be the Dadda my mother had told me so much about, the one who sent his love and kisses and the precious rag doll which I took to bed with me every night, I crept down the stairs. I just stared as everyone began hugging and kissing one another; my mother was crying.

Suddenly, I was spotted and the stranger held out his arms to me. I had been warned never to speak to strange men, so I held back feeling shy and hung onto my mother's skirt. Smiling warmly, he again beckoned me to come to him and my mother gently coaxed me forward. At first, I stiffened but his softly spoken reassuring words soon helped me to relax and realise that he was someone really very special.

Adjusting to civilian life and getting used to being a family of three took a while. With so many properties destroyed during the War, suitable rented accommodation was in short supply, so we continued to share the house with my grandmother and Sid, the only grandfather I ever knew. It was not until I was older that I realised they weren't actually married because my real grandfather, who I never met, was still alive and lived somewhere in the East End of London.

My mother took a job at the local sweet factory, which meant she sometimes had to work during the evening. On those days she cooked a hot meal for my father and me, which was kept warm between two plates over a saucepan of hot water. I always looked forward to Fridays, when she would bring home a large bag of boiled sweets.

My father went back to his old job at the Gas Works. He loved greyhound racing and would occasionally go to the local track. On those evenings when both parents were out of the house, I stayed with my grandmother until bedtime.

When I was about six or seven years old, my mother arranged for me to have private piano lessons. My first teacher taught the Smallwood Piano Forte Tutor method with its unconventional fingering, a cross representing the thumb. He also balanced penny coins on the back of my hands to improve my technique. My parents regularly went, with relatives, to the local Working Men's Club, which had a small dance band and I was encouraged to sing but had to stand on a chair to reach the microphone.

Summer holidays, taken at a Butlin's Holiday camp, gave an opportunity to enter talent competitions, which I sometimes won. On one occasion I became over-confident and insisted upon singing a song which,

*Singing at the Working Men's Club*

*Shaftesbury Junior School, front row second right*

unfortunately, the pianist who was to accompany me, did not know. He suggested, if I started, he would follow me, but it all went wrong and, acting like a prima donna, I stopped singing and flounced off the stage. I must have been about ten years old at the time!

The Carlton was rebuilt after the War and every Friday I used to rush home from junior school and beg my grandmother to take me to see the latest film.

Hollywood Musicals were my favourites, especially if they starred Doris Day, Jane Powell, Howard Keel, and Ann Blyth.

She did not always feel like going because her arthritis might be giving her trouble, but I would never take no for an answer. She usually relented and would take with her a bag containing an orange or apple, together with some sweets for us to eat during the performance.

On the way home from the cinema, we usually stopped at the local Pie and Mash shop, where my grandmother would order a bowl of jellied eels while I tucked into a hot meat pie and mashed potatoes covered in a hot parsley sauce. Occasionally we might meet my father returning home from the greyhound track.

Few people had television sets in those days, but my father was able to buy one at a reasonable price through an uncle who worked for a company which manufactured them. It was built into a large polished wooden box with a speaker on one side, and a nine-inch screen on the other. Several relatives were invited to watch the Coronation of Elizabeth the Second on June 2, 1953. All the grownups sat in a row on chairs with the children cross-legged on the floor.

Even though a large magnifying glass had been mounted in front of the tiny screen, it was difficult to follow the proceedings, particularly for anyone sitting at the end of the row. Also, the fact that the picture was in black and white, made it impossible to appreciate fully the magnificent spectacle and pageantry. Nevertheless, everyone enjoyed the occasion, caught up in the euphoria of once more being able to celebrate such a special event after so many years of misery and austerity.

The previous year, at the age of eleven, I had passed the 11 plus exam for a scholarship to the East Ham Grammar School for Girls. To celebrate, my father purchased a second-hand black Hercules bicycle which had a dynamo to power the headlight and rear lamp. Unfortunately, I did not have the pleasure of riding it to school for very long before he borrowed it to go to his work.

It was not until many years later I discovered that the school's curriculum had been part of a government experiment set up after the War to afford poorer children a higher quality education. Teachers were brought in from the private sector and the aim was to groom and encourage

Copyright ]          [ Ed. J. B. & Co. Ltd.

THE GRAMMAR SCHOOL FOR GIRLS

East Ham Grammar School for Girls

the more talented to aspiring beyond what traditionally might have been expected of them.

Several tutors were middle-aged spinsters, devoted to educating young ladies. Our Head Mistress, Miss Mitchell, was an attractive looking woman, elegant and soberly dressed, who always wore her greying hair in a bun. On the other hand, her Deputy, Miss Clifford, who taught Latin, was plain, and not as attractive; no matter what the weather, she usually wore long heavy woollen skirts, thick stockings and brogues. In complete contrast, our first Music Teacher, Miss Wroth, was young, very attractive and wore brightly coloured dresses. She also had a bubbly personality and everyone adored her.

My musical aptitude was soon recognised and encouraged, and I was introduced to classical music. At each morning's Assembly, while seated on the floor of the main hall, we were obliged to listen to a different classical recording, except at the beginning of every term when it was Bach's *Air on a G String*, a personal favourite of Miss Mitchell. Hubert Parry's *Jerusalem* was always sung at the end of term.

When my father died, I was thirteen. The funeral service, which took place in the Chapel of the City of London Cemetery, was a sombre, harrowing affair. My father had been very popular and many friends had joined members of the family to pay their respects, some having sought his counsel and advice.

Braving the unforgiving weather, everyone trekked afterwards to the graveside which was located some distance away close to the railway line. Watching as my father's coffin was slowly lowered into the freshly dug grave, was more than I could bear. Through my tears I noticed a photograph of a small child which had been placed on the headstone of the adjacent grave and I suddenly felt lost and alone. Putting her arms around me, my paternal grandmother whispered, 'always remember, God chooses only the best flowers for his garden.'

We had been close and he had always taken a keen interest in my education. I was going to miss him. Without the benefit of his advice, I had quickly to learn how to make my own decisions.

Since my mother was left with very little money, the school gave her vouchers to buy uniforms and patterned material in a choice of four colours to make into summer dresses. In addition to the daily Government-issue of one-third of a pint of milk, free school lunches were also provided.

Piano lessons were arranged gratis with a blind pianist Bill Cox. With his guide dog, a golden Labrador, by his side, he would sit in his chair and listen attentively while I played a set piece. Sometimes he stood, made his way over to the piano, and gently placed his hands over mine to be sure I was using the correct fingering. At first it made me feel nervous but after a while I got used to it.

Every class was obliged to take part in the School's Annual Music Festival and as one of only a few in my class who showed any musical talent or interest, I was given the difficult task of trying to persuade and train a group of classmates to sing madrigals.

One year I also composed a work for piano and voice entitled *On and on went the camel train*. Patricia Harding, who sat next to me in class, sang the words.

Always loving an opportunity to sing, I became a member of the school choir and was given the solo mezzo soprano part in Pergolesi's *Stabat Mater*.

English was also a favourite subject. In the Fifth Form, my class was fortunate to have Miss Herbert as our Teacher. She was strongly into theatre and organised trips to London theatres and the Royal Opera House, Covent Garden. It was during one of these outings, while seated in 'the gods', I heard for the very first time a performance of Wagner's opera *Die Meistersinger von Nuremberg* which, together with Cesar Franck's Symphony in D minor, featured in the syllabus of my GCE 'O' level exam.

Discovering I could also act, I was given the lead part in several school plays, one of which was *Alceste* by Euripides and my performance must

*As Alceste in the School play*

have been convincing because my mother actually shed tears during my dying scene. I was also given the title roles to play in two others by Euripides, *Iphigenia in Aulis* and *Iphigenia in Tauris*; and the maid in, *Le Malade Imaginaire* by Moliere.

By the time I had reached the fifth and sixth forms, Margaret Pye (unfortunately nick-named Magpie), had succeeded Miss Wroth and was responsible for coaching me through my GCE O and A levels Music exams.

My eclectic taste in music developed during my teens. In 1954 Rock and Roll suddenly burst onto the scene with *Shake, Rattle and Roll*, performed by Bill Hayley and his Comets. A group of us went to the local cinema to see the film *Blackboard Jungle* in which *Rock Around the Clock* was played. The music was so infectious it had everyone dancing in the aisles and became a sensation.

The next phenomenon was *Heartbreak Hotel* in 1956, when Elvis Presley took over the top spot and set us all rocking with *Hound Dog*.

Our school had a record player and some of the girls brought in records which they had purchased with their Saturday job pocket money. Every lunch hour would find a group of sixth formers in the hall, jiving in formation to Rock and Roll music. There was always an argument beforehand as to who should lead. While we practised Traditional Jive, another group, the Mods, would be trying out their own version. They usually listened and danced to modern jazz; which I found awkward, stiff and less abandoned.

I also became a fan of Traditional Jazz. Humphrey Lyttelton and Chris Barber were frequent visitors to a club several of us used to go to in Seven Kings. The fashion then was to wear a home-made mohair sack dress, which narrowed down severely at the hem, popper beads and winkle picker shoes. Consequently, jiving to upbeat Dixieland jazz was tricky, exhausting and very hot work, quite often causing our long necklaces to swing and unpop, scattering the beads across the floor. It was a relief to be able to cool down and just listen to brilliant Clarinettist Monty Sunshine's popular rendition of *Petite Fleur*.

I like to believe that I can still jive but, unfortunately, I have yet to find a good partner, so have to content myself with dancing alone around the kitchen or tapping my feet while watching the professionals on television.

In later life, my taste broadened even wider and I have grown to love Latin American music.

The school had a policy of encouraging students to reach out to other nationalities. I did well in, and enjoyed, French and German classes. While studying for O level GCEs in the Fifth Form, I was fortunate to have an opportunity to travel to Germany on a school exchange trip. A group of us, together with our teacher Miss Barraclough, took an overnight boat/ train from Victoria. It was for most of us the very first time we had ever travelled abroad and we were very excited and found it difficult to sleep in our bunks.

The Spillner family, with whom I stayed, were chemists and their house was situated next door to the pharmacy. The father, who had been interned in the UK as a prisoner during the first World War, spoke very good English, for which I was initially grateful, although he encouraged me to speak and improve my German. They had two children, Gerhard and Annegret, who was the youngest and with whom I became very good friends. Each day, in the summer heat, she and I travelled to school by bicycle, keeping to designated lanes, which had so far not been introduced into the UK.

The family were very keen I should experience German culture and visit as many places of interest as possible. There were car trips to Heidelberg, Stuttgart, Freiburg and the Schwarzwald. We also attended a performance of Wagner's *Parsifal*. Not having reserved tickets, we had to stand at the back of the stalls for something like four hours, in stifling heat as the theatre had no air conditioning.

*Annegret Spillner*

*With Francoise Lemarchand*

During the week I used to meet my English friends at school in Ludwigshafen, where we were obliged to attend classes conducted in German, which helped me to sail through my GCE 'O' level exam. My knowledge of German and French also became very useful during my career.

The Spillners were also very musical; the father played violin and I sometimes accompanied him on the piano. One evening, I remember, we played Schubert's *Ave Maria* together for friends, teachers and family members.

In order that I might have a record of my first ever trip abroad Herr Spillner gave me an old Kodak box camera in a leather case, the first I was to own and to cherish.

I so much enjoyed my month long stay with the Spillner family, which ended all too quickly. Everyone had taken so much time and trouble to teach me about life outside of my own culture and environment, which helped to prepare me for the future. I imagine it must have been quite a culture shock for Annegret when she stayed with my family later that year.

European trips were organised annually and sometimes requests made for families to accept foreign students to stay with them. My mother agreed to accept a French student from Paris whose name was Francoise Le Marchand. She was a big girl, at least six feet tall, and possessed a large appetite. One day she shocked my mother by asking if it would be possible to have horse meat for her evening meal! We only ever purchased horse meat from a knacker's yard, to feed the cat!

Sensing my mother's reluctance, Francoise offered to cook the steak herself. She put a knob of butter into a frying pan and when hot enough cooked the meat 'saignant' for just a couple of seconds. The sight of so much blood horrified my mother who had to leave the room. Francoise later remarked that, in her opinion, the reason the English lose their teeth early is because they eat over-cooked meat!

We were greatly relieved when she returned to France, otherwise I am sure my mother would have become a nervous wreck.

However, we did stay in touch and a couple of years later, after I had left school, I received an invitation from the Le Marchands to stay with them in Paris. I purchased a ticket on the newly introduced Air France Caravelle and, at the age of 18, excitedly embarked on my first foreign trip alone.

The family met me at Orly Airport and we drove to their apartment in the Boulevard de Clichy, not far from the Moulin Rouge. Madame Lemarchand had prepared a very appetising meal and when asked if I would like a second helping, I thought I would practise my French, but made a silly mistake by responding 'non merci, je suis pleine', instead of 'j'ai assez'. This obviously caused some amusement and realising I had probably made a faux pas, I blushed with embarrassment. Smiling, Monsieur Le Marchand, a news reader at Radio France, kindly explained that what I had actually said was 'I am pregnant', and not, as I had thought, 'I am full' in my translation from English.

My visit to Paris was a whirlwind of sightseeing, walking for many miles, so that the heels of my shoes eventually wore down. Coming across a street market, close to the Arc de Triomphe I found a stall selling LPs, and it was there I purchased my first 10-inch LP classical recordings of Cesar Franck's Symphony in D minor and piano concertos by Rachmaninov and Tchaikovsky.

# Choosing a Career

My father had always encouraged me to work hard but his ambition for me went no higher than to become a secretary. In those days this was nothing unusual for a girl from my background. It was expected that after leaving school one would get a job, probably locally, get married and have children; going to university was considered a complete waste of time and money.

A careers officer came to the school to give advice and arrange for some of us to spend a day at the London Hospital observing nursing staff and, in my case, to take a class of small children and try to teach them a new song. There was one little boy, probably no more than seven years old, sitting at the front, who kept winking and grinning at me, exposing two missing front teeth. I found myself blushing which seemed to amuse the rest of the class. Teaching the words first and then the tune was a big mistake because when I tried putting the two together, the words were already forgotten!

With no desire to become either a nurse or teacher, instead I chose in the Sixth Form to fit in classes for shorthand and typewriting whilst at the same time study 'A' level music, German, Commercial French and Economics and, like my contemporaries, leave school at 18 and get a job. Miss Mitchell was very concerned that I should not take this route and requested my mother to come to the school to discuss the situation and to try and persuade me to go on to higher education. My mother felt she was unable to advise and said I should decide for myself.

This was an important moment when I particularly missed my father but remembering his ambition for me, after completing 'A' level exams, I left school and got a job as a secretary. However, I did continue to have private piano lessons and take Royal Academy Music exams, up until I got married.

Lessons with my last music teacher, Mr. Belinfante a violinist, usually took place on a Saturday morning, at his house opposite West Ham Football Stadium. One particular Saturday, which will forever stay in my memory, is November 23, 1963. Just as I was returning home from a lesson, shocking news was being announced on the radio of President Kennedy's assassination the previous day.

With my shorthand and typewriting skills leaving much to be desired, I somehow managed to secure my first job as secretary to the Export Manager of Caribonum Limited, a carbon paper and typewriter ribbon manufacturer in Leyton.

Considered an advertisement for its products, the company insisted that every letter leaving the premises should be perfect, with no corrected typing errors. At the beginning, I found this very difficult to achieve, more than testing the patience of my boss, Mr. Dunne who, each day, found himself having to ask for everything to be re-typed. Gradually my skills improved and, after nine months, had reached the required standard. However, much to the disappointment of my employer, it gave me the confidence to move on.

I accepted a few short-term, secretarial positions before being engaged for almost five years as a Secretary/PA to the Export Manager of an international computer manufacturer whose offices were initially in High Holborn. The company merged with another and twice moved premises, firstly to Park Lane and finally to Putney Bridge. During this period, I was living with my mother and her second husband. Upton Park was my local underground station and the long daily journey travelling from one end of the District Line to the other became tedious.

My fiancé, David, and I often discussed the possibility of my finding another job much closer to home and he knew how much I loved music. By chance one evening on the way to meet me at my office, he bought a copy of the Evening Standard. During the journey he scoured the situations vacant section and came across an advertisement for an Assistant to the Warden of the newly established London Opera Centre, a post graduate training centre affiliated to the Royal Opera House, Covent Garden, for opera singers, stage managers and repetiteurs, which was located in a converted 1930s East London cinema in Stepney.

David encouraged me to apply and I was accepted for the position, not knowing, at the time, that fate was taking a hand and I was to embark on a varied and remarkable musical career, spanning more than forty years, which was to offer opportunities in the world of opera and classical music that I could never have imagined.

# David

David was the elder brother of Chris Hall, a member of a teenage group I used to go dancing with on a Saturday night. He was good-looking, charming and very much a lady's man! Whenever Chris organised a party at his parents' home, David would often be there, usually with a beautiful blonde Swedish girl in tow. He married Kirstin, one of his Swedish girlfriends, in Stockholm, having studied and memorised the whole ceremony in Swedish.

The couple spent the first year of married life living together in a rented upstairs apartment in a terraced house opposite David's parents. With his working shifts as a police officer with the Port of London, Kirstin was often left alone and unhappy and after only a year decided to return to Sweden and file for divorce.

For a few years I lost touch with the Hall family. Chris, who had meanwhile become engaged to Marie, I only met on the odd occasion. However, one weekend, between boyfriends, I happened to be at a loose end and they invited me to go with them to a local Jazz Club, failing to mention that David would also be there. We got on well and he invited me to meet him for a drink the following week at the Prospect of Whitby in Docklands. It was just before my 21st birthday.

The relationship developed and after a couple of years we decided to marry. In those days the Church of England was not allowed to marry divorcees, so we were happy when the vicar of the local Methodist Church agreed to perform the ceremony and wedding plans were made for April 1965.

As the date drew closer, several presents began to arrive from family and friends which included a pair of Witney blankets from my grandmother, but we were soon to receive a shock. With only a few weeks to go, the vicar informed us that David's Swedish divorce was not recognised in the UK.

In a state of panic, we contacted a Solicitor who referred us to a Barrister in Lincoln's Inn in the hope of finding a way around the law to enable our marriage to go ahead as planned. He explained that unfortunately it was not possible and advised David to file for a UK divorce, and that it was likely to take another two years.

Embarrassed, we had to let everyone know the wedding was postponed. My grandmother, angry with David, demanded the return of the blankets, which remained in their original packaging on top of her wardrobe until she died many years later. I should perhaps have seen this as an omen, but stupidly ignored the warning signs.

# 2 The London Opera Centre (1964-1972)

My mother had sometime mentioned that during their courtship days she and my father had visited the Old Troxy cinema in Stepney, which was opened in 1933 and with 3,520 seats was one of England's largest cinemas. As a result of wartime damage and the general decline of the area, the cinema closed in November 1960.

By 1963, the Arts Council of Great Britain had provided a £27,900 grant to set up the London Opera Centre to provide musical and dramatic training to young voice students who were offered two-year scholarships. It was to be located in the Troxy and managed out of the Royal Opera House, Covent Garden as a rehearsal space as well as an opera school.

In addition, the Centre was used for other aspects of stagecraft and technical training, scenery construction and storage. A 500-seat theatre was created in the balcony for occasional performances.

In June 1964, I joined the London Opera Centre and it was possible to take the relatively short journey by the bus, which stopped almost outside. My first impression of the building's exterior was that it had kept its original features, but once inside, having entered via glass swing doors, it no longer represented a cinema.

There was a very smart reception area with a large desk at which sat a receptionist called Cosette. Just behind the reception was the office of the

The Troxy Site of the London Opera Centre

House Manager. A grand staircase led to a large rehearsal room, library and the office of the Centre's Director James Robertson. Another staircase led to an upper level where workshops for stage manager students and a costume wardrobe had been created. The Warden's very smart suite of offices where I was to work, was situated at ground level off the foyer and gave access to the large noticeboard where weekly schedules and notices could be displayed.

James Robertson, CBE had been appointed Director following the resignations, some thought dismissal, of former opera singer Joan Cross and Ann Woods. James was the ex-Musical Director of Sadler's Wells Opera and before that had held a position with the Theatre de la Monnaie in Brussels. He was also invited as a guest to conduct opera and concerts in New Zealand.

Alan Bohn, the Warden (Bursar), a very quiet man who smoked a lot and disappeared at lunchtime returning some two hours later a little the worse for wear, was very kind and helpful and encouraged me to become involved with all aspects of the running of the Centre.

This entailed organising teaching and coaching sessions, arranging auditions, student finances and accommodation. We worked very well together but I was always conscious that Alan was a troubled soul and I later discovered he had been a member of the Fleet Air Arm and seriously injured in a flying accident during the War.

The Centre's House Manager, tenor Noel Gibson, whose singing career had never taken off, was happy to have been given an opportunity to manage the Opera Centre.

He was allocated a penthouse apartment, at the top of the building, where he also created an art studio for himself. In his spare time, he would often set off with his camera to the nearby London and St. Katherine Docks, which at the time were very active. He used the photos as subjects for his paintings, which he did on canvas with oils and a palette knife. The very large, finished works were hung all around the Centre, alongside portraits of famous opera singers from the past, and this acted as a gallery for potential buyers, of which there were many. I bought one of his paintings but with several moves over the years, I cannot recall what happened to it.

Noel was also particularly good working with wood and he created furniture for various departments, including a very large music library, which seemed to appear overnight! It then became necessary to hire a librarian and Oswalda Patrick, who had initially been engaged as a secretarial assistant, was given responsibility. She was Austrian and had met and married her English husband when he had been stationed in Austria with the British Army after the War.

They subsequently moved to the UK and had one daughter, but the marriage did not last. Although she was a few years older than myself, we became good friends and I helped her to find and furnish an apartment at Forest Hill in South London.

The library was situated next to James' office and over time, it became obvious Oswalda and James had become very close. He often visited her home, where she would cook him a meal and sometimes take care of his laundry. He happened to be married to June, but both had for some time led separate lives. They had a son who was studying at Oxford University.

Many years after I had left the LOC, I found out that James' wife had died and he had married Oswalda. The Centre had meanwhile closed and a New Opera School was set up in another location. James continued to conduct in New Zealand and Australia and Oswalda accompanied him. They eventually retired and settled in Llangollen in Wales, where James died in 1991 at the age of 79. Oswalda bequeathed all his scores, letters and other documents to the National Library.

The length of courses varied between one and three years, depending upon age and previous operatic experience. With one or two exceptions, usually those who came from New Zealand, most students had graduated from a Conservatoire, Music Academy, Music College or University.

Auditions for entry were frequently arranged before an eminent panel of judges, all of whom had distinguished careers in opera. One was Dame Eva Turner, whose career as a dramatic soprano had blossomed during the 1920s and one of the roles for which she was famous was that of the heroine in Puccini's opera *Tosca*.

There are probably more anecdotes about things going wrong in performances of that opera than any other. In the final Act Tosca was supposed to leap to her death from the walls of Castel Sant'Angelo, usually landing on a mattress. However, rumoured to have been an act of revenge for troublesome behaviour, the stagehands had thoughtfully improved her safety by replacing the mattress with a trampoline with the result that a flustered and still very much alive Tosca appeared two or three times from behind the wall!

The Peter Stuyvesant Foundation annually offered four scholarships, and I was given responsibility for setting up auditions in Music Academies and Colleges throughout the UK.

The judges came from both the operatic world and the Arts Council of Great Britain, and were joined by the sponsor's director, Michael Kaye. Usually, I sat with the judges and on one occasion, following an excruciating rendition of a famous operatic aria, one of them suggested perhaps I should either leave the room or, better yet, try not to express my feelings.

For various reasons there were a few mature students who joined in their late twenties, one of whom was famous Bass Robert Lloyd who studied at Keble College Oxford, became a history teacher at the Royal Naval College and lecturer at the National Police Staff College prior to taking a one-year course at the LOC in 1968, at the age of 28. After graduating he joined Sadler's Wells Opera (later to become the English National Opera) and in 1972 the Royal Opera House Covent Garden as Principal Bass and went on to have a successful international career, with appearances at the Metropolitan Opera in New York, La Scala Milan and Salzburg. He was awarded a CBE in 1991.

Australian soprano Joan Carden was born in Melbourne. At the age of 30, while studying as a private student at Trinity College of Music in London, in 1966/7 she won a Stuyvesant Scholarship. She stayed only one year, was given leading roles in the Centre's end of term productions and continued to have private singing lessons with her Australian teacher, Vera Harford. After graduating, she performed major roles at the Royal

Opera House, Covent Garden, Glyndebourne Opera, Metropolitan Opera in New York and German opera houses. In 1971 she returned to Australia, to join the Australian Opera as a principal until retiring from that company in 2003. She was awarded an OBE in the Birthday Honours of 1982. The Australian press called her 'The People's Diva'.

Through strong connections with the Royal Opera House and Sadler's Wells Opera, The Centre had access to some of the best producers and repetiteurs (opera pianist/coaches) and was able to invite some of the world's leading opera stars to give master classes e.g. Dame Joan Sutherland, Richard Bonynge, Sir Geraint Evans, and Tito Gobbi, very well known for his role as the villain Scarpia.

The old cinema had a vast auditorium and the main body was used for the Royal Opera Company's rehearsals, which gave the Centre's students a privileged opportunity to attend and observe major international artists at work. The back section had been converted into a paint studio, where scenery was painted for Royal Opera House opera and ballet productions. The large orchestra pit still housed an old grand Wurlitzer organ which formerly would have been elevated hydraulically.

On one occasion, members of the Opera Company were rehearsing Donizetti's *The Daughter of the Regiment*, with Joan Sutherland in the title role opposite Luciano Pavarotti who was making his Royal Opera House debut. Joan, a tall and rather well-built lady and always full of fun, having just finished a scene involving the chorus and still dressed in her regimental costume, approached one of the members who was rather short, picked him up and swung him around, causing the rest of the company to laugh and cheer.

At the end of each term, an opera production was staged in the auditorium to an invited audience. The operas to be performed were chosen specifically to involve as many female students as possible, since they outnumbered the males. Often there were two casts, each performing on alternate evenings; famous UK opera producers and conductors agreed to become involved, in addition to James Robertson; an orchestra from one of the London Music Colleges was invited to play in the pit.

One particular opera production stays vividly in my memory: Francis Poulenc's *Dialogues des Carmelites*. Set during the French Revolution, it tells the poignant story of an order of Carmelite nuns, who went singing to the guillotine. Kiri te Kanawa was given the role of Blanche de la Force and the last voice to be heard was that of the Mother Superior, whose role was convincingly taken by Scottish mezzo-soprano, Marjory McMichael. She gave such a moving performance it had the audience in tears.

The events became so popular that it was decided to move end of year productions to Sadler's Wells Theatre, which attracted critical acclaim from important music critics and gave potential operatic stars exposure. This gave me an introduction to professional management which involved promotion, ticket sales and public relations.

Decca occasionally hired the auditorium for major operatic recordings, one of which was Verdi's *Don Carlos* conducted by Sir Georg Solti. Teresa Berganza had been persuaded to come out of retirement and Grace Bumbry's voice was at that time in transition from mezzo soprano and this was to be her first major recording as a soprano. She had obviously been struggling and was very unhappy when I found her in the lady's room in floods of tears. After a while she composed herself and managed to get through to the end of the session. Baritone Dietrich Fischer-Dieskau, at the time suffering from a slight cold, and to protect his voice, continually sucked cough sweets called Cats' Tails, which he offered to anyone who happened to be nearby.

The COE students, who came from all over the world, were given opportunities to attend general rehearsals at the Royal Opera House and on several occasions were able to take advantage of the offer of complimentary tickets for actual performances. Members of the Centre's staff were sometimes given use of the Royal Box, since, not having the best view, it was very rarely used by the Royal Family. It had been lavishly equipped with chaise-longues, on which the sovereign of the day and guests had been able to recline with a glass of champagne and watch the production through a large ornate mirror strategically sited on the opposite wall. A curiosity was the Royal Lavatory, which was made of mahogany wood with steps leading up to it and, once seated, gave one the impression of sitting on a throne.

A request to pay an official visit, was received from the office of Princess Alexandra, a cousin of Queen Elizabeth. I was given the task of making all the arrangements. She was most gracious and wanted to meet everyone and showed particular interest in a rehearsal which was taking place for an end of term opera production. She enjoyed spending time afterwards chatting to some of the students and I later received a letter of thanks and appreciation on her behalf from her Private Secretary.

Granada Television ran a popular series of pre-recorded talent shows called *Opportunity Knocks*, hosted by Hughie Green. Two of the Centre's students were selected to take part and I agreed to act as their sponsor.

Although asked to arrive early at the studio there was much waiting around before someone came to usher us into a dressing room for a make-up session, followed by a camera rehearsal after which we were allowed a coffee break before the actual recording took place.

© The Troxy

*Sir Georg Solti conducting at the Troxy Site of the London Opera Centre*

There was a two-minute interview with myself and then my pair performed a duet called *Donkey Serenade*, made famous by film star Alan Jones, father of popular American singer Jack Jones. Their act was sandwiched between pianist Bobby Crush and a magician.

The votes of the viewers decided the winner and the result was an overwhelming win for Bobby Crush, who went on to have a very successful career in light entertainment. My contestants, although disappointed, admitted it probably had not been such a wise decision to have taken part in a programme which had an appeal completely outside their usual operatic comfort zone.

James had a sister, who was an orthopaedic surgeon at Oswestry hospital in Wales and sometimes he drove from London to visit her. It was on one of those occasions he met with a nasty car accident and fractured his hip.

Fortunately, his sister was able to get him admitted immediately into her hospital for treatment and as it was most likely he would be there for a while, Alan and I decided to pay him a visit.

The plan was to meet at Euston Station but, unfortunately, I got delayed and arrived just as the train was about to depart. Believing Alan had already boarded the train, I rushed across the concourse, past the barrier onto the platform and spotted the guard blowing his whistle and waving his flag. I frantically attempted to gain his attention and seeing me he gestured to jump into his van as the train began to pull out of the station.

After getting my breath back, I went in search of Alan, moving from one compartment to the next but it soon became evident he was not on board. There was nothing for it but to purchase a ticket and continue the long journey alone to Gobowen, changing to a local service for the final leg. Getting directions from the station, and with insufficient money to pay for a taxi, I made my way on foot to the hospital, where a bedridden James was pleased to see me, but disappointed Alan had not come.

Meanwhile, back in London, Alan had in fact waited for me but as departure loomed closer and I had not appeared, he began to worry, imagining I may possibly have met with an accident. He decided not to take the train alone and instead to contact my home. We did not have a telephone in those days, and when eventually someone was found to go to the house to check, no-one there.

He was at his wits end!

Oblivious to the chaos I had caused, I stayed for about one hour at the hospital, left as afternoon tea was being served to the patients, and returned on foot to the station for the return journey to London. Tired and hungry, I eventually arrived home late that evening to be greeted by a very worried but relieved mother.

When we met the following day in the office, Alan, obviously having slept very badly, was not in the best of moods. I tried to explain what had happened, but he made it plain he was not at all happy.

For personal and health reasons, Alan decided to resign and following his departure, I took over responsibility for running the department, although never given the title of 'Warden' or 'Bursar'.

It was while working at the LOC, I came across the name Placido Domingo. One of the Centre's tenor students, who had studied in the US, had heard him sing there and was so impressed with his voice he tried to copy him. Placido was not yet known internationally, having only recently arrived in New York from Mexico where he had grown up and performed with his parents' Zarzuela company before being discovered as an operatic tenor. Little was I to know at the time that he and I were to work together sometime in the future when he would perform and record with the London Symphony Orchestra and the Chamber Orchestra of Europe.

After completing their studies, several of the students went on to have very successful careers both in their own countries and invited to perform leading roles with the world's most famous international opera companies. Two New Zealand students, Malvina Major and Kiri to Kanawa, each in a different way, became involved in my personal life.

*Malvina Major*

# Malvina Major

Like her compatriot Kiri te Kanawa, Malvina Major was a 'Kiwi' and a student of Sister Mary Leo. In many ways they were rivals, both celebrities, having won several lucrative prizes in Australia and their native New Zealand, who went on to have international careers and were created Dames of the British Empire. However, that is where the similarities ended.

Malvina was a country girl and married a New Zealand farmer when she was very young. They soon started a family, forcing her to take time out from her career. But singing was her life and again beckoned. Sister Mary Leo told her about the London Opera Centre and suggested she, like Kiri, should use her prize money to pay for the course fees and her subsistence in London. She then had the difficult task of persuading her husband to leave his farm and accompany her to London to look after their baby. Once the decision was taken, it was first necessary to find suitable accommodation.

While waiting two years for his UK divorce, David lived alone in our home to be, a converted downstairs apartment in a house in Lewisham, owned by a family friend. Paul Person, a baritone who had earlier arrived, with his small family from New Zealand, to study at the Centre, rented the apartment upstairs. However, he did not stay very long because he was offered and had accepted a principal position with the New Zealand Opera Company. He decided to return home rather than complete the course and discovering through a mutual friend that Malvina was looking for somewhere to live, suggested she should take over the flat.

For a while, the living arrangement worked very well, until one day when they were both alone in the house, David approached Malvina in the hallway and made unwelcome advances which shocked and upset her. She immediately complained to James Robertson, who, without my knowledge, telephoned David's Chief Superintendent and insisted that he should be reprimanded.

By this time, the UK divorce had been made absolute and a new date set for the wedding which was due to take place within a few weeks. Alan decided to make me aware of what had happened before it was too late to change my mind. He was very kind and suggested I should carefully consider whether or not it would be wise to go through with the marriage.

As someone who once having set a course very rarely deviates from it and having already endured two years of waiting. I considered then was not the time to change. Instead, I made light of the situation. I was not prepared to accept what had really happened and suggested Malvina had perhaps been naive and probably made the situation seem worse than it actually was. The wedding went ahead as planned and I moved into the apartment, where we stayed long enough to save for a deposit to buy our first house in Bromley.

Although the atmosphere was cold and strained, we politely co-existed with Malvina and her family. She continued her studies and her husband found a part-time job, while they juggled, between them, how to look after their small child.

Malvina was a much more serious student than Kiri and quickly adapted to life at the LOC. Her talents were quickly recognised and like Kiri she was given leading roles in several of the Centre's opera productions. However, it was evident the couple were very unhappy. They never really settled or got used to being away from New Zealand and a rural way of life and were eager to return.

Prior to completing her course at the LOC, while performing in one of the end of term productions, Malvina was spotted by Claudio Abbado's manager who was very impressed and recommended her for the principal soprano role of Rosina in a new production of Rossini's opera *Il Barbiere di Sevilla* which was scheduled to take place at the Salzburg Festival. It was questionable whether or not her soprano voice was ready to take on such a taxing coloratura role or that she had the experience which might have prepared her for a situation when she would be performing for the first time, with seasoned professionals, at a major international festival, attended by the world's press.

As a consequence, although invited to repeat the role in the following year's revival of the opera, she did not achieve the success she had hoped for. Personally, I never understood why Claudio thought her suitable.

The episode shook Malvina's confidence and contributed to her decision to return to New Zealand. Back in her home country she threw herself into her career, singing principal roles with the New Zealand Opera company and giving recitals.

Sadly, her husband died young, but she stoically carried on with her career while at the same time managing the family farm. She later also took up teaching and, together with Kiri, set up a Special Trust to help aspiring opera stars, organising gala concerts which they both took part in to raise the necessary funds.

# Kiri te Kanawa

Kiri, the daughter of a Maori father and European mother, was adopted as a baby and raised in Gisborne, New Zealand. From an early age it was recognised that she had the rare gift of a beautiful voice and private singing lessons were arranged with a nun called Sister Mary Leo.

During one of his visits to New Zealand, James Robertson was invited to be a judge for the 1963 *Mobile Song Quest* competition and awarded Kiri second place to her long-time rival, Malvina Major. At the reception held afterward he was introduced to Kiri's mother and Sister Mary Leo, who took the opportunity to ask James whether he would, at the appropriate time, consider accepting Kiri as a student at the London Opera Centre.

Kiri went on to win many other major competitions both in New Zealand and Australia and consequently became a popular celebrity, with appearances on radio and television. Sister Mary Leo recommended that she should use her considerable amount of prize money to further her studies and promote her career either in the United States or the UK.

The nun wrote a letter to James, requesting a London Opera Centre syllabus and an indication of fees. In the same hand-written letter, she reminded him of the Competition and wished to inform him that, in the interim, Kiri had made considerable progress and, although most people considered her a mezzo soprano on account of the mellow quality of her voice, in her opinion she qualified as a heavy lyric soprano. James replied, 'I remember Kiri te Kanawa vey vividly, and I have no doubt that she would be acceptable as a student at the London Opera Centre... so we shall accept her without audition.'

On March 6, 1966, her 22nd birthday Kiri arrived in London with her mother and several trunks containing the many concert dresses she had accumulated.

They had rented an apartment in Richmond but, when Kiri realised the journey to the Opera Centre was likely take more than one and a half hours by car, she persuaded her mother to move to another in Forest Hill, South London.

Her first major purchase was a second-hand E-type Jaguar, in which, wearing a mini skirt and high white leather boots, she arrived on her first day at the LOC, causing quite a stir amongst her poorer fellow students!

Unlike most of her contemporaries at the LOC, most of whom had attended a conservatory, Kiri had not undertaken any formal training and found it very hard to fit in. She had difficulty making friends and felt lonely and unhappy, the only people she knew were James Robertson and Malvina Major, already in her first year at the Centre.

She had a beautiful face but was not very elegant-rather tomboyish and a little overweight. Some of the tutors found it a problem working with her, considering her lazy and unable to concentrate or cope with the necessary disciplines. She found learning languages particularly difficult, which resulted in floods of tears and requests to leave. The following day she would not come to the Centre and I had to call her on the telephone, to explain that was not the way to behave. After a great deal of coaxing and persuasion she eventually knuckled down, but it was always an uphill struggle. Most people forgave her histrionics simply because of a God-given gift of such a beautiful voice.

One of the Sadler's Wells Opera producers, John Blatchley, who used to come to the Centre to give coaching sessions and produce end of term workshops, despaired of Kiri and said he thought *we were wasting our time and she was never going to get anywhere!* I bet him £50 she would. John still owes me the money!

James was occasionally invited to conduct opera performances outside of the Centre. He received an invitation to conduct Bizet's *Carmen*, in Newcastle and proposed Kiri for the leading role which was to be sung in French. My command of French was of a reasonable standard, so I offered to give her private coaching sessions at my home, which she gratefully accepted.

Opera conductor, Richard Bonynge, husband of Dame Joan Sutherland, was invited to give a Master Class, with Joan in attendance. They were both impressed with Kiri's voice and Bonynge expressed the view that she was not a mezzo-soprano, but should, instead, tackle the soprano repertory. James heeded this advice and began gradually to expand her range upwards. She was initially given the title role in four excerpts from Donizetti's *Anna Bolena*, in an end of term production staged by Tom Hawkes. Australian soprano Joan Carden appeared as her rival, Jane Seymour.

During this period David was a CID officer with the Port of London Authority (although he later transferred to the Metropolitan Police Force and became a member of the Flying & Murder Squads) and many social evenings were organised in the London and St. Katherine Docks. Kiri was always willing to come along and, happy to sing popular arias to an attentive and appreciative audience, her only payment one or two bottles of whisky.

I recall one particular evening when in a smoke-filled room and accompanied by an out-of-tune-piano, she suddenly stood up and sang *The Lord's Prayer.* The effect was electrifying and one could have heard a pin drop.

David and I were married in March 1967. Chris was best man. My grandmother had refused to attend, although someone apparently did spot her standing in the large crowd which had gathered on the pavement opposite the church. As I entered the church and walked down the aisle on the arm of my proud uncle Terry, who had been very happy to deputise for his deceased brother, one of the London Opera Centre's repetiteur students, a young man from South Africa, played the popular Bridal March from Mendlessohn's *A Midsummer Night's Dream* on the organ.

While David and I were in the vestry signing the register we could just hear the strains of Kiri te Kanawa's beautiful voice as she sang two Schubert songs to a mesmerised congregation. My family, friends and I have always taken pride in telling people how fortunate we had been to have her sing at my wedding, several years before being invited by Prince Charles and Lady Diana.

The church organ came into its own with Widor's majestic *Toccata and Fugue* which was played as everyone exited the church.

Both performers and members of the Centre's staff were invited to join family and friends afterwards at the reception which was held in the staff restaurant at the London Opera Centre. Eugene, the Assistant Caretaker, who had previously worked as a chef, had insisted upon taking charge of organising a sumptuous buffet and later proudly produced a magnificent home-made wedding cake.

When it was time for everyone to leave, Kiri, who possibly had drunk more than one glass of champagne, found a typewriter in reception and typed a note, in which she described how much she had enjoyed the occasion, and then left it on the desk. The same evening, together with a friend, she went on a blind date and met her future husband, an Australian mining engineer named Desmond Park. They married later that year in Auckland, New Zealand, with the full paraphernalia and media attention usually given to a returning celebrity and national treasure.

After our reception, David and I spent a brief weekend at the historical Mermaid Hotel at Rye, one of the 'cinque ports', but our actual honeymoon took place later in September, when we flew by Pan Am to New York and took a Greyhound Bus upstate to Niagara Falls and on to Ontario.

One weekend, we were invited for lunch at Kiri's Surrey home which was situated in the middle of Patchesam Park golf course (Kiri was a keen golfer). It was there we met her adoptive father Tom, a New Zealand Maori, who was visiting alone, her mother having died. Kiri had expertly prepared the food herself, with husband Des only given permission to stir the accompanying sauce. She had the amazing ability to identify the ingredients of any dish she had previously tasted and replicate it without reference to a recipe.

*Signing the register, March 1967*

*Kiri te Kanawa, left (with LOC colleagues), at the wedding reception 1967*

*Kiri te Kanawa as the Countess in The Marriage of Figaro*

Kiri's attitude and behaviour in class had led other tutors to doubt she would ever have a significant career with a major opera company. However, she was spotted in the Centre's production of *Anna Bolena* by Basil Horsfield, a prominent London Agent, who agreed to represent her. When she completed her three-year course, he arranged for her to audition and she was accepted as a principal singer with the Royal Opera, Covent Garden.

Colin Davis, who had succeeded Sir Georg Solti as Music Director, was casting for a new production of Mozart's *The Marriage of Figaro*, together with resident producer, John Copley. Until then Kiri had only been given minor roles to sing but Colin thought she would make an ideal Countess. However, he faced strong opposition from John, who had previously worked with Kiri at the LOC and was exasperated with her.

After a great deal of argument and discussion, Colin finally managed to persuade him to coach her on a one-to-one basis. With considerable patience and hard work, the gamble paid off, the production was a great a success and brought Kiri critical acclaim and international recognition.

Several years later, the Chamber Orchestra of Europe were performing Mozart with Sir Georg Solti in the Alte Oper in Frankfurt and Kiri was invited as a soloist, together with mezzo soprano Frederika von Stade and tenor Jose Carreras, who had recently recovered from throat cancer.

We had not seen one another for several years, so it was good to have an opportunity between the rehearsal and performance to catch up.

David Fingleton, in addition to his duties as a Metropolitan Stipendiary Magistrate, wrote a weekly music column for the Daily Express and was Stage Design Correspondent of Arts Review. He had admired Kiri Te Kanawa since first hearing her sing in 1969 and had known her for ten years. He was commissioned to write her first biography *Kiri* which was first published in 1982. He came to my home to interview me about her time at the London Opera Centre.

The book launch took place in the Crush Bar of the Royal Opera House, where Kiri signed autographed copies for her many fans. I managed to secure two in which she wrote a personal message.

KENSINGTON PALACE,
LONDON. W. 8.

17th December, 1970

*Dear Th Robertson*

Princess Alexandra has asked me to write and thank you for a very enjoyable evening last week. Her Royal Highness was so pleased to have this opportunity of hearing the students of the London Opera Centre and she was most impressed by their performance. The Princess would be grateful if you would convey her thanks and her best wishes to them all.

Her Royal Highness would specially like to thank you for the arrangements you made for the evening which gave her the chance of meeting so many people. The Princess realises that this occasion must have given Miss Megennis a great deal of extra work as well and she would like you to convey her thanks also to her.

Princess Alexandra sends her best wishes for Christmas and the New Year to you all.

I too very much enjoyed the evening and would like to thank you.

*Yours Sincerely*

*Mary Fitzalan Howard*

Lady in Waiting

James Robertson Esq.

*Letter from the office of Princess Alexandra*

# 3  The Royal Opera House Covent Garden (1972-1973)

After eight interesting and enjoyable years helping to build the reputation of the London Opera Centre, I decided to move on, principally because of changes. The tenor John Kentish, who had previously worked with James Robertson as a principal singer with Sadler's Wells Opera and since retired, was engaged as Artistic Director and made it clear he not only wished to take over some of my responsibilities but also my office.

I found the situation hard to accept and decided to apply, and was accepted, for the position of Personal Assistant to John Tooley, General Administrator of the Royal Opera House, Covent Garden.

Sir David Webster had previously held the position of General Administrator since 1945 when the House was re-converted from having been a dance hall during the War. As the London Opera Centre was affiliated and accountable to the Royal Opera House, I had occasion to meet Sir David during the last decade of his tenure. However, his health was failing and John, who was at the time his Assistant, had already begun to take over the reigns.

Colin Davis, Sir Georg Solti's successor as Music Director, I already knew quite well. He could be impatient and sometimes impetuous. Board Meetings were held monthly in John Tooley's office and everyone would first have to pass through my office. Those meetings were often lively affairs and raised voices could sometimes be overheard. On several occasions Colin left the meeting early in a very bad mood and one day threw his papers on the floor of my office, complaining no-one listened to him or respected his point of view. Betty Scholar, his secretary, with whom I became good friends, seemed to be the only person who was able to calm him down.

The Board's Chairman was Lord Drogheda, who I found charming and always polite. On the other hand, another member of the Board, Sir Claus Moser, a Government Finance Minister, was a little too friendly. One day he told me that he was expecting some important papers to be delivered to the Treasury and asked if I would be kind enough to bring them personally after I finished work at 5 p.m.

When I arrived at his office, I discovered that his secretary had already left and there was no one else about. Sir Claus warmly welcomed and thanked me for the papers, then offered a drink, which I politely refused. He came close and tried to kiss me, but I fended him off, made an excuse I had to meet my husband, and headed for the door. He attempted to follow but, realising he had misjudged the situation, just shrugged his shoulders and turned away. Naively, I had not seen the warning signals beforehand.

Following that incident, whenever he attended Board meetings, I avoided making eye contact and kept my head well down as he passed.

Although I enjoyed working in the surroundings and atmosphere of Covent Garden, meeting many eminent people and famous artists in both the opera and ballet worlds, it soon became obvious the position was not what I had expected.

Paul Finlay, whom I had known previously at the London Opera Centre, where he had been a stage management student, was engaged to work alongside me, clearly to be groomed as John Tooley's successor. We were consequently in competition with one another and I found myself facing yet another situation when, as a woman, I was expected to play a secondary role. My pride was hurt because I considered I had moved on and become an experienced administrator.

Suspecting I was not happy, one day Paul produced a circular he had received from the Arts Council of Great Britain, which advertised the position of Concerts Manager at the London Symphony Orchestra. He suggested I should think about applying. At first, I rejected the idea as I had no experience of working with a professional orchestra but I gave it further thought, took the hint, accepted the challenge, and sent in my application.

Soon after I had joined the Royal Opera House a terrible incident occurred. One evening, it was getting late and David had not yet arrived home, which was not unusual. As a Metropolitan Police Detective, he was often required to work overtime and sometimes might end the day in a public house with his colleagues, who I always referred to as 'homo-socials'. I was just about to watch a programme on television when there was a knock on the door. Thinking David had possibly forgotten his key, I was surprised to see two men I did not recognise. They identified themselves as senior police officers and asked to come inside. Politely refusing my offer of a drink they suggested I might like to sit while they explained the reason for their visit.

David had been called to a disturbance on the upper floor of a rundown block of flats. As he reached the top of a flight of stairs, he had found himself confronted by a demented young man who threatened him with a knife. A struggle followed, during which David managed to disarm and eventually overpower him. Not realising he had been injured, he held on to the man until his colleague and friend, David Pickett, an advanced police driver, arrived to put on hand cuffs and call for assistance. While the prisoner was being bundled into the police van David suddenly noticed blood seeping through his coat and began to feel faint. His colleague managed to get him into his car, put on the siren and drove as fast as possible, passing through several red traffic lights, to hospital emergency, where it was confirmed that his condition was very serious and required immediate surgery. I was advised not to go immediately to the hospital, as there was nothing I could have done but to wait until there was further news.

The following morning, I telephoned the hospital and was informed the operation had gone well and I could visit any time. When I arrived, I found David sitting propped up in bed looking sorry for himself but managing to smile when he saw me. Fortunately, the knife had entered just a few centimetres away from his heart and he had been lucky to have survived. Both officers were highly commended, awarded bravery medals and hailed as heroes in the local and national Press. A photograph of The Police Commissioner visiting David in hospital, appeared in the London Evening Standard.

When David had fully recovered and returned to normal duties, the two comrades in arms decided to celebrate over a long lunch at a Holborn restaurant, which they frequently visited and knew the proprietor well.

The plan was to meet me afterwards at the Royal Opera House and drive together to Bromley hospital to visit Christine, David Pickett's wife, who had recently given birth to their daughter Claire. Both men arrived mildly inebriated and, although in the company of a police advanced driver, I was nervous throughout the journey and opened the car window to let in some fresh air. Christine was not amused when she saw the state of her husband and his friend and became even more annoyed when they bent over the cot, breathing alcoholic fumes over the small baby. Happily, it did not prevent us from being invited to be her godparents.

# 4 London Symphony Orchestra (1973-1976)

## Jumping in at the Deep End

My interview took place with the LSO's General Manager, Harold Lawrence, who had previously been a record producer in the United States. He had succeeded Ernest Fleischmann, who successfully steered the Orchestra to new heights and had since moved on to manage the Los Angeles Philharmonic Orchestra and the Hollywood Bowl. It was Harold who was responsible for the appointment of Andre Previn as Principal Conductor, believing he could open new doors by introducing classical music to the masses through television and recordings.

Within a few weeks of my joining, and just as I was getting to grips with my duties from the outgoing Concerts Manager, Harold dropped a bombshell by announcing his intention to return to the United States to take up his new position as General Manager of the New York Philharmonic Orchestra. He then broke the news that, since no successor was in view, I was, for the time being, to take over many of his duties. The Board had apparently decided not to replace him with another General Manager but to appoint Stephen Reiss as Administrator, principally because it was thought that when the Orchestra became resident in the Barbican additional management would be required.

The new arrangement was that Stephen and I would be concerned with administration and planning.

Then followed a whirlwind tour around London, with introductions to agents, recording companies, promoters and others in the music world, which really did feel like being thrown in at the deep end! Imagine, I had no previous experience of working with a world class symphony orchestra, so had to hold my nerve and quickly prove myself which was certainly not easy because I soon found out I had entered into a macho male dominated world.

Before the 1970s one of the few women to play in the Orchestra was the oboist Evelyn Rothwell, who joined in the 1930s and found herself regarded as an outsider by her male colleagues. She was not admitted to full membership of the Orchestra: the first woman to be elected as a member of the LSO was harpist Renata Scheffel-Stein in 1975, other British orchestras having left the LSO far behind. By the time of its centenary about 20 per cent of the LSO's members were women. The Vienna, Berlin Philharmonic and most American orchestras were all male. Their managers too were men and it took several years before the situation was to change.

The Board of Directors was made up entirely of male playing members of the Orchestra, some of whom were long serving. On the whole, I got along with most of them, in particular with Howard Snell and Kurt-Hans Goedicke.

Howard, who was the Orchestra's Principal Trumpet, served five times as Chairman. He also became involved in the world of brass bands and since the late 1970s has become one of its most influential and commanding figures. After leaving the LSO he took up conducting, founded the Wren Orchestra in association with Capital Radio, and invited me to become General Manager.

Kurt was born in East Berlin and grew up there during the Cold War. After graduating from university, he escaped to the West and eventually reach Ireland, where he married an Irish girl and acquired national status. He often made a joke about his name being changed to O'Goedicke in his passport. He secured a job with an Irish orchestra and later took up the position of Principal Timpani with the LSO, in which post he stayed for 34 years. Rather short in stature, Kurt was always immaculately dressed, his face shiny due to a liberal application of oil, and he could be easily identified by his expensive after shave lotion.

He once offered me a lift in his car to a rehearsal at the Royal Festival Hall. Before opening the door, he first wiped the handle and once inside the car took off his shoes, carefully placed them on the back seat which had been covered with a towel, put on gloves and started the engine. As the Timpanist, he and his instruments were usually positioned high at the back of the stage behind the rest of the Orchestra, just underneath the organ. Before the rehearsal began, I saw him lift one foot after the other onto a nearby chair and clean his shoes with a paper towel which afterwards was secreted behind one of the organ pipes.

Having, over the years, undertaken many overseas tour with the LSO, in particular to the US, he built up a sizeable fan club, mostly of young women, who treated him like a pop star. They would often just turn up and hang around backstage trying hard to gain his attention, much to the amusement of his colleagues.

Naively, at first, I was unaware of the many challenges which lay ahead, the more so as I progressed up the ladder into more senior positions. Again, I was competing in a man's world, where women were expected to play subordinate roles.

Andre Previn was in the middle of his successful TV series and there were major tours and recording projects already in the diary, which had to be fulfilled. The self-governing members of the LSO demanded a full monthly schedule. They were in competition with the other major London orchestras, all vying for lucrative recordings, with little regard for the fact that some conductors and soloists had exclusive contracts and, therefore, were not always free to work with them. The LSO had the best of all worlds, having principal conductor Andre Previn with his RCA/EMI/Decca recordings and BBC television series, and Guest Principal Conductors, Claudio Abbado, with a DGG recording contract and Colin Davis with Philips.

The London Concerts Board arranged planning meetings which were held every month at the Royal Festival Hall. Managers from each of the major London orchestras, including the BBC, would submit programme ideas and the proposed repertoire, after which dates were checked against a 'clash list' to avoid repetitions. Because Beethoven cycles were always popular, it was agreed that only one should be scheduled each season with a different orchestra.

Plans for the new Barbican Arts Centre also kept me occupied, as the LSO was to be the resident orchestra. To identify what would be required, both for concerts and office accommodation, I attended regular meetings with the Managing Director, Henry Wrong, in his office, which, at the time, overlooked a large hole in the ground, as archaeologists were still excavating the site.

Despite numerous acoustic tests and design revision by the architects, mistakes were later discovered; no provision had been made for a choir to be located behind the orchestra, which, subsequently, necessitated enlarging the apron stage, a consequence of which was to reduce the number of seats in the auditorium, with a potential loss of income; a further oversight, discovered later, was the lack of a facility for moving grand pianos.

The acoustic was not ideal for concerts because the hall had been designed as a 'multipurpose' venue and was more suited to the spoken word. It became necessary for further costly acoustic experiments to be undertaken and improvements made.

As 'resident orchestra' the LSO would have to give at least 40 concerts a season, of which half had to be repeated on account of limited seating capacity in the hall.

When the LSO staff eventually occupied their accommodation some years later, it was found to be smaller than originally planned and rather cramped.

The Orchestra's diary was a busy one, with a full concert and recording schedule. In addition to regular series of concerts in the Royal Festival Hall, out of town dates and overseas tours, the recording schedule also included film sessions with American composer/conductors. In January 1974, Rick Wakeman recorded live in the Royal Festival Hall, performances of his very successful *Journey to the Centre of the Earth*. In May 1974, a special album of music was recorded to accompany the hit Previn/BBC TV series that ran from 1971-1978. The year following my departure, John Williams came to London to begin recordings for the soundtrack for his very successful *Star Wars*.

In 1975, the legendary pianist Arthur Rubinstein, at the time having reached the great age of 88 years, came to London to be filmed playing three piano concertos (Chopin, Saint-Saens and Grieg) with the Orchestra and Andre Previn. All three were recorded during the same day, in the Fairfield Halls in Croydon.

This was not the usual recording session, with re-takes; each concerto was recorded as if it were a live performance, the soloist, conductor and musicians all wearing concert dress. The only difference, from any normal concert, was the absence of any audience. Fortunately, more than 40 years later, it is possible to view the performances on YouTube and I am happy to be able to relive those moments and be reminded of how impressed I had been by the demeanour of Arthur Rubinstein, a quiet, gentle man, elegantly dressed, completely absorbed in the music, in particular, his considered and serious interpretation of the Grieg concerto.

During my tenure, gala concerts were organised at the Royal Albert Hall, some in aid of charities, with artists such as Danny Kaye, Henry Mancini and Aram Khatchaturian.

Recordings and concerts were also undertaken with another great legend, Leopold Stokowski, who at the time was very old and could hardly walk. He was actually born Leonard Stokes, in London, but adopted a European accent when he spoke. He had first conducted the LSO in 1912, when he was already 30 years old, and the programme included Richard Wagner's overture to *Die Meistersinger von Nuremburg*. He was particularly famous for Bach transcriptions and of course for the soundtrack of the Walt Disney film *Fantasia*.

His concerts with the LSO usually took place in the Royal Albert Hall, for which he would request additional strings. He also had particular views as to how the musicians should be seated and would place the cellos and a larger than usual double bass section in lines high up behind the main body of the Orchestra, so that their sound would be better projected into the vast hall.

Deutsche Grammophon (DGG), scheduled a Beethoven Symphony Cycle, with Rafael Kubelik and individual symphonies were to be recorded with a different international orchestra and the LSO was allocated the First. There was no time to organise an actual concert and the complete work had to be rehearsed and recorded all on the same day. I remember the Orchestra finding difficulty with the introduction to the final movement but after some words of wisdom from the Maestro, and a few attempts, it was licked into shape.

For my final LSO project, I was pleased to have been able to organise a special recording for EMI. At very short notice, a window of opportunity had arisen for the Russian pianist Lazar Berman to record Rachmaninov's Third Piano Concerto. Between 1959 and 1971, he had not been allowed to travel abroad due to his marriage to a French national and as a consequence was not well known outside the Soviet Union. Claudio also happened to be in London at the time and was available to conduct. An LP of the recording remains part of my treasured collection.

## Musicians Union

Every professional musician was required to be a paid-up member of the British Musicians' Union. The LSO musicians were all free-lance and it was therefore important to have a body with muscle who would look after their interests.

All fees for concerts and recordings were set by the MU who would stipulate minimum rates for individual sections in an orchestra, i.e. principals, sub-principals and rank and file. It was left up to the Orchestra to decide whether or not they wished to pay a higher amount and, in fact, the LSO were very generous to their principal players in particular, with the concert master receiving the highest fee. The rates also varied between 'listed' London and Provincial orchestras and separate arrangements were made for salaried BBC orchestras and 'non-listed' orchestras, whose rates tended to be higher.

There were also rules governing the length of a rehearsal or concert and if, by any chance, they were exceeded, overtime would have to be paid. Conductors would be warned in advance of this rule and, if they got carried away and began to run overtime, the MU representative, who was usually one of the players, would interrupt and stop the rehearsal. Also a 15-20 minute break had to be taken during any three-hour rehearsal.

Similar rules were put in place for commercial recording sessions, which stipulated in addition that only 20 minutes of music could be recorded in a three-hour session. In the event a 'live' recording of a concert was taken, or sometimes a mix of two or more performances, the total number of 20-minute segments of recorded music, plus one, would determine the fee payable to each musician which would be in addition to their normal concert fee.

It was my responsibility to prepare costings and everything necessary to ensure adherence to MU rules. If I was in any doubt about a particular project, I would ask Stan Hibbert, who was in charge of the section dealing with classical orchestras, for his advice. He was always extremely helpful and we got along very well.

The structure and conditions were not as strict and complicated as those practised in the US, which made it an attractive and less expensive proposition for recording companies to record in the UK. They found London orchestras, like the LSO, to be particularly quick and responsive, and consequently many major high-quality recordings were produced.

## Salzburg Festival

One of my early assignments was to make the arrangements for the Orchestra's visit to the renowned Salzburg Festival. It was the first time a British orchestra had been honoured in this way and offered a two-week residency, in which to give seven concerts with five different conductors. This caused much excitement amongst the members of the Orchestra, but concern as to which repertoire should be performed and with which conductors.

Although Andre Previn had been successful with late nineteenth and twentieth century repertoire, the musicians were not always convinced by his interpretations of the classics and the Salzburg Festival was

Mit einer Sondermaschine der BEA traf gestern das Londoner Symphonie-orchester in Salzburg ein. Festspieldirektor Dr. Nekola (rechts) überreichte der Generalsekretärin und Managerin des Klangkörpers, June Hall (Mitte), einen Blumenstrauß. (Siehe auch unsere Kulturseite.)  Bild: Anrather

*Cutting - Arriving at Saltzburg Airport 1973*

reputed to be extremely conservative. Nevertheless, although risky, it was unanimously considered important to include one programme which consisted entirely of classical repertoire.

The musicians always found Brahms' scores challenging but, with the agreement of the Festival, the LSO Board decided to take the plunge and invite veteran conductor Karl Boehm to conduct a programme which would include one of the composer's symphonies. Much to everyone's surprise and delight, he agreed.

He had made his debut at this most prestigious of festivals in 1938, just after the Anschluss and appeared almost every year since, with the exception of the years immediately after the War.

While Mozart and Brahms were no longer core repertory for the London players, they certainly were for him, the Salzburg audience and the great orchestras he was used to conducting. Referring to his relationship with the Vienna Philharmonic Orchestra, he had previously written, 'I could hardly imagine any orchestra giving finer performances of the classical repertoire'.

He had first conducted them in 1933 with a programme which had included Haydn's *Haffner* and Brahms' Second Symphony. For the LSO to be playing both works under his direction, in a festival whose home orchestra was the Vienna Philharmonic, was certainly a very brave undertaking.

However, there remained two problems, how to handle Andre Previn who, as the Orchestra's Principal Conductor, would naturally expect to have first choice of programme and conduct the first concert, and who should lead for the Boehm programme. John Brown was the appointed LSO leader at the time, but he was Previn's man and it was considered preferable to engage a guest leader, someone who would already have had experience working with Maestro Boehm. It was eventually decided to invite Hugh Bean, former respected leader of the Philharmonia Orchestra who had all the right credentials.

For his programme, Andre proposed Shostakovich's Eighth Symphony and there was certainly apprehension about suggesting that work to the Salzburg Festival as it had never been performed there. It was agreed John Brown should lead for that concert and three others with Seiji Ozawa, Wolfgang Sawallisch and Claudio Abbado. The wide range of repertoire included Richard Strauss' *Till Eulenspiegel* (Sawallisch), Stravinsky's *Firebird* (Ozawa), Stravinsky's' *Sacre du Printemps* (Abbado) and concertos with Kyung-Wha Chung (Mendelssohn Violin), Henrik Szeryng (Mozart Piano), Leonid Kogan (Shostakovich's Violin) and Mozart and Mahler arias with Dietrich Fischer-Dieskau and British mezzo soprano Janet Baker.

A chartered plane flew the whole Orchestra and instruments to Salzburg. Andre and I travelled on the same flight and when we had disembarked from the plane, were greeted by the Festival's Intendant, Dr. Nekola and his assistant Dorle Schoerbeler, who presented me with a bouquet of flowers. Some of the press who were present, mistakenly assumed I was Mia Farrow, Andre's wife at the time, although I am sure she and I bore absolutely no resemblance.

The LSO's opening concert, conducted by Andre, was surprisingly well received by the conservative audience and critics, who considered the repertoire a breath of fresh air. For the first rehearsal of the Brahms, I sat in the auditorium, intrigued as the nervous musicians soon came under the spell of Maestro Boehm. I too was caught up in the moment, completely carried away by the intensity of the music with the second movement particularly moving me to tears.

Boehm and the Orchestra had initially been cautious, each having been warned that the other could be difficult. That caution, however, was short-lived. By the end of the rehearsal the Maestro too was captivated, saying to the Orchestra, 'We'll show von Karajan how to play Brahms.'

From a personal point of view, the whole occasion was impressive and overwhelming. It was my first season with the LSO and I had never before visited Salzburg. The beautiful and historic city was intoxicating; the glamorous Festival, which attracted the rich and famous and the world's greatest artists was a wonderful world to be part of.

It was the beginning of a warm relationship that would last until Boehm's death in 1981. He was made honorary president of the LSO and a set of recordings of the Orchestra under him, dating from that period, demonstrates what must be some of the finest playing in its history.

When in June 1975 he came to London to record with the Orchestra, it happened to be my birthday and at the end of a session, he presented me with a large bouquet of red roses and a boxed LP set of his recent recording of Beethoven's *Missa Solemnis*. On the inside of the lid he had written a very touching and complimentary message. The whole episode will certainly remain as one of the highlights of my long career.

The LSO's second visit to Salzburg took place in the summer of 1975. Following their previously successful collaboration, Karl Boehm was again invited to conduct, on that occasion a programme which featured the celebrated Russian pianist, Emil Gillels who performed the Schumann Concerto. A concert of works by Beethoven and Berlioz was performed with the up-and-coming young American conductor, James Levine, a prodigy of Leonard Bernstein.

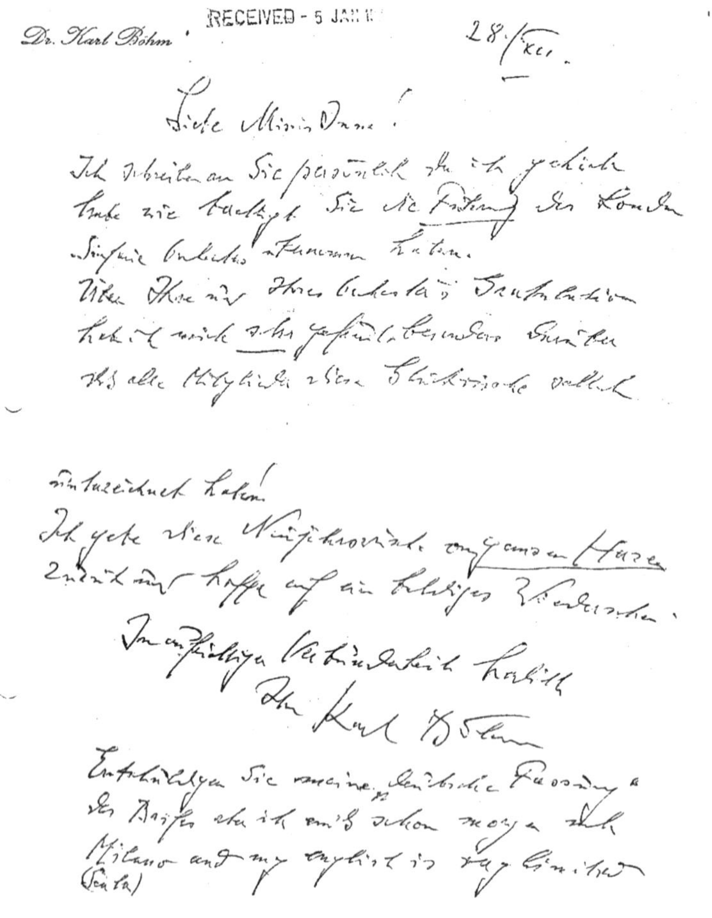
Dr. Karl Böhm

RECEIVED - 5 JAN

28./XII.

Liebe Miss June!

Ich schreibe an Sie persönlich da ich gehört habe wie tüchtig Sie die Leitung des London Symphonie Orchester übernommen haben.
Über Ihre und Ihres Orchesters Grußbotschaft habe ich mich sehr gefreut, besonders darüber dass alle Mitglieder diese Glückwünsche selbst unterzeichnet haben!
Ich gebe diese Weihnachtswünsche von ganzem Herzen zurück und hoffe auf ein baldiges Wiedersehen.

In aufrichtiger Verbundenheit herzlich
Ihr Karl Böhm

Entschuldigen Sie meine schreckliche Fassung des Briefes aber ich muss schon morgen nach Milano (Scala) and my english is very limited

Dear Mrs. June,

I write to you personally as I have heard how capably you have taken over the management of the London Symphony Orchestra. I was delighted to receive yours, and the Orchestra's, greetings (Xmas), especially so as all the members have signed personally.

I return these greetings from the bottom of my heart, and I hope for a WIEDERSEHEN soon.

With honest attachment, heartily.

Yours
Karl Boehm

*Letter from Karl Boehm with the English Translation underneath*

Andre Previn's concert included Prokofiev's Fifth Symphony and celebrated pianist Claudio Arrau played Beethoven's Third Piano Concerto. Leonard Bernstein also conducted a programme of Shostakovich's Largo from Symphony No.5, Sibelius Fifth Symphony, a Mozart piano concerto played and directed by himself, and one of his own compositions with choir, *Chichester Psalms*, specially commissioned in 1965 by the Chichester Festival.

The fact it was the only London orchestra at the time ever to have been invited to the Festival, with return visits firmly in the diary, rather went to the heads of the players, who believed this proved beyond doubt that in London they were *primus inter pares* (first among equals) which put them on the same level as the self-governing Berlin and Vienna orchestras. With this in mind, an approach was made to both orchestras with a proposal that the three might form some sort of association. It was never apparent, at least to myself, that the two European orchestras viewed things the same way but were friendly enough and for a while showed a courteous interest. Insofar as I can remember it went no further than a few social meetings over several glasses of beer.

## Rehearsal Venues

Finding suitable rehearsal venues was always a challenge, especially as all the four major London orchestras needed to find somewhere to rehearse prior to giving concerts in the Royal Festival Hall, where it was only possible to have a general rehearsal on the day of the concert. We regularly used Friends Meeting House, Baden-Powell House, Bishopsgate Institute and various London churches.

The Chairmen of the London Symphony and London Philharmonic Trusts worked tirelessly together to find a suitable venue with amenities which both orchestras could share. Mary Morris, Harold Lawrence's wife, a celebrated American international photo-journalist, spent a great deal of time researching deconsecrated churches in London and finally came across a neglected one in Trinity Square, close to Borough market in Southwark. The Georgian church had been built in 1824 and was badly damaged during the second world war.

A vigorous fund-raising exercise ensued and when finally sufficient funds were accumulated, work began in October 1973 on a major project to restore the church and convert it into a rehearsal and recording space. However, the previous night the building had been completed gutted by fire and a month later the contractors started the long job of almost total reconstruction. While underpinning the foundations, they were to make a grim discovery of over 500 coffins which were in a state of more or less advanced decomposition. Experts were called into deal with the situation and this macabre episode added £30,000 to the total bill.

A large, impressive library was constructed to house all the music scores of both orchestras and a vast storage space was created for large instruments and travelling cases. The original crypt was transformed into dressing rooms, recording studio and canteen/restaurant. A very fine office was also provided for the first Manager to be appointed, Terry Palmer, the LSO's former Personnel Manager.

Both orchestras scheduled most of their rehearsals in the hall and there remained sufficient space to allow other orchestras and recording companies to use it, which provided additional income towards the hall's running costs.

In 1975, the newly restored Henry Wood Hall was open for business, with an inaugural concert in the beautiful rehearsal and concert hall.

# Touring

Audience dress for concerts during this period was usually formal, when the men wore suits and ties and the ladies long evening or cocktail dresses. I attached importance as to how I should dress, both for business meetings and evening concerts, always making an effort not to wear the same clothes I may have worn on a previous occasion.

Through the generosity of one of the Orchestra's Trustees, Jack Maxwell, Managing Director of Richards Shops, I possessed a different long evening dress for every concert, in fact, too many to fit into my suitcase.

The solution, when touring, was to persuade the Orchestra's double bass players to agree for me to hang some of them in their instrument travel cases! As there were eight cases I had to remember in whose case I had put which dress!

The Orchestra received regular invitations to tour the United States and occasionally to take part in major European Festivals.

Stephen Wright, who was at the time Managing Director of Artists Agency Harold Shaw, approached me with an invitation from Madrid based impresario Alfonso Aijón, for the LSO to appear at the Granada Festival, which was to take place during the summer when temperatures were at their highest. As the concerts were to be performed in the open air, general rehearsals were scheduled early in the morning and the performances late in the evening, when the air would be cooler, which gave the musicians plenty of time to eat a leisurely lunch and to take a rest.

However, this had a soporific effect on some of the musicians.

Scaffolding had been erected with high platforms on which the Orchestra were seated. The brass section happened to be positioned at the highest level, with the trombones seated at the end of a line with the bass trombonist the furthest away.

With no guard rail and a sheer drop to the ground it was a dangerous position to be in. The symphony did not require the trombones to play until the final movement and watching from the audience I was nervously aware of the bass trombonist nodding off and became even more concerned when he appeared to be leaning towards the edge.

He must have been on auto pilot as amazingly he woke up just at the moment he was expected to play. Breathing a sigh of relief, I was able to relax and enjoy the rest of the performance.

# USA

The LSO's first tour to the USA took place in 1912. Due to a last-minute change, the musicians and instruments travelled on a White Star Line ship called Baltic, the original booking had been made on the Titanic. During subsequent years the Orchestra made many trips to the US, the thirteenth took place in 1975.

On several occasions, I had to endure unwelcome comments and advances, both in the office and on tour, especially on long tours to the US, which sometimes lasted three to four weeks. Trying to organise more than 90 chauvinistic musicians was no mean task.

During a tour of the US West Coast a concert was arranged in Tempe, Arizona. With temperatures around 100 degrees Fahrenheit, most of the musicians wanted to spend any free time around the pool. If I had information to impart it was therefore necessary to deliver it at the poolside. One particularly difficult musician, who one morning happened to be standing at the edge, sarcastically challenged me over some simple issue and I was sorely tempted to push him in.

I recall one occasion when, during an LSO tour of the West Coast of the United States, a newspaper journalist approached me for an interview, having discovered that I was possibly, at the time, the only known female international orchestra manager in the world. A bizarre, televised interview also took place in Aims, Iowa, sandwiched in-between items about the prices of wheat and cattle! While waiting to be interviewed, I found myself in the company of the local farmers, who must have found it strange to see me there.

Andre Previn usually conducted every concert, but there was one occasion when he cancelled at short notice. Fortunately Lukas Foss happened to be available and stepped in to replace him. Korean violinist Kyung Wha Chung had been engaged as the soloist in performances of Walton's Violin Concerto, which she had performed and recorded with Andre and the Orchestra, and was not at all happy with the prospect of performing the work with a different conductor.

Some concerts took place in the Hollywood Bowl in Los Angeles, the LSO being the first British orchestra ever to have performed there. It was quite an experience to be present at an open air concert in such a vast arena, with sound systems installed at critical points. Walking around during a rehearsal, I was able to gain an impression as to just how large it was and to gauge the distance between the audience and musicians, who seemed so far away. In spite of its size and being outdoors, the acoustics were remarkably good.

Coincidentally, many years later, I was actually approached by an American firm of headhunters, to be considered for the position of Managing Director of the Los Angeles Philharmonic Orchestra and the Hollywood Bowl.

In my teens I accumulated a large collection of jazz recordings, several with Andre Previn playing piano. At the time, I had no idea he was also an accomplished classical musician. Los Angeles was familiar territory from the days when he was engaged by the major film studios to compose and arrange scores and, on a free morning, he invited me to accompany him to a local market, where we came across a stall which sold jazz LPs. Sorting through the racks, he found an LP featuring jazz guitarist Barney Kessel playing arrangements of Bizet's opera *Carmen*. Andre proudly boasted that he was also featured on the disc and since I did not have the recording in my collection, offered to buy it for me.

One evening, Andre and I were in a hotel bar, having a drink with a few of the LSO musicians. In those days, I was a social smoker and Andre took two cigarettes from a packet and put them into his mouth, lit both, then handed one to me. I did not realise the significance at the time and took it willingly, but noticed knowing glances from one or two musicians.

I made an excuse to go to my room, which Andre mistakenly took as a cue and moved to the lift with me. I was so grateful the Orchestra's Deputy Chairman, Paul Katz, also got in with us. As I got out at my floor, Andre gave me a quizzical look, but stayed in the lift with Paul. Shortly afterwards the telephone rang in my room and it was Andre suggesting, 'perhaps another time'. I did not respond, and put down the phone, determined to be on my guard and avoid getting into any similar awkward situations in future.

During the third week of a long East Coast and Mid-West US tour, a concert was scheduled in the Detroit concert hall. The town was notorious for the amount of crime and for this reason the concert was scheduled on a Sunday afternoon, during daylight hours. As the tour bus approached the town, we were met by police mounted on motorcycles and escorted off the freeway.

There was also a constant police presence around the hall during the pre-concert general rehearsal. The fact that it was also a Sunday meant that many shops and eating houses were closed and this presented an enormous potential problem. Denis the CAMI Tour manager and I knew just how hungry and demanding the musicians would be. We searched the theatre but found the only items available were packets of potato chips and chocolate bars in a vending machine. Denis, whose task it was to find a solution, came to the rescue and decided to speak to one of the policemen, who directed him to a nearby hamburger and pizza kiosk.

With perfect timing, just as the rehearsal was ending, he returned accompanied by the policeman, both with armfuls of pizzas, burgers and cokes. They almost disappeared when, spotting the food, the hungry musicians descended upon them like vultures. How we ever managed to feed such a large number is still a mystery and reminds me of the parable of the five loaves and two fish!

## Hong Kong

An invitation was received from the Hong Kong Festival for the Orchestra and Andre Previn to give four concerts. With only a few days to go before the start of the tour, I received news that Andre had to cancel because he had contracted measles, which to me seemed odd as I had always assumed it was a child's disease.

Such short notice gave me the difficult task of having to find a suitable and acceptable replacement. Instead, it was agreed to invite two experienced international conductors, Bernhard Klee and Erich Bergel, neither of whom had previously worked with the Orchestra, and each was to conduct two repeat performances.

The musicians and instruments travelled on a British Airways charter flight. As one of the Orchestra's sponsors, a complimentary bar was provided. Another sponsor, J&B Whisky, also arranged for several crates of their best malt to be loaded on board for the long journey. Most of the musicians took advantage and it was not long before empty miniature bottles could be seen rolling from under the seats into the aisles, accompanied by loud snoring. By the time we arrived in Hong Kong, several musicians were so drunk they needed to be escorted off the plane.

During the tour, musicians in the brass section took it in turns to chat me up and at the following day's rehearsal had reluctantly to give thumbs down signals to their colleagues, to indicate they had no success.

Although disappointed, the orchestral musicians put their heads down and soon found a rapport with both conductors. I also did my best to make them feel comfortable and we soon became friends. Bernhard, who was married to Swiss soprano Edith Mathis, and I got on particularly well. Whenever he came to London to guest conduct other orchestras, we might meet and sometimes have a meal together. He very kindly gave me two paintings by Karl Korab, his favourite contemporary Swiss artist.

Following a lively performance of Beethoven's Seventh Symphony,

Erich Bergel invited me to join him for supper and we subsequently ended the evening in his hotel room, where he extolled the works of JS Bach, in particular *The Art of Fugue* and his last Cantatas. Erich's version of Die *Kunst der Fugue* is the result of his lifelong association with JS Bach's music. Indeed, when he was imprisoned by the communist government of Romania for conducting religious works, he survived in no small part by studying that particular work. He endeavoured to explain to me his theory of the mathematical basis on which they were composed, which I must admit I found difficult to follow but did my best to show interest and understanding.

The next day he asked if I would accompany him while he did some shopping and when we arrived at a jewellers, he offered to buy me a pearl necklace as a parting thank-you gift which made me realise he had misinterpreted my friendliness. Not wishing to hurt his feelings by refusing, I accepted but felt very uncomfortable as I was still married at the time. Some weeks later back in the UK, I received a call from his agent, informing me that Erich had asked him to let me know he was very much hoping to meet me again, I explained that it would not be possible and never heard from him again.

## Iceland

World famous pianist, Vladimir Ashkenazy, performed regularly with the LSO and Andre Previn both in concert and recording, and lived in Reykjavik with his Icelandic wife. Every year he organised an annual Music Festival in Reykjavik, to which he invited the Orchestra.

A charter flight was organised to take the Orchestra musicians and their instruments and we were met at the airport by Jasper Parrott, the UK Manager of both Vladimir and Andre. He could not wait to inform everyone that he had that very morning married pianist Cristina Ortiz.

Although the Festival took place during the month of June, the sky was overcast and there was constant drizzle. The concerts were arranged in a converted aircraft hangar with the audience seated outside on benches; almost everyone was dressed in a raincoat and carried an umbrella.

The performance began with an overture and was followed by a piano concerto with Vladimir as soloist. In the second movement his wedding ring suddenly flew off his finger and rolled under the piano. However, unperturbed, he continued playing and we had to wait until the interval before being able to scramble on hands and knees around the stage floor trying to find it.

The following morning happened to be free, so the ornithological members of the Orchestra, suitably attired for the inclement weather and clutching their binoculars, set off to bird-watch. Others, including myself, were given a tour of the vast underground central heating system powered by hot water from geysers. In addition to heating the roads and pavements, the geothermal energy also heats a large percentage of homes and outdoor swimming pools in and around Reykjavik. The mineral filled water is said to have healing effects.

We actually experienced two minor earthquakes while we were there. Apparently an average of 500 earthquakes occur in Iceland every week, most are undetected as they fall below M2 on the Richter scale. We were informed the reason is that Iceland is located on top of the Atlantic ridge. As the Eurasian and North American plates drift in opposite directions, Iceland is literally being torn apart, causing constant seismic activity.

# Gennadi Rozhdestvensky

The celebrated Russian violinist, David Oistrakh, had been engaged to play and conduct the Orchestra at the Royal Festival Hall, which was expected to be a major event in the London concert calendar, with every seat sold. Unfortunately, he died just before and we had to decide, quickly, how to proceed.

It was thought appropriate to invite Oistrakh's friend and colleague Gennadi Rozhdestvensky, a firm favourite of the musicians of the LSO, to conduct both concerts, as a tribute.

It was not an easy task, as I had first to enter into serious negotiations with the notoriously difficult Russian Agency Goskonzert. London Impresario, Victor Hochauser, who had experience and strong connections with Russian artistic life, agreed to act as intermediary, so a formal invitation was sent.

Following an agonising wait, a reply was received stating Rozhdestvensky would not be available. However, I happened to find out that at the time Gennadi was conducting in Washington, so it was possible for me to contact him personally and make him aware of the situation. He confirmed that, insofar as he was concerned, he had no other engagements planned and could be available and urged me to contact Goskonzert once again.

Rather than face another rebuff, I decided we might have more chance of success if an invitation could be sent from someone important in government and contacted Edward Heath, who was happy to help. It did the trick and Gennadi was given permission to come to London.

I met him at the airport and we drove directly to his first rehearsal at the Friends Meeting House. Tchaikovsky's Sixth Symphony was the major work to be rehearsed and when we arrived the Orchestra members were already assembled, tuning their instruments. I listened from the back of the hall, absolutely spell-bound. All he had to do was to raise an eyebrow, or twitch his nose, to get amazing results from the eager and attentive musicians.

The evening of the first concert there were long queues outside the Royal Festival Hall. Gennadi had earlier requested a television to be installed in his dressing room, so that he could watch a football match. From his fee, he purchased a television, washing machine and vacuum cleaner as those items were expensive or difficult to find in Russia.

Many years later, I was very pleased to have an opportunity to invite him to conduct the Chamber Orchestra of Europe in Bremen and the Barbican Hall in London.

# Leonard Bernstein

Leonard Bernstein's long association with the London Symphony Orchestra began in 1966 and lasted until 1990. Many notable performances were given with him, in addition to a number of recordings. In particular, his interpretations of Mahler symphonies were critically acclaimed, worldwide. In September 1973, he conducted the Second Symphony at the Edinburgh Festival with soloists Janet Baker and Sheila Armstrong, the Edinburgh Festival and London Symphony Choirs.

The day following the Edinburgh performances, the entire company transferred to Ely Cathedral for a CBS video recording of the work. Hugh Bean, who was guest leading the Orchestra for the project, lived in Beckenham, very close to my own home in Bromley and I offered to drive him to Ely. With the sky not yet light and a chill in the air, we left very early in the morning on the day of the recording and arrived a couple of hours later to see the Cathedral shrouded in a grey swirling morning mist.

Listening to Mahler's spiritual music in such a beautiful mystical setting, with trumpets positioned high up in the balconies and the two soloists' voices soaring above the Orchestra, gave me goose bumps. An invited audience attended the evening's live recording followed by re-takes and were requested to be as quiet as possible and to avoid coughing, as the acoustics were very lively and the slightest sound would have been picked up by the microphones.

Bernstein conducted concerts with the LSO during the Salzburg Festival, again, in 1975. He also developed a special relationship with the Vienna Philharmonic.

The Chamber Orchestra of Europe happened to be appearing at the Festival some years later, during the same period his recording company, CBS, placed publicity hoardings, no more than 50 feet apart, at practically every approach and intersection to the city.They said,'Leonard Bernstein, Wir Wilkommen Sie bei den Salzburger Festspielen.' Herbert von Karajan's musical rival and a firm favourite of the Vienna Philharmonic Orchestra, had come to town!

# Carlos Kleiber

In June 1974 the eccentric and reclusive conductor, Carlos Kleiber, was persuaded by the Royal Opera House to come to London to conduct Richard Strauss' opera *Der Rosenkavalier*. One of the legendary conductors of his time, famous for his infrequent but supreme interpretations, he had an unusually small repertoire for a major conductor, focusing on only a few symphonies, concertos and operas, demanding unusually long rehearsals. Believing this to be a rare opportunity not to be missed, the LSO directors requested me to make an approach for him to work with the Orchestra.

I managed to secure a ticket for a performance and invited Carlos to supper afterwards. He proposed I should meet him, after the performance, back-stage in his dressing room. Upon entering, I was confronted by a room full of sweaty wet shirts and underwear which had been draped or carelessly thrown over the table and chairs. Finding a vacant seat was therefore difficult, so I stood in a quiet corner waiting while he received his many admirers.

After everyone had left, it took quite a while for him to come down to earth, get organised and to pack his belongings, scores and batons. By the time he was ready to leave, it was already very late and I concluded the restaurant would most probably have closed.

Carlos suggested we should, instead, go back to the Savoy Hotel, where he was staying, and order room service. Looking around the room I was intrigued to notice on the coffee table and floor several CDs of recordings made by his father, the eminent conductor Erich Kleiber, whom he admired and tried to be almost as good as, or better. It was no secret that his father had an overpowering influence over him.

Steering the conversation towards the possibility he might conduct the LSO was particularly difficult, since he kept avoiding the subject. However, just before I left the hotel, he did promise at least to give it some thought. It was the early hours when I wearily drove home, not sure whether I had managed to achieve anything, but thinking it had after all been a fascinating and worthwhile experience.

I met him on many different occasions, sometimes when he attended Chamber Orchestra of Europe performances in Salzburg or Munich, where he lived. Each time, he would express his admiration for the Orchestra but never showed any interest to conduct. He attended the COE concert, in Munich, in 1983 and Claudio Abbado suggested to him, afterwards, that maybe it was time he should seriously think about doing so. His strange reply was, 'I do not know enough suitable chamber orchestra repertoire!'

He also said I should be in touch with him by post card, as he would not open letters. I complied with this request several times but always the reply was the same, 'in any case I agree only to conduct occasionally the symphony orchestras who can pay high enough fees and when I need money to support my family'.

As Carlos was also a fellow Cancerian, I usually sent him a birthday card, in the hope it would help to change his mind.

I once tried calling him on the telephone and a voice, which I recognised as his, answered 'the Maestro has gone shopping!'

Another meeting took place when he came to Salzburg to attend one of the COE's concerts, conducted by Nikolaus Harnoncourt. As an ardent admirer of Herbert von Karajan, it was a city he often frequented and while there would visit his hero's grave.

Some years later, I was in Berlin with the Chamber Orchestra of Europe and attended a Berlin Philharmonic Orchestra benefit concert which he conducted. There was a security alert beforehand and police arrived with dogs to search the hall but nothing was found and the performance went ahead. After the concert I went backstage to his dressing room to congratulate him. He made a bewildering comment to me, 'there was nothing chamber-like about that performance'.

In the queue of people waiting for an autograph was an elderly gentleman holding an LP, which he presented to Carlos to sign. It was one of his father's recordings and the fan was eager to explain he had been an admirer. Carlos looked surprised but was very gracious, smiled, chatted with the man for a while, and eventually obliged.

Unfortunately, he never conducted either the LSO or COE, and very rarely ventured from his home. His only few appearances and recordings were with the Vienna or Berlin Philharmonic Orchestras, and then no doubt because he needed the money!

# Sir Edward Heath

Edward Heath and I had four things in common, both were born under the sign of Cancer, had working class parents, received a grammar school education, and above all shared a love of music, which led to our paths crossing on many occasions.

Having won an organ scholarship to Balliol College, Oxford, he was generally recognised as an accomplished musician, but his ability as a conductor was somewhat dubious. Nevertheless, the London Symphony Orchestra Board decided to invite him to become an Honorary Member of the Orchestra, and to conduct Elgar's Cockaigne Overture at a Trust Fund concert in 1970. Another opportunity was given to him on June 9 1974, when the Orchestra celebrated its 70th anniversary with a Gala Concert at the Royal Festival Hall and he conducted the overture to Wagner's opera *die Meistersinger von Nuremberg.*

He had become Leader of the Conservative Party in 1965 and led his Party to victory in the 1970 General Election. In recognition of his having successfully negotiated the UK's entry into the European Common Market in 1973, Johannes Wasmuth, Director of the Bahnhof Rolandseck, invited him, together with Andre Previn, to perform two Gala Concerts with the LSO in Bonn and Cologne in April 1975.

*In discussion with Edward Heath during the LSO rehearsal in Bonn 1975*

Unfortunately, during his premiership, the country experienced economic decline, rising unemployment and strong unions flexing their muscles with strikes.

Heath legislated for a three day week, which proved so unpopular that he was eventually forced to dissolve Parliament and call a General Election, which took place in February, 1974. However, it resulted in a hung parliament, the Conservatives winning but without an overall majority and Heath, unable to form a coalition government, afforded Harold Wilson, Leader of the Opposition, a brief opportunity to become Prime Minister without a majority.

A second General Election was called later in October that year, which was narrowly won by Wilson's Labour party with a majority of only three.

Both humiliating defeats prompted the Conservatives to call for a vote of no confidence in Heath's leadership and for new elections to be held in February 1975 for Leader of the Party.

However, in view of the continuing high regard for him across Europe, it was nonetheless agreed to go ahead with the concerts in Germany.

Andre and I were invited by Mr. Heath to his office in the Palace of Westminster to discuss programmes. When we realised the meeting had been arranged for the week in which voting was due to take place to elect the Leader of the Conservative Party, we assumed it would be postponed. However, it went ahead as planned and Mr. Heath showed no signs of being concerned.

During the meeting Andre urged Mr. Heath to consider conducting the *Meistersinger* Overture again but he had other more ambitious ideas, his preference being to perform a work with a different tempo 'perhaps something in waltz time by Franz Schubert.'

No matter how hard we tried to dissuade him, he remained stubborn but, undeterred, Andre suggested that it might be best if he took some more time before finally deciding. Mr. Heath considered this for a moment, then requested me to call his office in a couple of days for his answer. I ventured to suggest that, since the leadership elections were imminent, it might have been better to wait until after the result had been declared. He replied with such confidence, 'no, no, it is just a formality.'

Sadly for him, he was not re-elected and when, as requested, I called his office, a voice answered, 'Mrs. Thatcher's office, can I help you?'

My immediate concern was how next to approach Mr. Heath and where I should contact him, since he appeared to have gone to ground. After several telephone calls, I managed to locate his secretary and eventually received an invitation to visit Mr. Heath at his West London Home, in Wilton Street. The meeting took place in his comfortable studio with its impressive library, many valuable paintings and his pride and joy, a beautiful grand piano. He seemed upset but good natured and finally, with an air of defeatism, agreed to conduct Edward Elgar's *Cockaigne* overture.

The following spring, the LSO arrived in Bonn for the first concert. In the late afternoon Mr. Heath took a general rehearsal in the concert hall and requested me to move around the auditorium to test the acoustic and balance.

The evening concert began with the overture which delighted the audience consisting, mainly, of European politicians, diplomats and other dignitaries. The Orchestra members were not actually following Heath's beat, instead relying on their leader, John Brown, to stay together.

Andre conducted the rest of the programme of works by Berlioz, Mozart and Prokofiev.

At the end of the concert, both conductors were presented with bouquets. As usual, Andre first gave individual stems to members of the Orchestra before tossing the rest into the audience.

Mr. Heath, who had been carefully observing this, tried to copy but his efforts were clumsy. Embarrassingly, he only managed to shed a few flowers and was left holding a small sheaf, not knowing what to do next. Looking perplexed, he awkwardly left the stage, still clutching the remaining flowers.

Afterwards, I went to his dressing room to offer my congratulations and, as I entered the room, tried to avert my eyes when confronted by a shirtless Mr. Heath, exposing a very pink upper torso. He asked me what he should do with the sad-looking bunch of flowers on the table. With tongue-in-cheek, half expecting him to give them to me, I suggested that, since he was staying at the British Embassy, he might give them to the Ambassador's wife. I next saw them being put into the boot of the Ambassador's car destined for the Embassy!

Johannes invited me to spend a long weekend at the Bahnhof Rolandseck, where he lived with his housekeeper. Construction of the Neo-Classical station building began in 1856. Completion followed in 1858 and it became the meeting place for bourgeois society, who liked to spend time and hold celebrations there.

Up until the Second World War, numerous personalities from society, politics and culture visited the station. Among the early visitors was Queen Victoria of England. Until the mid-1950s the station was largely forgotten. The once-so-magnificent station building beside the Rhine became increasingly dilapidated and was finally threatened with demolition. Johannes, a Bonn-based gallerist, discovered it in 1964. He

*Bahnhof Rolandseck*

took over the abandoned and ramshackle building and began to realise his dream of a place dedicated to art, converted to become a retreat for musicians and sculptors. It was situated on the banks of one of the most beautiful and magical sectors of the Rhine, with its legend of the Lorelei, who enticed sailors into its depths.

It was there I first met his assistant and curator, Annette Wolde, who gave me a tour of the gallery and showed me around an exhibition of contemporary sculptures. We were destined to come into regular contact several years later when she managed the Junge Deutsche Philharmonie Orchestra, in Frankfurt, and moved on to become responsible for the planning and organisation of concerts at the Cologne Concert Hall.

In November 1976, Mr Heath was due to launch his book 'Music, A Joy for Life'. Having some experience of performing in public with the LSO and with advice from his friends, including the Guardian's music critic Edward Greenfield, he needed little encouragement to write about his love of music.

He had also become friendly with the conductor Herbert von Karajan who, like him, was a keen sailor and Mr. Heath presented him with a copy of his earlier book on sailing.

They occasionally sailed together on Heath's boat Morning Cloud, when von Karajan would sometimes pass on some useful conducting tips, some of which, together with diagrams, Mr. Heath included in his new book.

The launch took place in the Great Room of Grosvenor House, in London, and, with a small group of LSO musicians, he conducted a performance of Wagner's *Siegfried Idyll*, which was followed by dinner and a book signing session.

We were often in contact. I enlisted his help with a difficult situation, when trying to persuade the Russian authorities to give permission for Gennadi Rhozdestvensy to come to London, at short notice, to conduct the LSO, in a memorial concert for his compatriot, the violinist David Oistrakh.

We also met in Aberdeen, during the International Festival of Youth Orchestras, and while I was working as General Manager and then Consultant for the European Community Youth Orchestra, of which he was President.

I later faced an embarrassing situation with the Mobil Oil Company and again sought his intervention.

Years later, when the Chamber Orchestra of Europe were performing at the Salzburg Festival, Mr. Heath was a visiting dignitary. We were both invited to a reception and making small talk, when he suddenly remarked upon the fact that he had never been invited to conduct the Orchestra. Fortunately, he did not ask the reason why, so I just smiled sweetly and quickly changed the subject!

Being asked whether or not I liked him is a question I found difficult to answer.

He was always friendly, very helpful, had a sense of humour, but appeared awkward and shy. He obviously felt comfortable in a musical environment, maybe a welcome release from the stress of political life. I got the impression he was a very private man and not someone it was easy to get to know well. People born under the sign of Cancer are said to have a hard outer shell but a soft inside!

# Andre Previn and Politics

Politics played an important part in the life of the self-governing LSO. There were several musicians represented on the Board of elected Directors, who resented Andre Previn and his style of music making, despite his being extremely popular with the concert-going public and enabling each musician to earn high fees from numerous recordings, television and concert invitations.

Many believed he was not the right person to conduct classical repertoire, considered the core foundation of any world class symphony orchestra.

Plots, mostly unsuccessful, were hatched to remove him.

The obvious candidates to replace him were Claudio Abbado or Colin Davis.

Colin had for many years hankered after the Principal job but only achieved his ambition many years later.

He did not have a major international career, having spent most of his time in the UK, at Sadler's Wells Opera and later as Music Director of the Royal Opera Covent Garden. The situation changed significantly after he developed successful relationships with the Boston Symphony, Concertgebouw and Dresden Orchestras.

Claudio, on the other hand, was already making a name for himself internationally and was invited to conduct concerts with the LSO during their first visit to the Salzburg Festival.

He also had a large following among the LSO musicians, who believed him to be the heir apparent.

Obviously aware of what was happening, Andre always appeared to be one jump ahead.

In Gramophone magazine James Jolly wrote:-

*'Abbado was in many ways the antithesis of Previn in terms of style and repertoire, bringing to the Orchestra a particular authority in the Austro-German classics as well as a commitment to the avant-garde.*

*From the Orchestra's point of view there were disadvantages to his appointment.*

*His relationship with the players was distant and he was unable to impose discipline on the Orchestra in rehearsals. He insisted on conducting without a score, and many times this led to barely avoided disaster in concerts.*

*Abbado had considerable international prestige, but this too had its downside for the LSO: he frequently made his major recordings with the Boston or Chicago Symphony Orchestras or the Vienna Philharmonic.'*

The Orchestra's Deputy Chairman, Paul Katz, and I flew to Salzburg with a framed collage of photos of the Orchestra members which had been taken with Karl Boehm and signed by each musician. The intention was to convey their admiration and to offer him the position of Principal Conductor. Although flattered to be asked, he declined, mainly on the grounds of age. He later became Honorary President.

Other possible successors were considered, one of whom was German conductor Eugen Jochum, who had become, by default, one of a few surviving revered conductors of the old school.

During the LSO's second visit to the Salzburg Festival in the summer of 1975, I was invited to lunch at the Jochum home in Bavaria. This was arranged by Robert Leslie, who was in charge of Public Relations for Deutsche Grammophon and acted as Jochum's Personal Manager.

On an Orchestra free day we hired a car and drove together with Guardian music critic Edward Greenfield. It was a beautiful hot sultry summer's day and spirits were high.

The house was situated next to a large lake and after lunch it was proposed we should all go for a swim. Unfortunately I did not possess a costume and Mrs. Jochum, who was several sizes larger than myself, offered to lend one of her own hand-knitted ones. Not wishing to offend, I reluctantly accepted, only to find, because it was too big, as soon as I got into the lake it began to fill with water making swimming very difficult. Confused and embarrassed, I struggled to keep it on when emerging from the water, conscious of being observed by my companions, who thought it all very amusing.

Maestro Jochum came to London to conduct and record Haydn *London* Symphonies, but the relationship did not progress beyond a couple of years.

Meanwhile, the plotting to remove Andre continued in the background. The chauvinist attitude endured and, although I was given the responsibility, it was always the Board's intention to have a male General Manager/ Managing Director, who would be someone with the right credentials to bring about Andre Previn's removal.

After first trying unsuccessfully with a triumvirate (including Ivan Sutton, ex-director of the City of London Festival, Stephen Reiss, ex-Managing Director of the Aldeburgh Festival and an expert on the Dutch painter Kypp, and me), John Boyden, a record producer who had made a success of the budget label Classics for Pleasure for EMI, was hired as Managing Director. Although he had no experience of managing a symphony orchestra, he made his views known that he had little respect for Andre Previn, so seemed a likely candidate to carry out the wishes of those who were keen to see his departure.

John relied heavily on my knowledge and experience and we managed to establish a good working relationship. He also brought with him, from Classics for Pleasure, a former colleague, Wilson Strutte, who was given the title of Public Relations and Press Secretary.

Until John's appointment, I had always accompanied the Orchestra on overseas tours, but it was decided he should make his touring debut on the forthcoming visit to Japan with Andre. It was also customary for an experienced music journalist to join the Orchestra on high profile foreign tours. Anna Motson, a freelancer, who was working for The Times newspaper, was invited but, unfortunately for John, he was not to know, until it was too late, she and Andre were friends.

At the time, plans were underway to move the LSO's offices from Museum Street, next to the British Museum, to a modern building in Argyll Street, opposite the London Palladium. With everyone away, I undertook the task of choosing furniture for my own and John's new offices. Jack Maxwell offered the services of one of his designers, to help with the decor, who was given artistic licence. One morning, I arrived to discover one of the walls in my office covered with beige hessian on to which had been secured sheafs of wheat and dried corn flowers. Although somewhat unusual and excessive, I quickly became accustomed to living with it.

The morning after the Orchestra's return from Japan, I went as usual to buy a newspaper at the railway station and spotted a headline in The Guardian, highlighting a scandal which had occurred during the LSO's tour. John, who was very naive and unused to the behaviour of musicians away from home, had been trapped into an interview with Anna Motson, while the plane was re-fuelling at Anchorage. All during the tour he had avoided being interviewed, but tired and jet-lagged, had let down his guard and moralised, criticising the musicians for what was in his opinion, their bad behaviour (heavy drinking and womanising).

Anna Motson, who we later suspected had conspired with Andre, wrote her article, but instead of giving it to The Times, had passed it to Tom Sutcliffe at The Guardian.

The LSO musicians felt betrayed and called an emergency meeting to discuss a course of action.

A full Orchestra meeting was later convened, ironically in the aptly named Waterloo Room of the Royal Festival Hall, and John was requested to attend. Realising the gravity of the situation, he asked if I would accompany him to Westminster Abbey, ahead of the meeting.

He obviously felt the need of some spiritual guidance as it was clear he had to pay a price, most likely his dismissal.

At the end of the meeting, after everyone else had departed, Anthony Camden, Principal Oboe, a supporter of Andre Previn, who had succeeded Principal Trumpet Howard Snell as the LSO Chairman, asked me to continue to hold the reins, until a new Managing Director could be appointed. I was given the title of Acting General Manager & Company Secretary, with assurances I would remain responsible for the day to day running of the Orchestra and any new MD would just be a figurehead, principally responsible for fund-raising.

That evening, David and I had reserved seats for a show at the Theatre Royal Drury Lane and, before the performance, decided to have a drink in the public house opposite, where to our surprise, we came across Andre Previn and Mia Farrow. Andre greeted me as though nothing had happened, but I was still upset from the events of the afternoon and, in an emotional outburst, accused him of conspiring to get John sacked and quickly urged a bemused David to leave.

The plotting continued amongst the various Orchestra factions. The Board of Directors arranged an 'away day' at the Selsdon Park Hotel, in Croydon, to discuss tactics. I took the minutes, which were strictly confidential to Board Members and me.

It was not long before the next MD was appointed, Michael Kaye, former Director of Peter Stuyvesant, the cigarette company and one of the LSO principal sponsors. Michael and I already knew one another, from when I worked at the London Opera Centre, several years before. In fact he and his wife, Kay, had attended my wedding and, for almost fifty years, I kept the green tray which they gave me as a present.

I had no confidence in Michael's ability to manage the LSO and felt resentment it had not been considered appropriate for me to be to be given the job. I could no longer tolerate the situation and decided to leave.

# Easier tempo for L.S.O. players

## By MICHAEL HICKLING

THE self-governing London Symphony Orchestra is now "running smoothly" after recent internal conflicts which originated in the players' dissatisfaction with arrangements during a recent tour of the Far East.

Mrs. June Hall. the orchestra's new acting general manager, yesterday promised the players an easier life when they go abroad. "We will try to make foreign tours easier with less travelling between concerts and fewer one-night stands," she said. Some players had blamed the managing director. Mr. John Boyden, for what they considered to be the disorganised badly scheduled tour of Japan and Korea. In an interview published when they returned to London Mr. Boyden accused some players of "beer-swilling irresponsibility."

### £5,000 LOSS

Mr Boyden was dismissed last week. Mrs Hall's appointment was announced last week and she will take over Mr. Boyden's duties.

At the ochestra's annual meeting on Friday, it was decided to leave the £12,000-a-year managing director's post vacant for the time being.

At the meeting it was revealed that the orchestra, which has an annual turnover of about £1 million made a loss last year of £5,000.

Mr. Howard Snell. chairman of the nine-man board which is elected by the other players, announced his reignation "for personal reasons." Mr Snell, the orchestra's first trumpet, led the unsuccessful attempt last August to terminate the contract of the principal conductor André Previn.

Mr. Jack Steadman. a former chairman. was re-elected to the board on Friday. He is strongly tipped to regain his old position.

### NOT DISCUSSED

He said yesterday: "Mr. Previn was not discussed at the meeting. His position is settled and is no longer a matter for discussion.

"The orchestra is now running exceedingly smoothly. The recent troubles are behind us and there are no lingering resentments."

---

*Article - Easier Tempo for LSO players*

# Woman made LSO chief

By Our Arts Reporter

Mrs June Hall, concert administrator of the London Symphony Orchestra, has been appointed acting general manager and company secretary. The appointment, announced yesterday in a press release headed "Business as usual", comes less than a week after the dismissal of Mr John Boyden, the orchestra's managing director.

Mr Boyden's dismissal followed remarks about members of the orchestra attributed to him in an article in *The Guardian*.

Mrs Hall, whose appointment is described as "for the time being", joined the LSO's management in May 1973, having previously worked in the administration of the Royal Opera House, Covent Garden, and the London Opera Centre.

Article - Woman made LSO Chief

In my new Office LSO Argyll Street

*Eugen Jochum*          *8 München 19 (Nymphenburg)*
                        *Brunhildenstraße 2*          18. 11.

Miss
June Hall
3, Burhill Grove
Barrow Point Lane
Pinner
Middle Sex

        Dear June,

                Your letter from Nov. 2. was a big surpri-
se für both of us, and we are very sorry , that You leave the
London Symphony! for us that will change the whole  athmosph ere
with the orchestra, what a pity!
                But we hope Your new position will make
You happy and so we wish You all the best for the future!
We hope that we shall meet again when we are in London next
time, You always know where to find us.
                With best wishes and greeXtings
                    sincerely Yours

*Letter from Eugen Jochum*

*Wiener Philharmoniker*
1010 Wien, Bösendorferstraße 12

Vienna, 12th November 1976

Mrs. June Hall
3 Burhill Grove
Barrow Point Lane
Pinner
Middlesex

Dear June,

Thank you for your letter of 2nd November. We will
be very sorry to loose "our man at the LSO", but of course
we do appreciate your decision.

On behalf of my colleagues and in my own name I would
like to send you our very best wishes for a good start
and successful career in your new position.

Kind personal regards,

Yours sincerely,

Prof. Paul Fürst

TELEFON: (0222) 65 65 25 – TELEGRAMME: PHILHARMONIKER WIEN

*Letter from the Vienna Philarmonic*

# The LSO on Previn

## Atticus
### ANTHONY HOLDEN

WHAT DOES the London Symphony Orchestra *really* think of its principal conductor, Andre Previn? Ill-informed rumours have abounded since August 1975, when an attempt to dethrone Previn by John Boyden, the orchestra's managing director, ended in Boyden's dismissal.

Now, at last, Atticus can provide an authentic answer. A document has come his way—and he is happy to afford Previn, who is unaware of its existence, this chance of perusing it. The document has hitherto been seen only by the ten members of the LSO's board (nine elected players and the new managing director, Michael Kaye). It formed a basis for discussion of Previn's future last month, just before he left to join his other orchestra in Pittsburgh, whence he will return in mid-March.

The author is, very fond of the word "situation," and various other abuses of the mother tongue, for which I must apologise. The document is, indeed, headed "Principal Conductor Situation." It reads on:

❛ The situation now begins to clarify itself in the following way:

**1. The Orchestra view** is that AP is over-worked and frequently ill-prepared, but they do not regard his removal as imperative. They appreciate his commercial value. Some members feel more strongly

than others about his continuing as Principal Conductor, but the general consensus is that the Board should try to reach a better contract situation. If this proves to be impossible, a parting of the ways would be accepted.

**2. The Board's view.** On the whole, that the Orchestra would prefer more distinguished musical leadership. On the other hand, they feel that AP has commercial advantages, but considter that any distinguished principal conductor would, in the long term, bring work possibilities. All directors agree that the present conductor situation must be revised, and some feel very strongly that AP's contract should be terminated.

**3. Management view.** AP has undoubted commercial attractions, both at the Box Office and in recording. His position with the Orchestra gives

Previn: Box Office draw

it additional publicity, which is almost certainly commercially beneficial, in that it makes the Orchestra newsworthy and interesting. However, artistic considerations must be the most important in the long term, and the management would contemplate a change with reasonable equanimity if it were really felt that AP's continuance was the major obstacle to achieving higher standards.

**4. The Recording Companies' view.** AP is assured of an interesting amount of recording work, at least in the short term. His appointment as Principal Conductor to the LSO has made him a recording star, and his TV work has also helped this situation. He has, therefore, benefited from his association with the Orchestra, but the LSO has also gained. If the association ended, it is reasonable to suppose that Previn's reputation would persist for at least a few years. The Orchestra would undoubtedly lose a certain amount of work which ❜ might pick up elsewhere.

Under the next section, the

Agents' View. Previn's European and American agents reveal that "AP would prefer to continue with the LSO, but there will be no problem for him to find alternative work in London, and the BBC would probably welcome him as Principal Conductor of their Orchestra. - AP wants to work with the LSO as long as possible, but is not interested in being 'kicked upstairs.'

"AP would like a new contract (for three or five years)...

A list of Points For Discussion follows, concluding: "The question finally is: do we want to stay with AP, and try and make it work better for the commercial benefits that it brings, with artistic improvements possibly lying in other directions, or, do we want to find an alternative course?

And their decision? Last month it was decided on the basis of this document, and quietly announced, that Andre Previn's contract, as principal conductor of the LSO was, being renewed for a further three years.

*Sunday Times Article on Andre Previn*

# 5  Marriage Breakdown

The timing of my departure also coincided with the breakdown of my marriage. David and I had been having problems for some time, which had begun while I was at the London Opera Centre. He worked long hours and often arrived home late, the worse for wear, having finished the day in a public house. His character seemed to change during the five years he was a member of the Murder Squad, attached to Brixton police station. He began to hold right wing bigoted views and refused to discuss his work. We found ourselves with little in common, there was a lack of trust and he was suspicious when I was working late. Like his father, he also had a bad temper.

Claudio Abbado and the La Scala, Milan Opera Company had been invited by the Royal Opera House, to give guest opera performances at Covent Garden. They were also to give a concert performance of Verdi's *Requiem* to which I was invited. After the concert, Gabriella Abbado organised a party at their Kensington home for some of the principal singers, including soprano Mirella Freni, Ruggiero Raimondi, myself and other friends.

By the time I left it was very late, but I had my car in town and eventually arrived home at around 2 a.m. to find a furious David waiting on the doorstep.

Our driveway was on a slope and just as I was trying to engage the handbrake, he opened the car door and attempted to drag me out. The car began to slip backwards, but somehow I managed to stop it. Uttering expletives and accusations of 'unacceptable behaviour', David pulled me out of the car and pushed me into the house. I lost my balance and fell to the floor.

The next day, I was due to attend Edward Heath's book launch at the Grosvenor House Hotel. My friend and colleague Wilson Strutte, had agreed to act as my escort. For the occasion, I purchased a new dress and because it had a very low neckline, decided to buy a gold necklace with a long chain. When David saw it he jealously demanded to know who had bought it for me and was not prepared to accept my explanation. Unfortunately, the dress also had short sleeves which did not completely conceal the bruises which appeared on my arm overnight. Wilson happened to notice them and became concerned.

Soon afterwards, I departed with the LSO for a major tour of the United States. Still emotionally upset, I found being several miles away helped to take my mind off my problems. Later, I discovered that, during my absence, David had attended a Port of London Police social event and, to the surprise of many of his ex-colleagues, he was with another woman!

The periods working away from home with many overseas tours, out of town and London concerts, all contributed towards the breakdown and I decided to leave. Meanwhile, My career was also taking a new direction, as I had been appointed General Manager of the recently formed European Community Youth Orchestra. Taking only a few personal items and my piano, I moved into a co-ownership ground floor apartment in Pinner, North London, where I stayed for a year.

John Boyden and I kept in touch. He was also unhappy in his marriage and still felt sore at the manner in which he had been dismissed. He harboured a grudge and a wish for revenge. To my lasting regret, during a visit to my Pinner home, I foolishly showed him a copy of the confidential minutes of the LSO 'away-day' meeting. A few weeks later, I was horrified and dismayed when The Sunday Times exposed the plotting which had taken place. There was naturally suspicion and speculation as to who had disclosed the information to the Press and I was a suspected culprit!

My biggest regret had been to leave my dog behind. She had been a loyal companion for almost ten years. We had only been married for a few months when one day David brought her to my office at the London Opera Centre, having found her in the police station, where she had been handed in as a stray. She was a mongrel terrier cross, about nine months old, a little lean with one floppy ear which had yet to stand up to balance the other. We named her Kilo because she had been found in K division. She gave us much pleasure and we enjoyed many adventures together chasing squirrels in Greenwich and Knole Parks or climbing hills in North Wales.

We helped to deliver her four puppies, two sets of twins, suspecting they had been sired by two different male dogs, which used to hang around the house when she was in season, a beagle called Bart, and Moggery a short legged long haired dachshund cross. We kept one of the beagle puppies, which we called Gram.

Our house backed onto the grounds of Bromley Court, a large hotel, and Kilo sometimes took off to chase a squirrel or fox. One day Gram, by then about nine months old, decided to follow her but ran in the wrong direction and was sadly knocked down by a car. The driver came to the house holding Gram's collar and clearly upset, told me what had happened. As David was away, at the time, on a Police Training course at Hendon, he kindly offered to bring Gram to the house. Kilo arrived home soon afterwards, saw Gram lying there, sniffed his bottom and just walked away.

Unable to hold back the tears, I carefully wrapped Gram in a blanket and gently laid him on the floor of the garage. Deciding I could not stay alone in the house, I put Kilo in the back of my car and drove across London to spend the night with my mother.

David arrived home at the weekend and had the unenviable task of digging a hole at the top of our garden. In drizzling rain and within the full view of our neighbours who were watching from their upstairs windows, with due ceremony, we buried our little Gram.

From time-to-time, David visited me in Pinner and brought Kilo with him. Late one evening, I received a phone call from him to tell me she had gone missing for several hours. She had eventually been found in a very sorry state at a local police station and, believing she might be dying, David had taken her home.

Although late and dark outside, unhesitatingly, I decided to make the long diagonal drive across London to Bromley, in Kent, to see for myself. However, much to my amazement, as soon as I entered the house, an excited dog rushed to greet me and danced around my feet. She had only been suffering from exhaustion and, hearing me arrive, had perked up. David tugged at my heart strings, by suggesting she might have been roaming the streets searching for me!

I resolved never to be parted from my dog again and agreed, unconditionally, to return home. Unfortunately, our marriage never really improved after that, in fact steadily worsened and I persuaded myself to stay only for so long as my dog was alive.

# 6  European Community Youth Orchestra (1977)

The ECYO which later changed its name to European Union Youth Orchestra, was the brainchild of Lionel and his wife Joy Bryer, and had evolved from the International Festival of Youth Orchestras which they had set up in collaboration with Lady June Haddo of Haddo House in Aberdeen. Presidents and Prime Ministers of all member European States were invited to be patrons, which included Edward Heath, who became the Orchestra's President.

The Chairman Lionel Bryer, a well-known South African dentist, practised out of their South Kensington home which was large enough to provide office space for the ECYO. His wife, an indefatigable American PR executive, tirelessly lobbied politicians and sponsors to gain financial support for the new venture. At the end of a working day, she often invited me to join her in her very comfortable sitting room for a large Bloody Mary, her favourite drink served in a tall glass with ice and lime.

My introduction to the organisation took place in Aberdeen during the Festival when both Edward Heath and James Judd conducted the young international musicians. Haydn's *Toy* Symphony, featured in one of the concerts and I was persuaded by James to play the cuckoo part, the first and only time I ever performed with an orchestra.

Back in London, I was immediately involved with the planning of auditions in each of the participating European Countries and setting up appointments with potential sponsors. Joy had earlier negotiated a travel sponsorship deal with Swissair, one of the conditions being that every journey had to be routed via Switzerland.

The plan was to have equal quotas from each participating European country. The first auditions were held in London and I well recall the session held for the wind section when a young red headed Scottish oboe player made a very favourable impression but was not accepted due to the UK quota already being full. However, he did succeed the following year. His name was Douglas Boyd; he was to become one of the founder members of the Chamber Orchestra of Europe and play an important role as a committee member.

After only six months, funds began to dry up and the Bryers were unable to continue paying my salary. Instead, we came to a new arrangement whereby I would receive a commission for any sponsorship I managed to raise. At this juncture I decided to become self-employed and continued working as a consultant until 1978, during which time, together with ex-colleague, Wilson Strutte, we set up our own arts marketing company, JHS International Marketing, and the ECYO as our first client.

I was given a target by Joy to raise sponsorship of £100,000. One of JHS's clients was the Greenwich Festival which was sponsored by Mobil-oil and, during a conversation with one of the directors after a concert, I had an opportunity to discuss the possibility of the company sponsoring the ECYO. He promised to give my proposal serious consideration and, within a few days, confirmed interest. I immediately informed Joy of what I thought was good news but was flabbergasted to be told that she had already concluded a deal with IBM and had failed to let me know. There was no apology, which made me extremely angry, as it had been my understanding I had been given the sole task of raising the money. The situation also presented a serious and embarrassing problem for my relationship with my client.

Edward Heath again came to my rescue. He was very understanding and offered to help smooth things over by inviting the Mobil-Oil Directors to a meeting at his Wilton Street home and promised to recommend the company for any future European project he might come across and consider appropriate.

I found the whole situation intolerable and decided to sever my connection with the Bryers. Joy and I managed somehow to remain on reasonably good terms, even when later I was involved with the Chamber Orchestra of Europe, whose membership included several graduates from ECYO.

# 8 The Wren Orchestra (1977-1978)

## 'The wren is a small British bird with a loud voice'

Howard Snell, former Chairman and Principal Trumpet of the LSO, with whom I had worked closely, was also keen to conduct. To this end, after he had left the LSO, he formed his own orchestra, made up of former colleagues, and called it The Wren.

Concerts were initially given in the Surrey area and on one occasion a member of Capital Radio's music staff attended. He was impressed and eager to become involved, and agreed for Capital Radio to promote and broadcast future concerts in London and surrounding areas.

Aware that at the time I was free-lance, Howard asked for my help, and I agreed to become a director and to work with Capital Radio, organising the concerts.

In June 1978, The Evening Standard's Adam Joseph interviewed me and wrote, *'helped by Capital Radio, who back the Wren to the tune of over £50,000 a year, June has taken it in less than two years up to the top league of orchestras'.*

At a concert of romantic Russian music performed at the Royal Albert Hall, more than 4,000 people turned up. The audience was not the usual one for classical music but was made up of family groups and young people who listened to Capital Radio.

That season the Orchestra, conducted by Howard, gave a series of

15 successful concerts in the premier London halls with programmes featuring Music from the Films and an evening of Gershwin and Copeland at the Royal Festival Hall.

An additional concert, sponsored by Mobil-Oil, was given at the Royal Naval College Chapel, Greenwich as part of the local festival. All the performances were recorded by Capital Radio and broadcast on Sundays in 'The Collection'.

The exposure won the Orchestra an army of young followers. However, just as the Orchestra was establishing itself, Capital Radio decided to buy into it and to make me their employee. Enjoying my independence, I declined and decided to move on.

# 8  JHS International Marketing (1978-1981)

JHS specialised in servicing the arts and was formed in the summer of 1978. It was set up so I was in equal partnership with Wilson Strutte. Initially, we worked from my house in Bromley, which I had recently moved back into, and on most days, Wilson travelled from London with his old English sheepdog called Beth, who always kept her distance from Kilo. Later, we operated out of an office close to Covent Garden and, at lunchtime, often grabbed a sandwich and drove to Hampstead Heath to walk both dogs around the lake.

Wilson had been Publicity Manager at the LSO, which talent and experience he put to good use. We offered artists, managements, promoters and sponsors what we considered a unique and comprehensive service that covered practically every facet of the business; concert management and promotion, advice on programme planning, booking a wide variety of artists on behalf of promoters, managing sponsorship projects for industry and acting as London representatives for overseas based organisations, which included the Hong Kong Philharmonic Society.

I used my contacts in the music world and we succeeded in arranging classical concerts for the Churchill Theatre, Bromley, the newly built Poole Arts Centre and the Greenwich Arts Festival, as well as promoting our own concerts in the Queen Elizabeth Hall.

Artists with whom we worked and promoted during this period included John Lill, Yehudi Menuhin, Claudio Arrau, Paul Tortelier, the Budapest Symphony Orchestra, The Royal Philharmonic Orchestra, The Palm Court Theatre Orchestra and others. We also raised sponsorship for the National Youth Theatre Company.

We managed sponsorship projects for British Airways and were asked by the Arts Council of Great Britain to raise sponsorship for a Wigmore Hall Summer Festival. The YWCA (Young Women's Christian Association) engaged us to organise and manage its 125th Anniversary Gala Concert at the Royal Festival Hall, in September 1980.

To emphasise the company's versatility, we were responsible for arranging an unusual cabaret at the Royal Lancaster Hotel, featuring the Wren Orchestra and the London Symphony Chorus, at a banquet given by the Mervyn Conn Organisation, in honour of the artists appearing in the 11th International Festival of Country Music. A special tour was organised for opera singer Benjamin Luxon and American folk singer and banjo player, Bill Crowfoot, to present their unique concerts of English and American folk songs throughout the UK.

We assisted in setting up and became directors of the Armenian Institute, a project instigated by the Armenian conductor, Loris Tjeknavorian, in conjunction with the Armenian church in South Kensington. Wilson and I had got to know Loris well at the LSO, when he was invited to conduct and record works of Aram Katchaturian.

With Loris Tjeknavorian

Just before his death, the composer was invited by the LSO to visit London, to attend a concert of his music performed in the Royal Albert Hall by the Orchestra and conducted by Loris. The concert was attended by Empress Farah Pahlavi, third wife of the Shah of Persia, an enthusiastic patron of the arts and supporter of the Armenian community in Iran.

Loris had been brought up in Iran, but left for America when the situation became difficult for his family to remain there, having lost most of their property and possessions.

Sometime later, I helped him to organise a tour of the Armenian communities with the Ambrosian Singers, which took place under the auspices of the Shah's wife. The London-based Group, none of whom could speak the language, had to learn Armenian chants phonetically.

By 1976 'Iran-air 'was hailed as second only to 'Qantas' as the world's safest airline and we booked to fly with them on a Boeing 707 to Tehran. However, my confidence was severely shaken when during the flight we suddenly encountered severe turbulence and the plane seemed to drop out of the sky. I was holding a hot cup of coffee at the time and had great difficulty trying not to spill it.

The concerts were held and enthusiastically received in various Armenian churches, located in major Iranian cities; Shiraz, known for its literary history and many gardens, a treasure-trove of Persian culture and gateway to Persepolis once capital of Iran; Isfahan, famous for its Persian architecture; Abadan and Teheran.

We were given a warm welcome from Armenian communities, each having laid on a magnificent feast which included rice cooked to perfection, slowly with butter, the like of which I have not since tasted. The clergy were most generous and hospitable and I was given presents of two beautiful prayer-decorated tablecloths.

I also had the privilege of visiting the heavily guarded vaults of a bank which housed the magnificent Royal Crown Jewels, and a tour around a large oil refinery in Abadan.

In Teheran I was intrigued and amused by the chaotic traffic. On one occasion, we were travelling down a busy one-way main street, which had four or five lanes, only to be confronted by a battered vehicle coming towards us from the opposite direction in the outside lane!

Another curiosity was to see the contrast between modern and continuing old customs whereby brightly dressed peasants drove their sheep, led by a black goat, along the side of motorways, passing abandoned tanks which no-one had thought to repair but instead had replaced with new ones.

Loris arranged a visit to some of the most interesting and beautiful historical sites, in particular a memorial in Persepolis dedicated to the massacre of Armenian communities by the Turks. A son et lumière was performed there, for which he had composed a Requiem commemorating those Armenians who had lost their lives.

JHS continued to operate successfully until I was asked to manage the Chamber Orchestra of Europe and Wilson decided to take up an executive position with his family's business.

# Wilson

My very good friend, Wilson Strutte, studied violin at college, although he did not pursue a career as a professional musician but, instead, joined EMI as assistant to John Boyden, who was in charge of the budget label 'Classics for Pleasure'. When John joined the London Symphony Orchestra, he brought Wilson with him to manage Public Relations and Publicity. We got along very well right from the outset and navigated our way together through the difficult political situations. He did not stay long after John and I had left the LSO and we decided to form JHS International Marketing.

We often met socially and had holidays together. During the period of my marital difficulties, he was my rock, always giving support.

He introduced me to a recording of Tchaikovsky's Violin Concerto played by the Italian violinist, Campoli, who was his idol. He was also commissioned to write a book about the composer and spent a year visiting Russia, researching and virtually re-living the turbulent events in Tchaikovsky's life.

Not having seen him for a while, I became worried and decided to pay him a visit at his London apartment. I was shocked to find him looking tired and wan, the ashtray full of half-smoked cigarettes. Several empty gin bottles lay scattered about the room. It was clear the Tchaikovsky experience had taken its toll. With the book finally published, he returned to being his former self and we celebrated in style. He even bought a beautiful white stallion, which he adored and called Tchaikovsky.

*Back stage at the Royal Festival Hall with Wilson Strutte right and the British Airways Sponsor*

Wilson also bought a large motor boat, on which we spent many enjoyable hours together, cruising the Solent or Lake Windermere.

After we disbanded JHS and both had moved on to other activities, we continued to keep in touch. Wilson moved from London to Lytham St. Annes in Lancashire, where he purchased a large house and converted one of the rooms into a recording studio. Knowing how much I enjoyed singing standard songs from the American Song book, he arranged orchestral accompaniments electronically on his computer. With a good supply of honey and lemon to ease my throat, we recorded several songs, although later listening to the tapes it was obvious it had been an effort trying to sing along to a non-flexible accompaniment! But we did have an enjoyable few days together and a couple of the songs turned out to be 'not half bad', although the tapes have since been lost over the years.

Wilson joined me in Salzburg, when the COE was playing for the Opera. As we planned to stay for three weeks, I rented a large apartment close to the Festspielhaus large enough to accommodate myself and some guests. Wilson already knew Christopher Smith-Gillard, the COE Tour Manager, through a mutual friend who had attended the same music college. He was a great fan of Julie Andrews and, on a free day, we took a *Sound of Music* Tour visiting places where the film was made. It was a glorious summer's day and, during the bus journey, we all joined in singing *Do Re Me* and *The hills are alive with the Sound of Music*, rushing across the meadow just as Maria did, in the film. We also visited the beautiful Cathedral at Mondsee, where the Von Trapp marriage was filmed, although the actual wedding took place elsewhere

On another free day, we drove together to Berchtesgaden, then boarded a special bus, for the ten-minute drive along a road cut into the mountain, which ended at the front of the tunnel leading to a golden brass elevator to reach the summit of Kehistein. The rocky outcrop rises 6,017ft above sea level over Obersalzburg and is where Adolf Hitler's Eagle's Nest, the second seat of power, had been built to celebrate the Nazi leader's 50th Birthday, initially as a teahouse and retreat and a place to entertain friends and dignitaries.

We were able to take in the 360 degree breathtaking views which Hitler enjoyed. Taking the elevator into the belly of the Kehistein to the underground living quarters 124 metres beneath the summit we were reminded this was the place where plans for war and mass murder were made.

When my marriage was faltering, Wilson was my rock and confidant. He invited me to join him for a few days in Malaga, to get my thoughts clear before deciding to take any action.

One day, after visiting Al Ham-bra, we decided to take the mountainous route back to the villa where we staying. It was like driving over a lunar landscape and we saw very little sign of life. Music was playing on the car radio and we were singing at the tops of our voices when, suddenly, I noticed that the fuel gauge was registering close to zero. Realising we were nowhere near a petrol station, I began to panic and accused Wilson of being irresponsible, by not filling the tank before we left. He told me not to worry, as he felt sure we would find somewhere soon to re-fuel. His excuse was that, as we were leaving the following day, he had not thought it worthwhile to fill the tank beforehand, as we would have had just enough petrol to get us to the airport and return the hire car.

We had been driving for some time, in the meantime, both of us becoming extremely worried, and were very lucky to come across what looked like a smallholding in the middle of nowhere. Amazingly, it had a small fuel pump. Speaking very little Spanish, Wilson somehow managed to persuade the owner to let us have enough petrol to get back to Malaga.

The following day, we were driving to the airport when again the fuel level fell dangerously low and ran out completely, just before we arrived. This led to further argument between us. Concerned we might miss our flight, we decided to leave the car by the roadside, take our bags from the boot, and walk the rest of the way.

Finally, deciding it was time for me to close the chapter in my life with David Hall, I searched for and found a small apartment, close to Beckenham Junction Station, which I was able to purchase with my small savings and a mortgage. Taking only a few personal possessions, my small upright piano and one or two kitchen utensils, I left behind a beautiful home, which I had lovingly furnished.

Wilson and his then partner, Trevelyan, offered to move the piano to my new home. As the apartment was situated on the first floor, with no elevator, they had the difficult task of negotiating the heavy instrument up two flights of stairs to reach it. Fortunately, I had a large kitchen/dining room and found the ideal place for and it at one end.

For twenty years Wilson and I did not see one another but always kept in touch, especially at Christmas and on birthdays. For some time he had not been in good health, eventually requiring home care, but that never deterred him from continuing to travel abroad, taking the odd cruise with Tim, his close friend. I kept my fingers crossed he would keep his promise to visit me in Cyprus and was pleasantly surprised when, one day, he announced he had actually booked a trip in April 2020, and we planned to celebrate his 68th birthday together.

Unfortunately, the world was plunged into a pandemic of Coronavirus and lockdowns, with international flights cancelled until further notice and everyone instructed to stay at home and self-isolate.

However, Wilson and Tim finally made the journey to Paphos in April 2023 and Charles and I arranged to meet them at their hotel. When we arrived we looked around and suddenly noticed someone waving. At first we did not recognise who it was, then it dawned on us, it was Wilson, hardly recognisable, his illness having taken its toll. Many tears were shed, and the twenty years just rolled away.

With his scoot-mobile safely installed in the boot of our car the four of us set off together to explore various interesting places in and around the Paphos area and where we lived.

Wilson obviously enjoyed his five day visit and promised to return very soon. However, as we were saying our good-byes, I had an uneasy feeling that this was to be for the last time, which was sadly confirmed when, just four months later, I received the news that he had died. RIP

# 9 Chamber Orchestra of Europe (1981-2006)

'A European Ideal'
'The best Chamber Orchestra in the world'
Daily Telegraph' 2006

The story of how the Chamber Orchestra of Europe was created has been well documented and is probably one of the great idealistic tales of the modern musical world.

It all started when a number of musicians, working for what was then called The European Community Youth Orchestra (later changed to European Union Youth Orchestra), had reached the maximum age limit and were ready to enter the professional world. About 45 of them had become friends and wanted very much to continue working together, so decided to form their own professional ensemble.

To give themselves time to pursue solo careers, they decided that their orchestra would meet for around 120 days, each year, and work only with the finest conductors. Having the idea was one thing, but they had no idea how to take it any further.

During an ECYO tour of Italy, one of the concerts took place in the Fraschini Theatre in Pavia and, while there, Claudio's assistant conductor, James Judd, mentioned the idea to Massimo Teoldi who was, at that time, the theatre's Director and concert promoter. He was very enthusiastic and agreed to give the musicians their first opportunity to perform as a Chamber Orchestra.

In the summer of 1980, the ECYO were appearing at the Salzburg Festival with Herbert von Karajan. James Judd, who, a few weeks earlier, played the organ at Peter and Victoria Readman's wedding, had persuaded them to cut short their Italian honeymoon. It was his plan to introduce some of the musicians to Peter, a financial adviser in the City of London and a former member of the Government's Think Tank, an obvious choice to help with the business side of setting up the orchestra. At first, Peter rejected the idea, but was persuaded to entertain it by Victoria and on their return to London sounded out possible sponsors.

Peter's business partner was the Honourable Jonathan Davis. Both men had met when they attended a course at INSEAD, an international business school. He had personal contacts with various livery companies in the City of London and approached the Merchant Taylors Company for their support. They agreed to loan their livery hall for a private concert, in which to launch the orchestra.

In May 1981, they took a gamble. Members of the embryo orchestra came to London from the Netherlands, Germany, Denmark, France, Italy and all over Britain. They rehearsed as best they could and camped out on the floors and sofas of friends. Luckily, Claudio Abbado was in London at the same time, working with the LSO. Since he was also the Music Director of the ECYO, he knew most of the musicians, very well. James encouraged him to come to the concert, even though he would not be able to make it until the interval. This he did and, much to the delight of everyone present, took the baton from James and conducted Mozart's Symphony No. 29.

If that first concert had not been an outright success the orchestra might have been still-born. The quality of the playing, and above all the enthusiasm of the players, impressed everyone and by the end of the party which followed, a sizeable sum had been raised in donations and sponsorship, with further amounts pledged.

Of course, it was an impossible dream. The players lived all over Europe. They were unknown, had no management skills and no money. How would they get together to rehearse? Who would pay them? Why would audiences want to support another orchestra, when Europe already had half-a-dozen superstar ensembles? Artistically and financially, the cause seemed hopeless!

At this point, Martin Campbell-White, Managing Director of the Artists Agency, Harold Holt, who had attended the concert, also agreed to come on board. A Charitable Trust was set up with Peter, Jonathan, James and Martin as Trustees. It was then decided to search for a professional General Manager, who could find engagements and establish the orchestra world-wide.

# Life begins at 40

A few weeks before my 40th birthday, I received a telephone call from Martin, whom I knew well. He asked if I would be interested in becoming the General Manager, with the object of establishing this new professional, idealistic, young, talented and dynamic group of European chamber musicians, as a world force in classical music.

At first I was reluctant and said that I would only consider the proposal on the understanding I could continue with my other activities. Martin suggested I should meet with Peter to discuss the matter further.

The meeting took place in Peter's office in Gresham Street, where he was working as a financial consultant to Commercial Union and British Airways Pension Funds. Without asking anything about my background and experience, he just said he hoped I would be willing to help. We agreed terms and I was given a vacant office, table, telephone and the assistance of his Personal Assistant, Liz Harris. I discovered, later, that the office and telephone were actually leased to an Arab client, who rarely visited.

An early course of action was to get to know some of the musicians. Several future members were still working with the ECYO at the time and were busy preparing Berlioz's *Te Deum*, with Colin Davis in St. Albans Cathedral. It was a beautiful summer's day when I went to meet the founding members of the group during their break, taking care to avoid meeting Joy Bryer.

The necessarily brief 'getting to know you' was held on the lawn, with Enno Senft (double bass), Douglas Boyd (oboe), Graham Oppenheimer (viola), Robin O'Neill (bassoon) and Roger Tapping (viola), the musicians who, together with other colleagues, had the original idea of forming their own orchestra and were the true founders of COE. Suddenly, we noticed Joy Bryer approaching in the distance, so all kept our heads low until she passed by. We chatted for a short while and then agreed to schedule our next meeting in Pesaro at the end of July.

In order to assist with getting the Orchestra started, Martin had interested the newly established Rossini Opera Festival, in Pesaro, into engaging the Orchestra for a new production of *La Donna del Lago*. The conductor was to be a close friend of Claudio Abbado, pianist Maurizio Pollini, who had undertaken a personal challenge to research the hitherto little-known opera. Since it was his first foray into conducting, the organisers had understandably been nervous and reluctant to engage a well-known professional orchestra but were happy to take a young, talented group as guinea pigs.

*COE musicians on the stage of the Teatro Communale Pesaro Italy*

James Judd and Victoria Readman made all the hotel and travel arrangements and settled the Orchestra. On the day I arrived, my first encounter was with the trombone section, who were returning from a rehearsal. Just as I was descending the spiral marble staircase in the hotel, I lost my balance and slid, headlong, down the stairs, with my skirt flying over my head. Embarrassed and flustered, I stood up, straightened my dress and introduced myself to the bemused musicians.

The project in Pesaro proved a very successful exercise for the COE, even though there were problems working with Maurizio. His approach to rehearsals was, in many ways, similar to how he might prepare a work for the piano, always starting at the beginning and working through, unlike experienced opera conductors who would be economical with time and artists' patience by rehearsing in sections. This was frustrating and time-wasting for everybody.

Eventually, things settled down and the performances went very well.

The results also proved it had been a wise decision to invite the COE, whose talents were recognised and much appreciated and in turn led to regular re-engagements. Their energy and commitment won the hearts of the Italian audiences, who called them 'bambini'.

Maurizio's method of working was, again, to cause even further problems when, two years later, the exercise was repeated, with the additional pressure of a live recording for Fonitcetra.

As before, rehearsals were chaotic, fraught, and often went into overtime. Tempers became frayed and my life intolerable. There is a famous photo in the Orchestra's archive of an angry Principal Horn, Jonathan Williams, well known for quickly losing his temper, nose to nose with Maurizio who, unfortunately at the time, had his leg in plaster, due to an accident, so could easily have lost his balance.

Complaints were made to me by the musicians, along with demands for additional payments. Upset and worried, I walked alone around the streets of Pesaro, trying to work out a sensible solution to the ever-growing problem between conductor and musicians. Offering a bonus finally succeeded in calming things down.

Several re-takes were scheduled following the performances and, instead of focusing on the sections of the opera which involved the same artists and/or chorus, Maurizio, once again, insisted on starting at the beginning and working through. I learned, afterwards, he had personally edited every recording and re-take session, totalling 60 hours, and when, having finally consented to the recording's release, it had quickly to be re-called, because he was not completely satisfied.

The whole exercise proved too costly for Fonitcetra, the company went into liquidation and ceased operations.

Further editing of the tapes ensued and sometime later a new recording was released on the RCA label. On the other hand, several successful European concert tours were undertaken, with Maurizio directing from the piano.

In spite of the problems, the Orchestra formed a close relationship with the Rossini Festival and, for many years, received regular invitations, giving opportunities for the young musicians to work with eminent conductors and soloists, including Claudio Abbado, who became the Orchestra's Artistic Adviser.

# Establishing the Orchestra

Back in London, with communications having to be carried out either by telephone or letter, I used my own portable typewriter and Peter's cumbersome telex machine; accounts were manually entered into a ledger. It was not until sometime later that life became so much easier with fax machines, electric typewriters and computers.

Jonathan Davies, son of a Welsh baronet whose family had made a fortune from coal mining in Wales, also shared the office. He administered the Margaret Davis Charitable Trust which donated money to COE and he was a keen supporter. Peter often cynically accused him of being 'inherited wealth', whereas he boasted his fortune had been made through hard work! The Trust possessed a valuable Stradivarius violin which was given on loan to the Orchestra's Principal Violinist. Using his connections, Jonathan was also able to make a deal with the budget airline carrier, Dan Air, to provide cheap air travel, a valuable asset, since the musicians came from many different European countries and were required to travel to the first city of any tour for the rehearsal period and concert. Dan Air also provided low-cost charter flights to transport the whole orchestra for the rest of the tour.

He also volunteered to oversee the COE accounts, with the assistance of *Goodie* (real name Ann Nelson), who worked part-time and acted as *Girl Friday* for himself and Peter and would, whenever required, prepare and serve in-house business lunches. She was also jokingly blamed for having mis-handled the travel arrangements for Peter and Victoria's honeymoon otherwise they possibly might never have become involved with COE.

From its inception, it was agreed the COE would be run on democratic principles. The musicians would have a say in artistic matters, but financial and management responsibilities would be left to the Chairman Peter Readman and myself as General Manager. Six Orchestra members were initially elected as part of the Committee, together with Peter and myself, to form an executive. The musician members were elected annually and the number was eventually reduced to four. Ideas for repertoire and artists were proposed and discussed. Inevitably conductors and soloists also had an input, as in many cases did the promoters who were buying in, which often led to compromise and the necessity to satisfy all interested parties.

It was always the COE ideal to remain independent, both financially and artistically and a conscious decision was taken not to appoint a Music Director, but instead to work with a small number of established musicians on a regular basis, each specialising in different areas, and with whom the COE could grow and develop.

To further demonstrate its democratic credentials, it was unanimously agreed that all committed members of the Orchestra, irrespective of their position in the Orchestra, would be paid the same concert fee and subsistence. However, to keep the Leader and other Principal players satisfied, concertos, chamber music and recordings were offered, for which they received an additional fee.

For the first couple of years, I worked alone on a part-time basis. From the outset, I valued the important contribution made by the playing members of the Orchestra Committee, who after all, considered the Orchestra to be their own.

Initially, I found myself in an awkward situation, which had quickly to be addressed. Peter made it clear he wished to be involved on a day-to-day basis and to give his wife Victoria a meaningful role. Their enthusiasm was to be admired, but I had become a hardened professional and needed to convey this, without offending either of them. Victoria possibly understood, because soon things began to improve. I was also glad to have the support of Liz Harris, Peter's PA, who was a good ally and knew exactly how to handle him.

My other concern, at this juncture, was we only had James Judd to conduct. Although very able, he was known at the time as Assistant to Claudio and had yet to establish himself as a conductor in his own right. Unfortunately for him, I was also biased. I had got to know him when he had been a student repetiteur at the London Opera Centre, where he was outshone by several of his contemporaries, some of whom had received bursaries from the Royal Opera House and went on to have successful careers.

Without international recognition, I was not convinced I could sell the Orchestra. The musicians voiced additional reservations. They were young, headstrong and idealistic, thinking it more important to play with like-minded musicians, famous or otherwise. However, I pressed home my point and they gradually began to accept the argument they could only achieve their goals and be recognised internationally by initially working with well-known popular conductors and soloists, and by doing so would encourage concert promoters to take a financial risk.

It is possible James had originally thought to be more closely involved with the Orchestra's plans and development, which in turn might have helped him to progress in his own career, and such a rejection would inevitably have been disappointing. It also presented Peter with a personal problem, as James was a family friend as well as a Trustee and the person responsible for introducing him to the project. Happily, over time, he pursued a successful career conducting and recording with orchestras abroad and in the UK.

# Keeping the Show on the Road

With an almost empty diary, it was important to keep everyone on board. The only other engagement in the diary was a return visit to the Rossini Opera Festival in August the following year for performances of *Tancredi* and *Stabat Mater*, succeeded by two orchestral concerts conducted by James in the Pesaro Conservatorium and Rimini Concert Hall. After a free day in Rimini, when the musicians were able to relax, it was time to begin a tour with Maurizio Pollini as piano soloist and director. Three concerts were scheduled in Turin, Florence and, finally, at La Scala, Milan. The programme consisted of works by Mozart and Haydn.

During the tour, I received a call from the producer of BBC television's lunchtime programme, *Pebble Mill*, asking if I and a couple of musicians would agree to appear on one of the programmes. However, the proposed date was the day after the tour ended in Milan and was not ideal but Principal Double Bass and Committee founder member, Enno Senft and Lebanese Principal Flautist, Wissam Boustany agreed to take part.

I remember arriving home late in the day, very tired and having to get up very early the next morning, to catch a train to Birmingham. The interviews seemed to go well and both musicians, although very tired, equipped themselves very well and played their solos perfectly

We had to think of self-financing projects and with very little income I agreed to forego my fee, for a few months, until we had secured sufficient funding. John Boyden, who had returned to classical music recording following his departure from the LSO, suggested we should issue an LP of popular classical works conducted by James Judd. He persuaded Monty Lewis, who owned the budget label, Pickwick Records, to take the distribution, accessing the budget market which included Woolworth, WH Smiths and major supermarkets.

A contract was agreed, based on a royalty, with a cash advance to cover the musicians' expenses. With two-thirds living in different European countries, it was necessary to pay for travel and accommodation, so European members of the Orchestra were encouraged to stay with London-based colleagues, or to share hotel rooms.

To prepare in advance, the repertoire to be recorded was included in a private concert on March 15, 1982, in Merchant Taylors Hall, for Friends of the Orchestra. Two recording sessions took place the following day in Barking Town Hall and the COE red bird was featured for the first time on the LP cover and later on CD.

Additional dates began to appear in the diary. A request was received to perform a concert in late September, which was to take place in the

Fairfield Hall in Croydon, South London with guitarist Julian Bream and conductor John Eliot Gardiner. Rodrigo's *Concierto d'Aranjuez.* was included in the programme and recorded the following day for RCA in St. John's Smith Square.

An invitation was received from the City of London Festival to perform a concert in the Baltic Exchange. We invited Alexander Schneider to conduct the Orchestra in works by Haydn, Bach, Handel and Mozart and our young star violinist Marieke Blankestijn and Principal Oboist Douglas Boyd, performed Bach's Concerto in C minor for oboe and violin. A repeat performance was given the following day in the Baltic Exchange for the Friends of COE.

Meanwhile, Claudio, who had encouraged his young musicians to go ahead with their project of forming a new orchestra, had been playing a waiting game and was kept informed of its progress. Considering the time to be right, James and I decided to make an approach and successfully persuaded him to conduct the Orchestra on a major three-week European tour, in October/November 1982, which was to be preceded by a private performance for European Bankers in St. John's Smith Square.

The first concerts of the tour actually took place in Croydon's Fairfield Hall and the Barbican in London, both sponsored by Rank Xerox, and were followed by performances in several major European cities, all of which, with the exception of Paris, were sponsored by ICI Europa.

With Claudio at the helm, I had no difficulty in negotiating a very successful tour from both artistic and financial points of view. It proved so successful that it helped to sow the seeds of a strong and lasting relationship, with many prestigious overseas projects and recordings, which lasted more than eight years.

Lord David Sainsbury through his personal Trust, supported the Orchestra virtually from the beginning, both in terms of direct funding and sponsorship of COE own label recordings. Later we were also able to attract large companies to sponsor special projects and tours. Among the earliest was Rank Xerox, who provided a couple of electric golf ball typewriters and importantly a van to transport the instruments (hitherto we had to hire a vehicle), in addition to supporting European tours.

ICI and BOC came on board later and sponsored major tours, in Europe, the USA and Japan, as well as recordings. With sponsorship from ICI we were also able to launch the COE own label, using the little red bird logo and embarked on a series of recordings, some featuring soloists from the Orchestra and conductor Alexander Schneider.

# Choosing an Identity

Choosing a suitable name for the Orchestra took some time. Ideally it might have been called European Chamber Orchestra, which could be shortened to ECO, but the English Chamber Orchestra already claimed prior ownership.

We also thought it important to have a logo which could easily identify the Orchestra. Celebrated artist Philip Sutton was commissioned to submit ideas.

Armed with sketchbook and pencil he attended several rehearsals and concerts and later invited Peter and myself to his studio to view the final result, which was a series of oil paintings featuring colourful exotic birds. A bird had been the chosen subject on account of its ability to cross boundaries. The final choice was the little red bird, somewhat resembling an ibis, which has appeared in publicity all over the world, on posters, programmes and recordings. The rest of the paintings were later featured on LP and CD covers of COE's own sponsored recordings.

'A Classic Collection'
World premiere recording of
The Chamber Orchestra Of Europe
James Judd

Beethoven: Overture 'Prometheus'
Mozart: Divertimento in D
Rossini: Overture 'The Barber of Seville'
Fauré: Pavane
Wagner: Siegfried Idyll

*COE first commercial recording with new logo featuring the little red bird*

## Progress

In the event, the 1980s proved to be a very good time in which to establish the Orchestra. There was no hint of recession; businesses were thriving and sponsorship was plentiful, although achieved against much competition and through hard work; audiences were healthy; the recording industry was spending a great deal of money (over) producing and duplicating repertoire: importantly the 'European ideal' was fresh and attractive; supporting European youth was appealing, giving me an incentive to make my former colleagues aware of the Orchestra. One of the first to be contacted was my old friend Alfonso Aijón, with whom, since my LSO days, I had remained on very good terms. His positive response gave me confidence. He said he would be happy to arrange concerts in Spain, purely on my recommendation, and without first hearing the Orchestra.

With the subsequent participation of major international artists, many of whom I had come to know well during my long career in music, I was able to secure concert engagements and international tours in the most important, high profile, concert halls throughout Europe.

Being able to negotiate good fees and sponsorships, without the need of any government support, the Orchestra became financially independent, making annual surpluses. This made it possible to take on additional staff and to pay the musicians reasonable fees.

The first member of staff to come on board was Henrietta Sullivan, who was engaged as my Assistant, followed, shortly afterwards, by Christopher Smith-Gillard, who had previously worked as stage manager with the English Chamber Orchestra, and became our Tour Manager.

We moved into a suite of offices in a beautiful period building in Laurence Pountney Hill, owned by one of Peter's business associates, and were able to pay a contribution towards the rent.

Jonathan and I shared an office, which had a sloping old oak floor, constantly causing our chairs to roll to one side which did nothing for our postures. Henrietta shared another office with Peter's PA. When she later married Piero, an Italian restaurant owner, various replacements were found as an interim measure, because we had promised to keep the position open, until she could return on a part-time basis.

One day in 1986, I received a letter from a young man called Simon Fletcher, who had recently left York University and was seeking employment in the Music Industry. I was intrigued and impressed by his self-confident approach and his belief we could do no better than to offer him a position. It made me smile and, curious to meet this young upstart in person, I responded by asking him to attend an interview. There was an immediate rapport between us (another Cancerian!), and he came on board as Personnel and Planning Manager, also responsible for the Orchestra's library.

Julie Pickles was later engaged as my able Assistant and Travel Manager, and together with Simon and Christopher, continued to work alongside me, until my retirement.

As our small staff increased in size, it was decided to find larger premises and we first moved to a suite of offices in Lincolns Inn Fields, where we stayed for a few years, and subsequently moved into 8 Southampton Place in Holborn, taking the basement and ground floor of the building for which the COE paid the total amount for the rent and, as a registered UK charity, received a rate rebate.

By then Peter's own business was based in the US and he only required one office for himself and his PA. Jonathan occupied one of the basement rooms from which he could oversee the Orchestra's accounts, while administering his family trust.

# Artistic Influences

The challenge was always to invite conductors and soloists with whom the musicians of COE could make music at the highest level, some specialising in particular repertoire.

Throughout the late 1980s and early 1990s, the COE was riding high, achieving critical acclaim wherever it performed. Rumours of its success soon spread to other Italian cities. Claudio, now very committed and making time for regular periods to work and record, encouraged his colleagues Salvatore Accardo, Bruno Canino and of course Maurizio Pollini, to work with the orchestra and for promoters to offer engagements. Milan based artists manager, Patrizia Garassi agreed to arrange and negotiate Italian tours.

Several tours were undertaken with Salvatore as soloist and conductor, in Italy and London, where he conducted the Orchestra in a BBC Promenade concert at the Royal Albert Hall and recorded Paganini and Bach Violin concertos.

Soon we began to work regularly with artists such as Nikolaus Harnoncourt, Paavo Berglund, Alexander Schneider, Heinz Holliger and Andreas Schiff, who were always delighted to accept invitations to work with the Orchestra.

For them it was a special and enjoyable experience away from their usual routine each having strong ideas and personalities sufficiently different to give an ideal mix, and without whom the Orchestra would probably not have survived. They certainly did not earn their bread and butter with us.

On the periphery were celebrities, Sir Georg Solti, Lorin Maazel, Murray Perahia, Maria-Joao Pires, Helen Grimaud, Gidon Kremer, Mitsuko Uchida, Myung-Whun Chung, Emmanuel Krivine, to name but a few, all of whom gave time from their own busy schedules to work with COE, both in concert and recording.

Having so many major artists and recording companies on board resulted in more than 200 recordings, several of which won international awards.

In January 1985, James Galway's London Manager, Michael Emmerson, persuaded him to work with the young musicians and he agreed to perform concerts in the UK and to make some recordings for RCA. Unfortunately, during the sessions for Mozart's Flute and Harp Concerto, with Marissa Robles, there was an unpleasant exchange over tuning between him and Principal Oboist, Douglas Boyd. James' golden flute was tuned to Continental A, which was higher than that of the oboe and it was not possible for either musician to reach an acceptable compromise. Consequently, the recording was never issued but another, featuring works by Claude Debussy, was more successful.

Artistically, Claudio was principally responsible, from the beginning, for shaping and developing the Orchestra's romantic style, using modern brass instruments, French horns and trombones with valves, timpani with plastic heads and the strings playing with vibrato.

However, in 1985 another important figure, Nikolaus Harnoncourt, was to have a profound and lasting influence. He was well known for his early music performances with his own orchestra Concentus Musicus of Vienna, who played in an authentic way, and Nikolaus insisted the COE should do the same, i.e., strings with no vibrato, trumpets, horns and trombones without valves, and timpani with skin heads. With the exception of the Principal Timpanist, most of the musicians were very receptive to his requests. A strong relationship was formed with him, which continued for many years, producing exciting performances and prize-winning recordings.

Although the musicians were generally very adaptable, sometimes, especially when, having recently performed with Nikolaus, it took time to change styles. Claudio, in particular, showed his irritation at having to work hard to make changes.

Other conductors and soloists had similar experiences, one of whom was pianist Murray Perahia, a perfectionist. He was at first reluctant to work with COE as conductor/soloist, having previously had a very good working relationship with the English Chamber Orchestra, whose style was more conventional and to his liking. During COE rehearsals he repeatedly insisted upon more string vibrato and sometimes got exasperated when it took too long to achieve the desired result.

Heinz Holliger, one of the world's finest oboists, also worked with the COE as a conductor. In one of his programmes he chose to include Schumann's Symphony No.4, a work the Orchestra had previously recorded with Nikolaus. However, during the rehearsals Heinz made of point of expressing to the musicians his disagreement with Nikolaus's interpretation, believing his to be closer to what the composer had intended. Heinz was also a prolific composer and was commissioned to write a special work to celebrate the Orchestra's tenth anniversary, which was performed in St. John's Smith Square.

# Orchestra Personnel

Committee meetings usually took place on tour over lunch in advance of a full Orchestra meeting. On those occasions, I took the opportunity to give updates on schedules and future plans and we would discuss programmes, artists, logistics and personnel matters. Occasionally, discussions became heated and there would be clashes of personalities. If Peter happened to be visiting he would also attend, or when the Orchestra were working in London, he sometimes invited Committee members to his home for a meeting over coffee.

It took me a considerable time to get used to being questioned, sometimes quizzed, by the young musicians who, unlike myself, had little knowledge or experience of managing a professional Orchestra. During an early full orchestral meeting which took place in New York, I encountered what I conceived to be so much hostility, and threatened to walk away.

It has often been said that dogs and their owners tend to show similar personality profiles. I have come to the conclusion musicians' characters often resemble the instruments they play. Those who play string instruments with lower registers, for example cellos and double basses, tend to be less highly strung than their violin colleagues. Violas have a middle register and fall somewhere in between. Some viola players often begin their careers playing the violin but for various reasons switch instruments; the section as a whole is often subjected to unkind jokes within orchestral circles. Members of the Brass section are sometimes brash and argumentative whereas those musicians who play wind instruments are usually more pragmatic. Consequently, I had more difficulty working with a violin Committee member than a double bass player. For me, the ideal committee would have been made up of only members of the Woodwind and Double Bass sections!

One particularly wise and very likeable founder member of the Double Bass section was a German musician called Lutz Schumacher. While on tour, in Italy, he met and subsequently married Rosie, a local girl who was almost half his height. They made their home at Lake Como and raised two beautiful children.

Unfortunately, tragedy stuck, firstly when their son had a fatal accident while working in a theatre and, a few years later, following a short illness, Lutz died, still a relatively young man.

His loss was greatly felt by the shocked members of the Orchestra, who all rallied around to give both moral and financial support to Rosie and her daughter, Alessandra.

Run as a democracy, matters concerning all aspects of Orchestra personnel are dealt with by the players themselves e.g. auditions, deciding who should play, discipline, etc. However, personal loyalties sometimes come into conflict, making it hard to take difficult decisions.

Some musicians have experience working in other orchestras, where Unions are consulted to resolve disputes. Once, it was decided to ask a British member of the trumpet section to leave and he threatened to sue and involve the Musicians Union. Several unpleasant meetings took place and I tried to calm things down. But the situation was never resolved satisfactorily and, so far as I am aware, that player remains a member of the Orchestra.

Chamber Orchestra repertoire does not usually require trombones. However, when programming larger more romantic works, for the sake of continuity and to maintain a high standard, special membership status was afforded to those trombone players who would commit to play whenever required. The section comprised UK and Scandinavian musicians.

For several years there was harmony, but one British member was often argumentative. His behaviour was, on the whole, tolerated but when it was discovered he had been engaging in politics within his own section and it was unanimously agreed his own playing had deteriorated, the Leader of the Orchestra found an excuse to complain to the Committee, with a request that he should be asked to leave. As General Manager, I was given the unenviable task of writing a letter terminating his membership, the only occasion when this occurred.

He and I had previously always got along very well and in fact he had come to my defence when, during an Orchestra meeting in New York, I had almost walked away. He took the decision very badly and vowed never to speak to me again or have further contact with any member of COE.

The Orchestra's Principal Viola player had been intimidating a fellow German player in her section and mischievously causing problems for the management with intrigues and innuendos. She was requested to attend a meeting with the Orchestra Committee to discuss the issues but resented my presence and insisted I should leave the room. Receiving very little sympathy, she left the Orchestra soon afterwards and subsequently made a very successful career as a soloist and chamber musician. She also happened to be one of Claudio Abbado's favourite musicians.

# Touring

Unlike the LSO, which has its base in one city, its own concert series, receives public funding, and undertakes major overseas tours perhaps once or twice a year, touring with COE involved being away from home and on the road, living out of a suitcase, for a week to ten days at a time, sometimes twice every month. Tours were mostly arranged outside of the UK and could only be viable with a minimum of six concerts and certainly, in the early years, each was performed in a new city or country.

With most of the musicians living in a different country, arranging for everyone to arrive in time for a first rehearsal had to be planned very carefully. Julie, our Travel Manager, worked closely together with Simon and Chris and developed a good relationship with an international London-based travel agent, so we rarely encounterrd any mishaps.

Instrument transport also had to be arranged. Paperwork was a headache, expensive and time-consuming. During the early 1980s it was obligatory to obain carnets for all instruments which had to be cleared through customs at the border of every European country we passed through.

It was not until May 1987 that a new European Convention of Common Transit was agreed, which permitted the free movement of goods between the 28 member States and the Four EFTA countries, .

In the early days, we hired a large van, which Chris volunteered to drive, sometimes accompanied by a British member of the Orchestra. When Rank Xerox came on board, as one of the Orchestra's early sponsors, they provided funds to purchase our own van, in addition to donating two golf ball typewriters for Henrietta and myself.

A UK company called *Transport to the Stars*, was later regularly engaged. It was owned and operated by 'Bonzo', whose real name was Ian Bonner. He was well-known and worked with several orchestras and groups. Ian and a co-driver would first collect those instruments which were stored in London, drive to the first venue and stay with us for the rest of the tour, transporting the instruments and assisting Chris with stage management. On a free day, some of the musicians made personal purchases which Bonzo was more than happy at the end of a tour to take either to London, or make a detour en route to deliver to someone's home.

We usually hired timpani and other percussion instruments in London but, occasionally, had no choice but to hire locally particularly when working with a conductor like Nikolaus Harnoncourt, who for classical repertoire always insisted on using original timpani with heads made from animal skin. Such instruments were more frequently located on the Continent, but often tended to be old, well-used, with noisy pedals and not in very good condition, as well as very expensive.

Our Principal Timpanist, Geoffrey Prentice, at the time a vegetarian, initially refused on principle to play those instruments, suggesting we should instead find a replacement willing to do so, but he was eventually persuaded to change his mind when a colleague asked if he wore shoes with leather soles. He was also a perfectionist, never satisfied and always complained.

Nonetheless, being a true professional, he did his best and would be seen prior to every rehearsal and performance carefully tuning the instruments, keeping one ear close to the head, while turning each key handle.

He was delighted when, with increased sponsorship, we were able later to buy our own unique sets of timpani and travel cases, which Ian stored for us in between tours. Interestingly, several years later, Geoffrey was often to be seen devouring a large steak!

When travelling on long plane journeys, it was necessary to fly the instruments. Specially designed insulated aluminium travel cases were custom made for the double basses, other large instruments, timpani and music scores, all built to withstand airport handling.

Smaller string and brass instruments were usually allowed to be put into the overhead lockers with hand luggage but, on a flight to Biarritz, not appreciating their fragility and value, Ryanair insisted everything had to go into the hold. An exception had always to be made for the five very valuable cellos, from which their owners refused ever to be parted. For all flights, no matter how long, individual seats, at full price, had to be purchased  for them, even though the instruments were not able to take advantage of any complimentary onboard refreshments. It must have appeared curious to other passengers to see five cellos with safety belts fastened installed in their own seats.

The Orchestra has always been expensive, due to the necessity of always having to to break even and whenever possible make a surplus. Fortunately, during the early years this was easily achievable, having  a strong Deutsche Mark as the currency in which we earned most of our fees, and some of our expenses paid in a weaker Sterling.

With the addition of sponsorship and charitable donations, we were able to build up a substantial working capital fund, which in turn helped to subsidise operations and kept the Orchestra competitive during lean years. For early tours, I could count upon the assistance of the Orchestra committee members, who between them took responsibility for compiling hotel rooming lists and roll calls for buses and distributing subsistence payments.

Although a member of the European Union, Italy had not yet adopted the Euro and the Italian Lira had been devalued every few years, resulting in several millions having to be divided into large wads of notes for each musician. Enno Senft usually accompanied me to the bank to collect the money and we both used to stare in awe as we watched the bank tellers making their calculations on abacuses!

One of the viola players, Stephen Wright, volunteered to act as stage and transport manager and librarian, in addition to playing in the Orchestra. He earned my everlasting admiration and appreciation, all the more because he was dyslexic. Although he had difficulty with composing and writing notices, amazingly he had none when reading the musical notes in a score.

Choosing good and affordable hotels on tour was initially a challenge and the musicians were encouraged to share rooms.

As time moved on it became possible to allocate single rooms as appropriate and doubles for couples. In those cities where we became regular visitors and stayed for longer periods, e.g. residences, I was able to negotiate a good deal and hotel staff usually recognised and welcomed us.

For most engagements, the organisation and payment were undertaken by the promoters.

However, an awkward situation arose during one Italian tour. The musicians were already on the bus about to depart for the airport when I was rudely confronted by the hotel manager, who threatened to keep everyone there until his bill had been paid. I stressed it was not my responsibility and suggested he should speak with the concert promoter with whom he supposedly had an agreement.

He continued to argue, then called the police, and I was requested to accompany them to the police station.

Not relishing the thought of languishing in a prison cell, and conscious of the time, I began to worry we would miss our flight, Henrietta, who spoke fluent Italian, had meanwhile arrived to interpret and, seeing my discomfort, jokingly promised to visit.

At least I was allowed access to a telephone and, after several attempts, managed to locate the promoter. He apologised profusely, saying there must have been a misunderstanding and promised to settle the hotel account immediately.

I was duly released to re-join the anxious musicians who were still waiting at the hotel.

We only just made it to the airport in time!

# Australia

An invitation was received from the Perth Festival, in Western Australia, for the COE to perform four concerts in February 1983, with possible additional concerts in other major Australian cities and Singapore. The Festival's Director, David Blenkinsop, who previously had been Concerts Manager of the Birmingham Symphony Orchestra, and already a huge fan of the Orchestra, had the ambition to bring new exciting orchestras and artists to Perth.

Unfortunately, there were only sufficient funds to pay for the musicians' travel, hotel and subsistence and David still needed to persuade other Australian cities to take a concert to help cover the Festival's own costs. I therefore reluctantly asked the young musicians to forego their fees but happily, excited to be embarking on their first major overseas tour, everyone agreed. David proposed that Polish conductor Jaczek Kapzyck and blind pianist Bernard D'Ascoli should be engaged for the whole tour.

Arriving at the hotel after the very long journey, broken only by a touchdown in Hong Kong, and not stopping to unpack or take a rest, the first thing everyone wanted to do was to rush like lemmings to the nearby beach and dip their swollen ankles in the sea.

We were based, for ten days, in the lovely city of Perth. All rehearsals and four concerts were scheduled to take place during the Festival. In between, an out-of-town concert was arranged in a cinema in Geraldton, a port north of Perth.

The venue seemed remote. The acoustic was very dry and the conditions far from ideal, which made us apprehensive as to what kind of audience to expect. The hall was almost full, mostly with local people who probably came to enjoy the rare occasion.

There was little to see and do, very few places to eat and the only curiosity was a Russian tanker moored at the port! We were all very glad to get back to Perth.

The Orchestra was scheduled to fly from Perth to Adelaide, where recent forest fires had devastated much of the surrounding countryside. Just before we were about to land there was an electrical storm and the plane was diverted towards Melbourne. We had almost arrived when a message was relayed to the captain informing him there had been heavy rain and it was safe to return to Adelaide. We eventually landed very late in the evening and were greeted by a wonderfully multi-coloured sky, the rain having helped to douse the fires.

The day after the Adelaide concert we flew again, without incident, to Melbourne, for a performance in the 'Barry Humphrey's' Concert Hall.

Crossing the large foyer, to access the hall, there was no way of avoiding the very large glass case displaying 'Dame Edna Everidge' memorabilia.

The weather was extremely hot and humid and the residents of Melbourne, dressed in very little, some exposing large areas of flesh, were seen out for their Sunday walk. This was my first experience of widespread obesity in a major city.

The tour gave a rare opportunity to meet up with four of my old classmates I had not seen in a long while. Rita Cannon had been living in Perth, with her family, for many years. After raising her four children, she studied at the University of Western Australia and attained her English degree.

She became a theatre critic attached to the University, and had a regular radio show; she actually interviewed me for one of her programmes. During some free time, she invited me to visit her home and took me on a tour of Perth to see koala bears, kangaroos and wallabies.

Patricia Harding was living in Sydney. She and I used to sit next to one another in class and we had fun taking part in the school plays and performing as a duo, during the annual music festival. She too had emigrated many years before with her husband, Peter, and raised a family there. Knowing how much she appreciated music, I invited her to the concert, in the beautiful new Opera House. She came backstage to meet the conductor and soloist and we had supper together afterwards, the intervening years just rolled away.

*Making friends with a kangaroo in Perth, Australia 1983*

*Dancing on the Sydney Opera House steps with Artist Agent Joeske van Walsum*

*School Friends Reunion in London with Patricia Harding centre and Berta Sayers, right*

*COE musicians at the Sydney harbour bridge, 1983*

The following day, we moved on to Singapore, for the last concert of the tour. While there, I was fortunate to meet up with another good friend, Berta Sayers, who was living as an ex-pat with her banker husband Roger. They were about depart for the UK, so I was pleased not to have missed them. The humidity level was extremely high and we had two days to take in the sights and visit interesting places, such as the bustling market places with many offerings of delicious street food. Some members of the Orchestra took advantage of a free half-day by organising a boat trip to an island, which made me concerned they might not make it back in time for the evening concert.

While I was away in Australia, my beloved dog Kilo was, finally, put to rest. She was sixteen-years-old and had been my constant companion, particularly since my return to the marital home. Before I left for the tour, she had been showing signs of deterioration, not wishing to eat, her bladder failing and her eyes beginning to cloud over with cataracts. To his credit, David did not break the news she had died until after my return home and, in the meantime, had buried her in the garden. I was miserable and decided the time had finally arrived to leave for good. With my small savings and a mortgage, I purchased a one-bedroom apartment in Beckenham and threw myself into buying furniture and supplies, my piano the only major item I had brought with me.

*Kilo*

At this point I began to drop Hall from my surname in favour of my maiden name.

Roger Graef, a personal friend of Peter and a keen supporter of the Chamber Orchestra of Europe, is probably best known for his films, most notably *The Police*, a series broadcast by the BBC.

While doing research for a new book entitled *Talking Blues*, he approached me for an interview about my life as the wife of a police officer.

The book was subsequently published in 1989 and is a collective portrait of the police in the late 1980s.

The many contributors, both serving officers and wives, speak with painful and impressive frankness about the demands of the work and the dangers of policing, in an increasingly violent society.

# Europe

When touring throughout Europe, we found the most comfortable and reliable way to travel was by train, first class, particularly during winter, when bad weather rarely interrupted timetables. I tried always to organise the concerts to take place, strategically, en route. However, there were occasions when there was no alternative but to take a plane.

At the beginning of December 1999, we were on a tour with Nikolaus Harnoncourt which began in Berlin, and continued afterwards to Frankfurt, Cologne and Paris, from where, the following day, we were due to travel to Amsterdam and on to Vienna. Immediately after the Paris concert the instruments were loaded onto the truck to be transported by road overnight and the musicians returned by bus to the hotel for the night.

However, the weather deteriorated and we woke up to heavy snow showers. There was a slow precarious bus journey to the airport and we arrived to discover that all flights had been delayed or cancelled and no information as to when it would be possible to depart. The bad weather worsened and we were stuck for several hours at Charles de Gaulle, watching as planes were de-iced only to ice up again. Concerned we would not make it in time for that evening's concert, frantic, at times heated, conversations took place with ground staff trying to explain the urgency for our departure.

An exasperated official sarcastically informed us 'everything possible was being done but the weather conditions were outside their control'.

*Enjoying a hot cup of coffiee while waiting for a train during a cold winter tour*

Surprisingly, Nikolaus, who had remained calm and in a good humour throughout, just seemed to accept the situation and go with the flow.

Slowly, the weather began to improve and we eventually received the good news that a plane was available, but it was already mid-afternoon.

We arrived at Schipol airport, with no time to spare, drove to the hotel, quickly deposited suitcases, and continued straight to the hall for a short rehearsal, very relieved to see the instrument truck being unloaded at the stage-door. With only a brief interval to freshen up, eat a few bananas for energy, the wind players to check their reeds and clean teeth, then change into concert dress, the performance, somehow, began on time.

With adrenaline running high, tiredness forgotten, the musicians played their hearts out and the concert proved to be one of the highlights of the tour.

With little time to relax, a well-deserved meal was much appreciated after the concert. There was an early start, the following morning, to take another plane to Vienna for the final concert of the tour in the Musikverein. Austria, already in the middle of winter, had experienced seasonal heavy snow falls, but was used to coping efficiently with such bad conditions.

On this occasion, the instruments travelled in the hold and were met, at the airport, by another van which transported them to the concert hall. The plane landed, safely, on schedule and, with the roads cleared of snow overnight, we arrived at the hotel in time to have lunch and relax before the evening concert.

In March 2005, a project was organised with Andras Schiff as soloist and conductor. The eight concert tour began in Paris and ended in London's Royal Festival Hall. In between, performances took place in Lucerne, Cologne, Budapest, Milan, Feldkich in Austria and Vaduz in Lichtenstein.

During the tour one of the Austrian violinists Martin Walch, who had a reputation for always complaining, had been annoying everyone and finally managed to upset the Feldkirch hotel staff.

It was necessary to take a two hour bus journey from Feldkirch to Zurich airport, to catch a flight to London, and Martin asked the hotel staff to prepare a snack for the journey, to include some boiled eggs. He professed to suffer from travel sickness and insisted on sitting at the front of the bus next to Andras, who had asked to travel with us.

After about an hour, Martin made a move as if to crack an egg on the dashboard but, receiving a stern and disapproving look from the bus driver, had second thoughts and instead tapped it on his knee. This drew the attention of everyone on the bus and to their delight and shrieks of laughter, the contents of raw egg splashed out over Martin's trousers and hands; the hotel staff had their revenge!

*Claudio Abbado and the COE receiving the Freedom of the City of Modena Italy 1982*

On another occasion, we were travelling by bus to our next destination when, suddenly, there was a commotion behind me. I went to find out what was going on and came across two musicians struggling with one of the Swedish violin players, trying to restrain him, because he was having a diabetic seizure. Frantic efforts were made to locate something sweet and to persuade him to drink some orange juice, but he was fading fast into unconsciousness. He did not appear to have any insulin with him and, having to act quickly, I asked the driver to find the nearest hospital. Trying not to exceed the speed limit, we arrived, just in time, for the medical staff to take over and revive him.

There was a further incident, with the same musician, who collapsed in his hotel room and was ranting and raving behind a locked door. Fortunately, he was heard by a friend, who called the hotel management to open the door. He began to fight with everyone and, with difficulty, someone managed to force something sweet into his moth and he eventually calmed down. Thereafter, a close watchful eye was always kept on him.

Early starts and long travel days, with a concert planned the same evening, proved tiring for everyone. After checking into an hotel, the priority was to eat a good lunch and retire, in the afternoon, for a few hours' rest. We stayed at one hotel that was undergoing refurbishment and extension. Worried about the noise, I asked for the work to be halted, at least for a few hours in the afternoon, so as not to disturb the musicians. Unfortunately, no instructions were given to the man who was driving a bulldozer and excavating the grounds outside. The noise was so loud, I decided the only thing to do was for me to confront the oncoming vehicle and wave my arms about to make him stop. Peace was restored and I was later hailed as a heroine by some musicians, who had been watching from a window.

## USA and Japan

The Orchestra toured the USA on seven occasions during my time with COE, and five to Japan, including a Wind Soloists Tour.

The US authorities required visas and work permits, all of which necessitated form filling, visits to US embassies and waiting in long queues with passports.

The passports of those living in and around London could be collected and dealt with by a member of COE staff, while others, who lived in different European countries, had to make their own personal visits to an Embassy or Consulate where they lived; often, this involved long journeys and endless hours waiting.

There was also a great deal of paperwork and forms to be completed for the Tax Authorities, to avoid tax being deducted unnecessarily from our fees.

The first USA visit took place in February 1985 and was organised by Douglas Sheldon of Columbia Artists Management, with whom I had worked at the LSO.

Claudio Abbado, James Judd and Alexander Schneider shared the conducting. The tour commenced in Greenville and Atlanta, followed by Washington, New York, Boston, Pittsburgh, Kalamazoo, Chicago, San Francisco and finally Los Angeles.

It was the middle of winter and there were heavy snow falls, especially on the East Coast and Mid-West. We experienced delays, when aircraft had to be de-iced, and were actually snowed in at Kalamazoo almost missing the flight to bitterly cold Chicago, where Lake Michigan was frozen over.

The second, in 1986, also in February/March, was, again, organised by Doug Sheldon, with Claudio conducting all performances. The tour began with rehearsals and concerts in Connecticut and Yale Universities, prior to Carnegie Hall in New York, progressed through Boston, Washington, Chicago, Salt Lake City, San Francisco and Los Angeles, from where the Orchestra flew to Osaka to continue the tour in Japan, organised by Peter Gelb, a CAMI colleague of Doug's.

On that occasion the weather was kinder, although very cold, particularly in New York and Chicago. However, it was springlike in Osaka and we were able to visit one of the beautiful Buddhist temples surrounded by trees full of cherry blossoms and pagodas accessed by small painted bridges over rippling streams.

The concert in Osaka was attended by Prince Naruhito, heir to the Japanese throne, who succeeded his father to become emperor in 2019. Afterwards, he came backstage, where I introduced him to Claudio and members of the Orchestra before attending a magnificent banquet which had been organised by BOC, (British Oxygen Company).

It was while in Osaka, I experienced my first taste of green tea. Barbara Shorter, who was in charge of Public Relations for BOC, our tour sponsor, one morning invited Chris and myself to join her in her hotel room, where she had her own supply.

We later attended a tea ceremony together in the hotel. Seated in a circle on the floor, we were served by beautiful Japanese ladies wearing heavy make-up, traditional black wigs decorated with ornate combs and dressed in brightly coloured kimonos, their small feet tightly bound and forced into wooden shoes which made them shuffle around.

I was later taught how to make a good pot of tea by Japanese international pianist Mitsuko Uchida when she invited me to her London home for a meeting to discuss plans for a European tour.

She explained that the water should reach a certain temperature and not be allowed to come to the boil, a lesson I never did take on board.

The next tour to Japan was in March 1991, the COE's 10th anniversary year. We were invited to perform a Schubert Symphony Cycle with Claudio over five concerts in Tokyo's Suntory Hall and were joined for the project by Murray Perahia who played all five Beethoven piano concertos.

Two prior concerts were performed in the Symphony Hall and the tour was again sponsored by BOC.

The COE was invited to Japan on three more occasions, twice with conductor Emmanuel Krivine. The first in 1997 when he was joined by Martha Argerich and Mischa Maisky, and the second in 1999 with Japanese violinist Akiko Suwanai; I did not accompany the Orchestra on that occasion.

During the first tour, everyone was very excited to be travelling, for the first time, by high-speed bullet train from Osaka to Tokyo, passing the magnificent 3,776 metre high snow-capped Mount Fuji, as we sped through the countryside.

However, the tour, itself, was fraught with difficulty. Arguments broke out between Krivine and Maisky, who threatened to cancel.

*Claudio in conversation with Crown Prince Naruhito (Emperor of Japan since 2019), Osaka 1986*

*Presenting COE musicians to Crown Prince Naruhito, Osaka 1986*

Martha, a friend and neighbour of Mischa, and I tried to calm both down and a truce was called. There was also a contretemps between the leader of the Orchestra and one of the first violin players, in which, unfortunately, Krivine took sides, only helping to inflame the situation.

Martha, on the other hand, was very good natured throughout and played like a dream. She has always been a favourite of mine and going to her dressing room, after one performance, I couldn't resist the urge to take hold of both of her hands and kiss them. She thought I was mad. After a concert she was seldom able to sleep and would often stay up most of the night, sometimes socialising with members of the Orchestra.

For one of the concerts, the audience consisted principally of university students. Because music was included as part of their curriculum, it was compulsory to attend. Most had probably got up very early that morning to attend lectures then, later in the day, took advantage of a couple of hours' free time to go shopping before attending the concert. They were observed wearily entering the auditorium, holding large bags containing their purchases and upon finding their seats immediately slouched into them, falling into deep slumber, some resting their heads on a neighbour's shoulder. The music was accompanied by gentle snoring and it was the applause at the end of the performance which finally woke them up. Like clockwork dolls, they all sat bolt upright and politely clapped their hands. The conductor and musicians, amused by such extraordinary behaviour decided to play a 'Brahms Lullaby' as an encore!

In Tokyo, we stayed in the Ana Hotel. My room was situated on the 34th floor and I had already gone to bed when the first tremors were felt and the room began to sway. I was lying there wondering what to do when an announcement came over a loudspeaker above the bed, first in Japanese, then in English, telling everyone not to use the lift and to stay calm. I decided to stay put, thinking that if this was to be my last moment on earth it was better to die comfortably in bed.

The quake lasted only for a few minutes and thankfully registered a moderate M 6 on the Richter scale. Tokyo is built atop the triple junction of the Eurasian, Philippine Sea and Pacific plates, and its 12 million metropolitan residents feel earthquakes almost every week. Most are small and cause little damage.

# Hong Kong

In January 1988 I had a second opportunity to visit and explore Hong Kong, when the COE was invited to give four concerts as part of the annual Festival with violinist Oscar Schumsky, three with him as soloist and director, the other featuring Principal Clarinettist, Richard Hosford. Two chamber concerts were also performed by the Wind Soloists of the Orchestra.

After the excitement of arriving with the plane almost touching the rooftops as it came in to land, being in residence for two weeks gave everyone ample time to enjoy visiting places of interest including an excursion to the New Territories and the daily markets which sold all kinds of exotic foods. Witnessing animals cramped in cages and the killing and gutting of fish was not a pleasant experience. Daily boat trips were taken on the ferry from Kowloon, passing small fishing boats bobbing about in its wake and seeing much activity on the decks of small wooden houses built on stilts.

*Jumbo floating restaurant Hong Kong*

*Visiting a Hong Kong Street market with Christopher Smith-Gillard*

*Lunch at the British High Commissioner's Residence, Hong Kong*

One day everyone was invited for lunch at the British High Commissioner's residence up on The Peak, where we were lavishly entertained in the beautiful garden, and later given a tour of the house. Another invitation was received to join one of the Festival sponsors, a Hong Kong businessman, at his palatial home for supper.

Seated around a very large round table, set with chopsticks, small bowls, and crystal glasses, we were introduced to several different courses of wonderful traditional Hong Kong cuisine.

Finally a large dish of rice was placed in the centre, from which no one attempted to take anything. We had been forewarned that to have done so would have been considered impolite and an insult to the host and an indication of our appetites not having been entirely satisfied.

## Families

Romantic relationships blossomed between members of the Orchestra, some resulting in marriages which endured, others were not so successful. There were also second-time around partnerships. It was not long before there was the patter of tiny feet. In some instances, this caused a conflict of interest particularly for the female members of the Orchestra, most of whom wished to continue their careers. One day, Peter and I were confronted by two of the married musicians who had a small baby, and wanted to bring him on tour. They not only considered it our responsibility to provide accommodation for a nanny, but also to make a financial contribution towards her travel. Anticipating there would soon be others in a similar situation, we agreed and decided to make it a general policy for future European engagements. With an ever-increasing number of children, collapsible buggies would be seen travelling with the luggage and eventually a creche was created.

Whenever the COE was in residence for a long period, for instance an opera project which often took place during the summer, many musicians brought their families, either with a nanny or sometimes grandparents. It was therefore much cheaper and more convenient to rent houses rather than hotel rooms. It also became cost effective to share nannies.

The policy was later extended to the Beethoven Symphony Cycle in New York. The Orchestra's Leader, whose partner was the Principal Clarinettist, decided that only one of them should fulfil the engagement and the other would stay at home to look after their small daughter. The conductor, Nikolaus Harnoncourt, would not have been at all happy to accept a substitute Leader so we had no choice but to make an exception and offer to pay all expenses, including travel, for a nanny to be present the whole tour.

It took some persuading, but finally both musicians agreed to take part. Performing complete Beethoven cycles, twice, took its toll on the string players, particularly the cellists, and it was therefore also necessary to engage a physiotherapist to be on hand.

Early in 1990, Deutsche Grammophon was in the process of building its CD catalogue and wished to record the Bach *Brandenburg Concertos* without a conductor. It was agreed, as part of a sponsored series, to make the recordings with the COE and to schedule them in the Snape Maltings concert hall, in Suffolk, home of composer Benjamin Britten. The Principals of the Orchestra were put in charge of the artistic content.

During the week-long engagement, two of the participating musicians embarked on an affair. Both were married at the time to someone else, one of them actually to another member of the Orchestra.

That summer, the Orchestra was taking part in the Salzburg Festival with conductor Michael Tilson-Thomas. One of the concerts was scheduled in the Felsenreitschule with a Principal of the Orchestra as the soloist in the concerto. I went backstage to wish him luck beforehand and, while I was still in his dressing room, his wife suddenly burst into the room and chose that moment to admit to the affair. Although obviously shocked, he somehow managed to compose himself and demonstrated true professionalism, by going on stage and producing one of his best performances.

Thereafter, the atmosphere was strained between the two opposing musicians who happened to sit next to one another in the Orchestra and over the years had become very good friends. Interestingly, both went on to have successful conducting careers. Eventually, the couple were divorced. The wronged husband eventually married a member of the cello section, a very close friend and a founder member of the Orchestra. The ex-wife was turned down for full membership with the Orchestra and only invited to play occasionally, as a deputy; she found work with other orchestras and later moved to Italy and married the COE's ex-Principal Horn player.

## Social Life

Because COE was an itinerant orchestra, each project had a beginning and end, with intervals in between when everyone would travel back to his or her respective country. With most having worked together for many years, it was just like greeting or saying farewell to a close friend or family member.

The COE musicians worked and played hard. No matter in which city they happened to be performing, someone would always provide a list of the best eating establishments, having done careful research ahead of the tour. The favourite time for a party was either on a free evening or after the final concert of a tour and, particularly, just before Christmas.

In the early years, Pesaro was a popular regular summer residency. For the first couple of occasions the Orchestra stayed in hotels but later on it was decided, and proved cheaper, to rent villas and apartments which the musicians shared and allowed for family members to visit.

This resulted in many dinner parties and gave those musicians who loved to cook, an opportunity to show off their culinary skills.

Interestingly, many of the dishes had an Italian twist and local produce was used to the full.

Henrietta, Chris and I shared a very large apartment and one evening a few friends were invited to learn how to make, and afterwards savour, Principal Trombonist Simon Wills' delicious take on Spaghetti Carbonara which naturally was accompanied by some very fine Italian wine.

On free days, those musicians who took advantage of the weather and the Adriatic Coast, with its sandy beaches, often arrived for a rehearsal the next day, either looking like lobsters or, for the lucky ones, showing off their newly acquired tans.

One December, a Christmas party was organised at the end of a Berlin residency. As usual, a piano was provided and I remember singing *Girl from Ipanema* accompanied by Enno Senft. There was also recorded music for dancing and Jean-Bernard Pommier, who had been engaged as conductor and soloist for the concerts, invited me to dance a jive, more like a jitterbug. Encircled and encouraged by musicians all clapping and whistling. I was thankful he did not go so far as to try throwing me over his shoulder!

Some artists, with whom the Orchestra developed close relationships, occasionally invited the whole Orchestra to a restaurant for supper e.g. Claudio Abbado, Maurizio Pollini, Andras Schiff and Murray Perahia. Always the best wines were served and inevitably a member of the Orchestra would burst into song while others harmonised. This was usually followed by banging on the table and chanting for me to sing, with vocal accompaniment.

Paavo Berglund, Alexander Schneider, and the violinist Gidon Kremer generously invited everyone to their homes after a performance.

Gidon's apartment was situated at the end of a street in an old district of Paris. Since it was not close to the concert hall, we hired a bus to take everyone there.

Unfortunately, there were cars parked on either side of the narrow street, making it too difficult for the bus driver to negotiate. He was about to reverse, when several of the musicians told him to stop, got out of the bus and proceeded to bump the cars onto the pavement. With the route cleared and everyone cheering, the bemused driver put the gears into forward and continued to Gidon's apartment.

Ferrara was also a very popular Italian residence The City also boasts a culinary tradition dating back to the Middle Ages, with typical dishes such as 'cappellacci di zucca', They have a particular shape of a hat (hence the name) with a soft pumpkin filling, whose sweetness creates an exceptional sweet and sour taste.

*Settimo's Trattoria* was a special favourite eating establishment where many parties took place. The friendly and enthusiastic staff put together a football team to challenge a keen Orchestra side. Not all of the participating players were physically fit which caused me to worry one of them might get injured and be unable to play in the concert. It only required a ball to hit the mouth of a wind player and that would put him or her out of action for a couple of days. Finding suitable replacements on tour was never simple.

Sometimes a few musicians, led by Tour Manager Christopher Smith-Gillard, might organise a cabaret and on one occasion, after a concert given in Ferrara with conductor John Eliot Gardiner and soprano Anna Antonacci, a supper party was arranged in a local restaurant. A programme was put together which included myself singing *Que sera sera*, arranged by Chris with a small chamber group to accompany me. I changed some of the words, to reflect my relationship with the musicians, and encouraged everyone to join in the chorus. One musician commented afterwards on my vague resemblance to Doris Day and John Eliot said I was a star!

The Lonely Goatherd in Geneva

The COE was on tour in Switzerland with a concert scheduled in Geneva, home of the Principal Flautist. One free evening, he proposed that everyone should decamp to his favourite restaurant and asked me to join them. After a good meal and plenty of wine, it was time for some musical entertainment and the question was asked if anyone knew *The Lonely Goatherd* from the *Sound of Music*. Without thinking, I put up my hand and there was no going back. I was encouraged to climb onto one of the tables and did my best to yodel with my companions joining in the chorus. That incident reminded me very much of when I was young and had to stand on a chair to reach the microphone.

Two members of the French Horn section were fond of jazz and I sometimes found them in a dressing room improvising together, with one playing the piano, and if I recognised a song I would join in.

In June 1996, the Orchestra's annual visit to the Styriarte Festival in Graz coincided with the European Football Championship. England and Germany, for many years arch rivals, were scheduled against each other in the semi-finals on June 26. A rehearsal of Schumann's opera *Genoveva* with Nikolaus Harnoncourt was scheduled to take place that evening and the football enthusiasts would have missed the match. Whether or not Nikolaus was a football fan we shall never know but he was understanding and agreed to put the rehearsal forward to the afternoon.

A large television set was installed in one of the Hotel Weitzer's meeting rooms, with a generous supply of beer, water and soft drinks. Chairs were divided into two sections, one for England supporters and the other for those who supported Germany, which included not only the German members of the Orchestra, but the entire Teldec Recording Team.

As the match progressed, the cheering and groans increased in volume and tension mounted as the score was a draw at full time. A penalty shoot-out followed, which again ended in a draw and for those who were watching it was agonising as the game continued to sudden death. With all five of the England regular penalty takers already utilised, number 6, Gareth Southgate (later to become Manager of the National team) was the next to step up.

Everyone held their breath and then followed a cacophony of despair around the pitch as his attempt was easily saved. The English musicians could hardly believe it and sat in stunned silence, as they watched the sixth German player take his turn, willing him to miss. England were out and Germany had reached the final. The jubilant Germans jumped up and down and hugged one another, while the dejected English just remained seated in disbelief.

Vienna featured regularly in the Orchestra's calendar. A few musicians actually lived and worked there. One was Australian cellist, Howard Penny, who had many friends and contacts and, often, was lucky enough to receive invitations to prestigious cultural events.

Vienna's annual New Year Ball season provided an occasion for young debutantes to come out and be presented to High Society in one of the city's magnificent palaces. They would all be dressed in extravagant white ball gowns, displaying family jewels and be accompanied by handsome young men in military uniform.

It was for one of these grand occasions that Howard managed to get invitations for myself and a few friends. Fortunately, since the Orchestra was already in Vienna for a couple of concerts, I happened to have with me a long black evening skirt and a turquoise sequinned top.

With Howard as my escort, we made a grand entrance into an opulent ballroom, brilliantly lit by enormous crystal chandeliers hanging from an ornately gilded and painted ceiling. The invited male Orchestra members wore their concert tails, white shirts and bow ties.

We were transported back in time. When a polka was announced, Principal Oboist, Douglas Boyd, asked me to join him and together we energetically pranced up and down the room, jumping and skipping in time to the music, while at the same time trying to avoid the other dancers who moved more elegantly around the floor, the girls with one hand on the shoulder of their partner and the other holding up a skirt sufficiently high enough to discreetly reveal a white diamond studded shoe.

Howard also had friends in Salzburg. The COE had been invited to perform two concerts with conductor Marc Minkowski in the Grosses Festspielhaus on New Year's Eve and New Year's Day. With freezing temperatures and regular heavy snow falls, it necessitated having to wear winter boots and warm clothing. Each day, the Salzburg authorities deployed large snow ploughs to clear the roads, creating large blocks of compacted snow which were then loaded onto lorries to be transported away. Everywhere the beautiful and historic city was adorned with seasonal colourful decorations and pretty lights.

The Orchestra musicians were very excited to be there and the first concert on New Year's Eve was enthusiastically received by the knowledgeable audience with a standing ovation. To celebrate, everyone had supper afterwards in a nearby restaurant, during which, in order not to be overheard, Howard quietly informed me that Charles and I had been invited, together with special guests and Salzburg dignitaries to attend a celebration at midnight in the castle ramparts.

After climbing a long winding stone staircase, we arrived at the top, out of breath, and were immediately greeted with a glass of ice cold champagne, poured from a bottle which had been chilled in the snow. While the champagne continued to flow, we looked out over the ramparts, almost speechless, as we gazed in awe at the panoramic view - everywhere covered with thick white snow, glistening in the moonlight shining through a clear sky, studded with millions of bright twinkling stars.

When the cathedral clock struck twelve, the convivial atmosphere suddenly erupted into cheers as church bells tolled both near and far and the sky was filled with multiple moving shapes and vivid colours accompanied by a cacophony of crackling sounds, as fireworks were set off from all over Salzburg and the surrounding villages. All the guests began moving around, kissing or shaking hands and wishing everyone *Glucklies Neues Jahr*. We just savoured every magical moment, as though caught up in a fairy-tale wonderland!

Another year, during a tour of Spain with Claudio Abbado, a concert was arranged in Valencia. Charles joined us for this part of the tour as he had an old friend living there he had not seen for some time and who had recently opened a restaurant.

We agreed to invite Claudio and the Orchestra members there for supper after the performance.

A sumptuous meal was served, accompanied by a great deal of wine and sangria, but with spirits very high things began to get a little out of hand and before long sounds of breaking glass were heard outside. Worried about possible damage, we went to investigate the cause of all the commotion and found Claudio, smoking one of his favourite Cuban cigars, having his idea of fun with some of the musicians, as they threw glasses at the wall! I suggested to Chris, our Tour Manager, that it was perhaps time to round everyone up as quickly as possible and get them on the bus back to the hotel.

The Scandinavian musicians were the hardest drinkers, often staying up late into the night and it was usually extremely difficult for them to wake up early the next morning to take the bus to the airport.

I warned that anyone who was not punctual would be left behind and have to make their own way. This did in fact happen to one of the Danish violinists, who had to pay for a taxi to the airport and arrived only just in time to check in.

Long charter flights could also be a problem, especially when alcohol was flowing on board. We were travelling back to Europe from Japan and as usual the 'Scandis', as we liked to call them, seated together at the back of the plane with their cans of beer, slowly became inebriated and fell asleep, snoring loudly.

As we were approaching the airport Chris went around the plane to make sure everyone was awake, only to find one seat empty, the Danish violinist once again. No-one could offer an explanation, so Chris asked one of the stewards to help search for him. It was eventually noticed that one of the toilet doors was locked and had to be forced open. Upside down on the floor with his feet on the toilet seat was the missing musician, fast asleep, unaware of where he was. Chris managed to wake him and got him back to his seat just before the plane landed in London.

During an early Spanish tour, we were forbidden to return to a particular hotel because some of the then very young musicians held a party in one of the rooms and decided to throw the balcony furniture onto the beach below.

As the musicians got older and became more mature, at least most of them, thankfully such events became a rarity.

# Lebanese Adventure

In-between tours, I worked in the UK and took the train from Beckenham Junction station to my office in London which, at the time, was situated in Lincoln's Inn Fields. To supplement my income I had trained as a Financial Consultant and although the course covered all aspects of financial planning, I decided to specialise in Home Income Plans for the elderly.

One morning, while waiting for the train to arrive on Platform Two, I became aware of a handsome, smartly dressed man, staring in my direction. Our eyes met and he mouthed good morning. I shyly looked away and was relieved when the train arrived. It was too soon after my marriage breakdown and I had no interest or desire to enter into a new relationship.

With long intervals in between, mostly due to my being away on tour with the Orchestra, we only occasionally came across one another. 'Good morning' progressed to sitting together on the train and getting into conversation. He told me his name was Charles and I seized on an opportunity to try and sell him a Personal Pension Plan. Although he seemed interested at the time, I was to learn, later, that he bought one from another company.

After completing his training in the United States, Charles had become a flight engineer with Trans-Mediterranean Airways, a Lebanese freight company but the civil war in his country, which had been expected to last only a few months, had made it necessary for him to relocate to Heathrow Airport in the UK. However, it continued for 15 years, forcing the Airline to cease operations and issue redundancy notices to its employees. Charles remained in the UK and found employment with a Lebanese publishing house based in central London, which was where he was working when I met him.

He eventually plucked up courage to invite me to join him for a drink but I declined. A year passed, during which time he apparently did not give up hope. Finally, I agreed to have dinner with him. It was the eighth of the month, a number which was to have future significance.

We began dating and, not longer afterwards, David and I agreed a financial settlement which enabled me to sell my small apartment and purchase a new larger one with two bedrooms in the same area.

As I was about to go on tour, Charles offered to pack everything into boxes while I was away. When I returned, he helped me to move in, unpack, and stayed on. He never did occupy the apartment he had only recently bought and completely refurbished.

We had been living together for two years, sold both apartments and bought a house together, during which time my divorce was made absolute. Having refused his marriage proposal several times, one evening he delivered an ultimatum 'if I had not changed my mind after three years it may be the right time for us both to move on'. I had one year to decide!

My friends had concerns about my becoming involved with a Lebanese, several of them not even knowing where Lebanon was, often confusing the country with Libya, and believing women were treated as second class and not allowed to mix with the men. There had also been recent terrorist attacks attributed to Lebanese guerrillas and as far-fetched as it may seem, one friend suggested Charles might even be a spy. I repeated this to Charles, who played along, mischievously hinting that it might in fact be true! This prompted me to decide that the best way forward would be to find out the truth for myself and visit war-torn Lebanon.

Due to the dangerous situation, the Foreign Office were warning British citizens not to travel there. The Lebanese Ambassador, an acquaintance of Charles, gave assurances we would be safe, provided we avoided no-go areas and kept to the Christian side of the country. Beirut airport was situated on the west-side of the city and occupied by Syrians, therefore off limits. The only alternative was to fly to Larnaca in Cyprus and take a boat to the Lebanese Christian port of Jounieh.

April 1988 was more than eventful and certainly a month never to be forgotten. We celebrated my mother's 70th birthday on the 7th, and the following day embarked on what was to become our strange Lebanese adventure.

I was already viewing the prospect with curiosity and trepidation, particularly as three days before we were to depart, we heard on the radio that there had been another plane hi-jacking by suspected Shi'ite pro-Iranian gunmen, who had taken over a Kuwaiti Airways flight en route from Bangkok to Kuwait. On board were 112 passengers which included three members of the Kuwaiti royal family. Lacking fuel, it was forced to land in Iran, where negotiations took place for the release of some of the passengers. Three days later, the plane again took off, with the intention of landing in either Beirut or Damascus but were refused permission. After seven hours and lacking fuel, the Cypriot authorities finally agreed to let it land at Larnaca airport. I telephoned BA, to ask if our flight was still scheduled. They confirmed it was but warned to expect a great deal of activity and security at the airport.

As we disembarked at Larnaca, we could see the hi-jacked plane, positioned at the end of a runway next to the sea, with the hostages still inside. With armed police and flashing lights everywhere, we quickly made our way to the arrivals hall. Asking for directions to the boat, we were informed it had already left and there would be no other available until after the weekend. Apparently, the Cypriot Captain had decided to set sail earlier as he wanted to return in time to celebrate Easter with his family. It certainly wasn't planned but, due to circumstances beyond our control, we were left stranded and forced to spend Orthodox Easter in Cyprus!

Thinking quickly, Charles proposed we should find a taxi and ask the driver to take us to an hotel. After showering, feeling refreshed, we decided to take a walk, but found most shops closed and only a small number of restaurants were open.

We headed towards the Port, believing we might find more life there, and came across a young man selling tickets for a boat trip to view the hi-jacked plane with the passengers still inside.

We were impatient to leave and the long weekend seemed to pass very slowly. I was already feeling a little nervous, since I was soon to meet Charles' mother, Josephine, and his relatives for the first time.

Tickets were secured on an overnight crossing, the following Monday, for the next stage of our journey. The boat was crowded with many passengers who, like us, had missed the Friday crossing. We were allocated a cabin in the bowels of the ship, right next to the engine room, making it impossible to sleep, so decided instead to spend the night upstairs in the passenger lounge.

Luckily, we found a vacant table, and ordered something to eat and drink. Trying to blank out the noisy chatter all around us, we were just settling down to read our books when Charles felt a tap on his shoulder. He looked up to see a smartly dressed young man, whom he did not instantly recognise. Before becoming a flight engineer, Charles had been a physical education instructor and a celebrated captain of the Lebanese National Volleyball team and it transpired the young man had been one of his students. They chatted for a while and the young man gave Charles his business card saying that we could contact him anytime during our visit. Without looking at it, Charles put the card into his pocket.

Arriving early the next morning, the port of Jouneih was bathed in bright sunlight. The harbour was full of luxury yachts bobbing on the gentle waves, their masts clanging in greeting. It was hard to imagine there was a civil war going on. As we got closer, we could just make out members of Charles' family, excitedly waving on the quayside.

We were directed to Passport Control, in the arrivals hall, and, as usual, Charles and I split into separate queues. He was still using his Lebanese passport, which often caused problems when we travelled together in Europe, and several times I had urged him to apply for a British one.

To my surprise, I managed to clear passport and customs controls very quickly and went to wait on the other side of a glass panel. After a while, I could see that Charles was having a problem and arguing with an official who was gesticulating for him to go back. Because he did so much international travelling, for his work, which required visas, it had been necessary to renew his passport on three occasions and he had decided only to bring the most recent one with him, leaving the others behind in the UK. Unfortunately, one of them contained the original exit stamp from Lebanon and due to this irregularity, the official would not let him enter the country and was about to send him back on the next available boat.

I began to feel uneasy at the prospect of possibly being alone in a foreign country occupied by a foreign power, my own government not guaranteeing my safety and, except for only a few words, not being able to speak any Arabic. I need not have worried on that score because I soon found out almost everyone spoke English and/or French.

Peering through the window, I spotted the young man who had earlier introduced himself. The official saluted him, and they went into deep conversation. The next thing I saw was Charles being escorted by him through passport control to join me on the other side. He explained he was Personal Adviser to the Lebanese President and had been requested to return urgently from the United States. After thanking him profusely and promising to stay in touch, with a sigh of relief, we proceeded to the arrivals hall where we were warmly welcomed by Charles' vivacious favourite cousin Therese, with whom we were to stay.

Driving through the Christian area of Lebanon, I was surprised to see modern buildings, shops with the latest Paris fashions, busy market traders, and people going about their daily lives, appearing as though completely unaware of the war. Certainly, there were no camels or any desert, instead, it was a modern, western-style society, where most people spoke at least three languages, sometimes including them all in the same sentence.

On the large terrace of the penthouse apartment, which overlooked Jounieh Bay below, we were greeted by the whole family who had gathered to welcome us. They had not seen Charles for several years and were curious to meet his English girlfriend. Displayed on a very large table was an amazing assortment of wonderfully appetising Lebanese meze dishes, cleverly preserved over the Easter break, which, I was informed, was breakfast and, one by one, each family member coaxed me into trying something from every dish. It was evident that a great deal of effort had gone into making an impression.

All the while, Josephine sat silently, observing my every move.

*Playing a joke with Charles, Lebanon 1988*

*Charles and my wedding day April 8 1989*

Eventually, the ice was broken and we entered into conversation in French and one of her first questions was to ask whether I spoke any Arabic. I said I knew only a few words, which she encouraged me to recite. Not appreciating their meaning, I innocently repeated expletives which Charles often uttered while driving, which clearly shocked her, while other members of the family tried to stifle their amusement.

Fortunately the awkward situation was saved by one of Charles' cousins who produced a portable radio playing Arabic music. She and her husband were both members of a professional Lebanese folk group and began to dance. I found the intoxicating and evocative rhythm irresistible and joined in, trying my best to copy their movements with my own version of a '*belly dance*', which finally produced an approving smile from Josephine. Experiencing warm Mediterranean hospitality and living in close proximity to the people, I saw no sign of women being treated as second-class.

It was during this visit, I finally accepted Charles' proposal of marriage. As we both considered eight to have become our lucky number, we decided to marry on April 8th the following year.

Therese insisted upon travelling to the UK, to take responsibility for the flowers and introduced us to a local Armenian jeweller, who made our wedding rings and a three ring bracelet from the same piece of gold.

Garo, Therese' husband, had been a well-known and respected oriental carpet dealer and godfather to the local Armenian community.

He also had enemies and was assassinated the day after the couple returned from their European honeymoon, leaving his young wife a widow and pregnant. She inherited some land, rented apartments and the florist business, which she managed.

Sadly, a few months before our wedding, at the age of 32, Therese died from breast cancer, leaving her 11 year old daughter, Caroline, an orphan.

Unfortunately our UK house was burgled twice and most of our valuables and jewellery were stolen, including the new wedding rings and my mother's engagement and dress rings, which she had entrusted to me. Luckily I happened to be wearing the bracelet. Feeling guilty and not wishing to let her know the truth, I told her that everything had been put into a bank safety deposit box.

Charles and I went to Hatton Garden to choose an engagement ring and purchased two new wedding rings, which my mother always assumed were the originals.

We continue to celebrate on the eighth of every month, usually over a candle-lit dinner.

## Cyprus Re-visited

My first visit to Cyprus, in 1988, had not made a very good impression. However, I was to have an altogether more pleasant experience when, in September 2004, the Chamber Orchestra of Europe was invited to take part in a Festival. It was at the end of a European Tour and concerts were planned in Nicosia and Limassol.

Together with the conductor, Emmanuel Krivine, we flew from Amsterdam to Larnaca and on, by bus, to Nicosia, where the first concert took place the following day in the Strovolos Municipal Theatre. At this point in the tour, Charles came to join me because, afterwards, we were to fly to Lebanon to visit his family.

Everyone was accommodated at the Hilton Park Hotel and, on a free morning, the musicians took advantage of the large swimming pool before going in search of the best restaurants in town for lunch, always an important priority on tour.

Cyprus had not yet adopted the Euro, so it was necessary for daily subsistence to be paid in Cypriot pounds, the amount increased to take into account the high cost of living.

Backstage, after the first concert, we were introduced to a young Cypriot conductor, who was obviously very keen to work with the Orchestra. He handed me his curriculum vitae and kindly offered to take Charles and myself, the following morning, on a sight-seeing tour of the Island. A very proud Cypriot, he showed us some wonderful archeological sites and churches, all the while describing and explaining their significance. Suitably impressed, Charles and I agreed to return for a holiday at the earliest opportunity.

The following day we relocated to the Ajaxa hotel in Limassol for an evening concert in the Rialto Theatre. Afterwards everyone was invited to a traditional restaurant, treated to a meze, local wine and entertained by resident musicians who played popular Greek and Cypriot music. This gave an opportunity for the COE musicians to relax and let their hair down in the knowledge they were to fly home the next day.

# Residences

The Orchestra did not have a permanent base and, in order to survive financially, touring was out of necessity the principal activity. Constant touring was not desirable and very expensive; as travel, hotel, per diems and occasionally hall hire costs for the rehearsal periods had also to be factored into fees.

It was therefore important not only to interest sponsors, but also to establish residencies in several different locations where hotel, local transport and pre-tour rehearsal facilities could be provided.

## Pesaro

Italy was always a favourite and the natural home of the COE. It was after all where the idea of forming the Orchestra was conceived. With strong Italian connections, engagements in cities and towns throughout the country featured prominently in the diary and won the support and hearts of Italian promoters and audiences.

The COE's first professional engagement took place in the new Rossini Opera Festival in Pesaro with performances of *La Donna del Lago*, conducted by the pianist Maurizio Pollini.

The relationship flourished for several years with the Orchestra invited back regularly to perform Rossini operas with eminent conductors and artists, among whom was Claudio Abbado. Rossini overtures were often played at the end of his concerts and were always popular.

Opera performances with Claudio proved to be the most enjoyable and satisfying projects, in particular *Il Viaggio a Rheims*, also recorded live for DGG, and repeated at the Festival two years later. During the rehearsal period members of the Orchestra became very friendly with the singers and had ample time and opportunity to study their characters in the opera.

After the final performance, a party was organised for everyone who took part and some of the musicians staged a costumed parody of a scene from the opera, accompanied by Chris on the piano. Cellist, Howard Penny, chose one of the arias sung by a principal soprano. Red in the face, he somehow managed to cope with the high coloratura without choking.

The recording of the opera received numerous international awards including *Gramophone Record of the Year 1986,* first issued as a boxed LP set and later on CD.

# Venice

With the last performance of *Viaggio* having taken place in Pesaro, the Orchestra moved on with Claudio to Venice. It was September and the city experienced heavy downpours which flooded St. Peter's Square and duck boards had to be erected for pedestrians. With so much water, it was difficult to see where the quayside ended and the Canals began!

An invitation had been received from the Biennale Festival to participate in a production of Luciano Berio's opera *Prometheus*, to be performed in the Arsenale. The large building, devoid of its canons and artillery, leaving just a brick shell, allowed for a set, representing a huge boat, to be constructed, so big, that it left little room for the audience.

The musicians were seated apart in different areas of the boat and those whose view was obscured, consequently found it difficult to see the conductor. The composer was often present at rehearsals and requested the musicians to produce unusual sounds e.g. the trombonists were asked to spit into their instruments!

Situated in the district of San Marco in the centre of Venice, the beautiful Teatro La Fenice, *The Phoenix*, is located on an island surrounded by canals. Built on the site of a former theatre, which had been destroyed in a fire, it was opened in 1792, and became a famous and renowned landmark in the history of Italian Theatre.

Many Opera World Premiers have since taken place there. In 1930, The Venice Biennale introduced the first International Festival of Contemporary Music.

The COE was invited to give a concert in the Teatro with Claudio in February 1994, with a programme of works by Rossini, Schubert, Schoenberg and Haydn. It was Carnival time, Venice was heaving and it was difficult to move around. The hotels in the Centre were all full with tourist who had travelled from around the World to take part and mix with the locals in the parades, masquerade balls, music and parties, with everyone eager to show off fantastic costumes and masks. In the past, the reason given was to hide any differences of class or status. The musicians were found accommodation on the outskirts of the city, so it was it necessary to travel to the Teatro by *Vaporetto* (water bus). The instruments had also to be transported by barge, which had the difficult task of negotiating the busy canals and low bridges while, at the same time, avoiding numerous gondolas.

The Teatro was twice destroyed by fire, the first time in 1836, the second in 1996, when only the exterior walls were left and it did not re-open until 2004. Two electricians were accused and charged with arson; apparently for not receiving any money for their work.

## Ferrara

Ferrara, famous for its castle and moat, is located in the northern region of Emilia Romagna, once home to the Estense court (who ruled the city from the 13th to the 18th centuries). The court, on the bank of the River Po, was one of the most formidable cultural powers during the Renaissance. Under the Este domination, Ferrara experienced its golden age, hosting the most important contemporary artistic and literary figures and playing a key role in many fields.

A strong relationship was forged with Claudio Abbado's daughter Alessandra, who was very active in Italian artistic life and one of her ambitions was to start a festival in Ferrara. She also happened to be an admirer of COE, and aware of the search for a new location.

The Teatro Communale had been renovated and an art gallery already established, so she approached me with her idea of inviting the Orchestra to have a residency and the use of a beautiful specially converted convent as accommodation for the musicians.

I invited Alessandra to London, for a meeting with myself and Peter, to discuss details. For us, it was a very interesting and exciting proposal which we wished to take further, as soon as possible. Alessandra stressed the importance of bringing the mayor of Ferrara on board, as he was eager to establish his city as an international artistic and musical centre and wanted to develop tourism. Subsequently, meetings were organised with him in Ferrara and, while there, I was given a tour around the convent, which was in the early stages of renovation.

The city of Ferrara, provided annual funding together with local sponsorship for two fortnightly series of concerts and the occasional opera production. It was also hoped, and indeed expected, that Claudio would be involved and other famous artists encouraged to perform there. I believe we more than succeeded, in every respect, certainly aided by the enthusiasm and support of Italian audiences.

Mauro Meli was engaged as Artistic Director. At first, it was difficult working with him but, eventually, with Alessandra's continuing support, we found a mutually acceptable working pattern. Alessandra was given responsibility for press and promotion, in addition to organising art exhibitions in Ferrara's other historic buildings.

The COE gave its first concert in Ferrara in April 1989, conducted by Claudio, with pianist Maria-Joao Pires who performed Schumann's Piano Concerto. Unfortunately, for the first couple of seasons, some of the COE principal players made little or no effort to make themselves available.

To supplement their incomes, they were busy with other projects in their home countries, so Ferrara was not their priority. In addition, it was not easy to persuade major artists to become involved, many never having heard of Ferrara!

However, as word began to spread, the situation changed and Ferrara became a second home.

Apart from several successful projects, many happy moments were shared there, including parties in local restaurants, a favourite being *Settimo*.

In February 1992, at the end of a period of concert performances of the highly successful *Viaggio a Rheims*, a DGG studio recording of *The Barber of Seville*, conducted by Claudio, was scheduled in the Teatro Communale. Placido Domingo flew in, specially, to sing *Figaro*, a baritone role and an early departure from his usual tenor repertoire, although he had recently begun to sing Heldentenor roles, using the lower register of his voice.

His co-star, singing the part of *Rosina*, was the American soprano, Kathleen Battle, reputed to be a difficult and a demanding prima donna. This certainly proved to be the case.

Not only did she exasperate everyone by insisting upon re-take after re-take until satisfied with her own performance (even though Claudio and the recording producer had been perfectly happy with earlier takes), she was also not at all content with her hotel accommodation. She demanded to change rooms several times, and, when she finally chose one which pleased her, she insisted that all the furniture should be removed and replaced.

Luckily, acceptable items, which had originally been used in an opera production, were found in the Theatre.

Two years later, a memorable production of *The Marriage of Figaro* was staged in a beautiful setting and directed by Dr. Jonathan Miller. Claudio conducted the performances with a star cast which included American soprano Sylvia McNair as *Susanna*, Margaret Price as the Countess, Lucio Gallo as Figaro, and frequent visitor to COE's musical life, Ruggiero Raimondi as Count Almaviva.

*Don Giovanni*, (Mozart), also conducted by Claudio, was staged in 1997, with Simon Keenleyside in the title role and Bryn Terfel as Leporello.

Both singers became good friends with members of the Orchestra and could often be seen enjoying a meal together in one of the local restaurants or joining in a morning keep fit class arranged by Howard Penny.

## Cagliari

Some years later, Mauro parted company with Ferrara Musica and moved to Cagliari, his hometown, to take charge of the Opera Company. He regularly invited the COE to give concerts in the Opera House, there, which usually followed appearances in other Italian cities.

In October 1997, concerts were arranged in Ferrara, Milan and Cagliari with veteran conductor Giancarlo Guilini. To be performing with someone who had a long and distinguished career and possessed a mesmerising, almost spiritual, charisma was for the musicians a memorable occasion This was especially true during the performance of Schubert's *Great C Major* Symphony which took place in the Catholic church of Sant' Agostino in Milan, when the tall, handsome aristocrat often closed his eyes during the performance.

After the Cagliari concert, Mauro invited Maestro Guilini, my husband, Charles and me, to join his family and friends for supper at his house. The Russian pianist, Mikael Pletnev, who had performed and directed concerts in the same period with the Orchestra, was also invited and spent pleasant moments with Charles sharing jokes and learning how to write his name in Arabic.

## Paris

During rehearsals and performances of the revival of *La Donna del Lago* in Pesaro with Maurizio Pollini, I was paid a visit by Brigitte Marger, who had just been appointed to the position of Director of the new Cite de la Musique in Paris, an arts complex built on the site of an old abattoir. The concert hall was to be the new home of the Ensemble Modern, the brainchild of Pierre Boulez, and it was Brigitte's desire to balance the musical content by also having a resident classical orchestra.

She believed the COE, together with Claudio Abbado, would fit the bill perfectly.

For obvious reasons, Brigitte had not wanted a modern work in the programme, which would have defeated the object of inviting the COE to perform alongside Ensemble Modern. However, for his first concert, Claudio chose to include a contemporary composition by Sylvia Fomina, which Brigitte felt obliged to accept, as it was his express wish.

The work was composed for electronic music, requiring equipment to be sited around the hall. Apart from it being difficult for the Orchestra to play, no-one really liked it or thought it a great work. The composer attended the rehearsals, looking Goth-like, dressed in black, with long black hair, heavily made-up eyes and a very white face.

Subsequently, the relationship with the Cite flourished and continued for many years. Even with changes in management, following Brigitte's retirement, the COE continued to give regular concerts there, with occasional appearances at the Theatre des Champs Elysees.

# London

Although the idea of forming the COE was conceived in 1980, it formally came into existence in May 1981 and later that year the newly built Barbican Centre in London was due to be inaugurated by HM Queen Elizabeth.

Henry Wrong, who was to be General Administrator, had attended the COE first concert in Merchant Taylors Hall and was so impressed, he invited the COE to give a trial concert in September.

We were fortunate, for several years, to have continuing strong support from the Barbican's Artistic Directors, Anthony Lewis Crosby and Cecile Latham Koenig, who agreed to give the COE two annual seasons each of four concerts. In addition, through its funding from the City of London and the Arts Council of Great Britain, it was possible for them to pay realistic fees. The exposure in turn assisted in interesting sponsors, including the Sainsbury Foundation, Rank Xerox, ICI and BOC.

Many memorable concerts were given in the concert hall. In particular, one stands out. Nikolaus Harnoncourt agreed to conduct a performance of Beethoven's Ninth Symphony on April 20, 1991, and Martha Argerich was engaged to play the First Piano Concerto. Philip Langridge was to have sung the tenor part but, unfortunately, was unable to get to the hall in time, as he was stuck on a train, somewhere in the west of England. With only a few hours to go before the performance I frantically tried to find a replacement, someone who Nikolaus would have been happy to accept. Luckily, Robert Tear happened to be in town and was planning anyway to attend the concert. He needed little persuading to step in, at the last moment, and was given a standing ovation.

Occasional concerts were also given in the Queen Elizabeth and Royal Festival Halls. However, with the departure of Anthony and Cecile, combined with changes in management on the South Bank, together with the financial crisis, appearances in London slowly began to disappear, with only invitations from the BBC to appear in Promenade concerts at the Royal Albert Hall. The COE continued to give annual concerts in St. John's Smith Square to an invited audience of friends and supporters.

One of the COE's main sponsors BOC, in addition to giving money towards major tours and recordings, also supported various charities, one of which was the British Heart Foundation, whose patron was Princess Diana, Princess of Wales. The COE was invited to give a performance in one of the livery halls in London, which Princess Diana attended. Afterward she met the performers and various dignitaries and, prompted by my husband Charles, was introduced to me.

We made small talk for a while discussing some of the personal difficulties experienced when touring and being away from home, something she understood and with which she sympathised. We both agreed it was essential to have aspirin in our luggage!

Lady Valerie Solti, widow of Sir Georg asked me to reserve seats for her at a Friends' concert to be held at St. John's, Smith Square. One of her guests was the Duke of Kent, another cousin of Queen Elizabeth. Before the concert, I was chatting with Charles and my mother when suddenly I spotted the Duke, who had arrived early, alone, and appeared lost. He seemed relieved when I went over to him, introduced myself and made small talk until Valerie and her other guests arrived.

Charles and I were honoured to receive an invitation to a Garden Party at Buckingham Palace, attended by Her Majesty Queen Elizabeth and the Duke of Edinburgh.

## Berlin

The subject of residences was often discussed during Orchestra general meetings. Dorle Sommer, a German viola member, who was living in Berlin at the time, mentioned that the new Philharmonie building, which was to have the Berlin Philharmonic as the resident orchestra, also required a resident chamber orchestra, for the smaller Chamber Music Hall, as the Philharmonic Orchestra had been forbidden to play there by its Music Director, Herbert von Karajan.

Everyone agreed this should be followed up as soon as possible, so a meeting was convened in Berlin with Peter, myself, Berlin Festival Director, Ulrich Eckhardt, and Senator

A strong argument was put forward, as to the value of having a European Orchestra in Berlin, which was striving to be identified as the Capital of Europe, and the COE was an ideal candidate. The Senator was persuaded and promised to do his best to convince the Senate of the plan's merit. Following several meetings, representations and presentation of acceptable programmes and budgets, it was finally agreed to grant a contract, initially for three years, commencing in 1988. The Orchestra was to be in residence annually for two series each of four concerts with the proviso that Claudio should conduct at least once every season.

Early visits took place with the Wall still in existence. On a free day, together with Chris and a few musicians, I took the U-bahn to Friedrichstrasse and the heavily guarded Check Point Charlie. I remember standing in a long queue in the rain, while papers were processed and passes issued.

Upon entering East Berlin, the surroundings changed drastically, such a contrast to affluent West Berlin, which still had a 30's decadent air about it.

There was a distinct impression of deprivation and poverty; the sad-looking, tall, grey austere blocks of apartments, standing side-by-side with other derelict buildings, still bore signs of conflict. Streets were almost deserted, except for the put-put noises of an occasional Trabant, and ancient battered buses spewing out black smoke from their exhausts, the principal means of transport.

Finding a decent restaurant was an almost impossible task. There were street vendors selling hot-dogs but one could not help wondering what they might have consisted of.

After the Wall came down in 1989 and the process of re-unification began, slowly, everything changed. The COE was in residence just afterwards and several musicians made their way to the fast-disappearing wall and managed to dislodge a few pieces to take home as souvenirs.

Throughout the term of our contract with the Berlin Senate, many successful projects were realised and the COE achieved support from a loyal following amongst the Berlin public. The prestigious venue also attracted famous conductors and soloists. Using state of the art recording equipment installed in the hall, high quality recordings were made of the concerts, destined for the COE archives.

A special project was arranged with Rudolf Barshai, who had worked closely with Russian composer Dimitri Shostakovich and arranged some of his works for chamber orchestra. In March 1989, COE gave the premier performance of his arrangement of the Chamber Symphony for Winds and

*COE rehearsal in the Kammermusiksaal Berlin*

*With Senator and Frau Hassemer left Claudio and Elmar Weingarten in the foyer of the Kammermusisaal Berlin*

Strings, Opus 73a, in the Kammermusiksaal. His string arrangement of the Chamber Symphony Op.110 was performed two days later, followed by DGG recording sessions of both works during the subsequent three days. An arrangement of Chamber Symphony Op. 83b was performed in a Berlin concert two years later.

Rudolf generously invited me to his Swiss home. The house had a magnificent view of a lake and snow-capped mountains, said to have been the inspiration for Richard Wagner when he composed his famous Ring Cycle. I spent a most interesting and enjoyable weekend being lavishly entertained. His wife, a very good cook, introduced me to what I thought at the time to be a revolutionary potato peeler, a simple metal device, which many years later I was able to find in most hardware stores in the UK!

During the visit, Rudolf, an accomplished string player in his own right, spoke about his association with Shostakovich, from whom he had learnt a great deal and gained permission to compose arrangements of his works.

The arrangement in Berlin lasted for several seasons, with three-year-contract renewals until Ulrich Eckhardt, who had meanwhile taken additional responsibility as Managing Director of the Berlin Philharmonic Orchestra, fell out of favour and resigned.

He was succeeded by Elmar Weingarten, his former assistant at the Festival, whose powers and responsibilities were drastically diminished. Berlin politics had  changed and Senator Hassemer no longer had influence.

Consequently, the number of COE appearances decreased and contracts were not renewed. Under a new arrangement, the COE no longer had exclusivity and other Groups were invited to perform in the Kammermusiksaal.

## Cologne

The Cologne Philharmonie Concert Hall opened its doors in September 1986. To get as close as possible to achieving a perfect room acoustic, it was designed in the form of an amphitheatre, with seating for 2,000 people. There are no walls in parallel to each other, so as not to produce any echo. Size and padding for the seats were also designed so that the acoustic remains constant, whether or not a seat is occupied. However well designed, it does have a problem, in that the hall is situated beneath a public walkway and noises can be heard in the hall. For this reason, the town square is closed during performances.

Robert Schumann's Third Symphony, *Rheinische*, inspired by his visit to Cologne, was performed at the opening and a few majestic chords from the last movement of the same symphony are played over a tannoy, before the start and after the interval of every concert to summon the audience into the hall.

Cologne featured regularly, as part of a COE tour. The Intendant of the Philharmonie, Franz-Xaver Ohnesorg, became a supporter and enthusiastically invited the Orchestra to appear on four occasions, annually, linked into tours which included Frankfurt, Berlin, Paris, Vienna, London and towns in Italy.

He had a full money chest, successfully raising sponsorships for very high-class, high profile artists and orchestras to appear from around the world. Fortunately, the COE fitted very well into his scheme of things, and in turn was introduced to many internationally famous artists.

Eventually, Xaver moved on to become Director of the Berlin Festival, and, later, General Director of Carnegie Hall in New York, where it was his ambition to introduce European highlights into the season. While there, he put forward the proposal that the COE and Nikolaus Harnoncourt should be invited to perform two Beethoven Symphony Cycles in the Hall. However, many of his ideas met hostile resistance from the Board and he was forced to resign and return to Europe, where he disappeared

*After concert supper with Maurizio Pollini left and Peter Readman in Cologne*

for a while.

It must have been very hard for someone of his standing and ego, having risen to the heights of his profession, to fall in such a humiliating way.

While still in charge at Cologne he began what has since become a tradition, to invite artists backstage after a concert to sample the locally brewed 'Koelsch' beer, a light ale served cold in traditional 0.2 litre tall and cylindrical Koelsch glasses. This was a kind gesture very much appreciated by thirsty musicians. I tried it a few times but was careful not to have a second glass as it had a high alcohol content.

Xaver's assistant in Cologne was Annette Wolde whose role was to organise and negotiate concerts. She and I had first met in Bonn at the Bahnof Rolandseck when organising the LSO concerts with Edward Heath. Prior to moving to Cologne, she had been in Frankfurt managing the Junge Deutsche Philharmonie and Ensemble Modern, having succeeded Karsten Witt, their founder.

Annette played an important role alongside her boss, Andreas Moehlich Zebhauser, in successfully collaborating with the COE for a shared residency and regular concerts in the Alte Oper. We worked closely together for many years, although she could be difficult over the choice of artists and programmes, as her preference was for modern repertoire.

## Frankfurt

The Alte Oper in Frankfurt was extensively damaged by bombing raids during World War II in 1944, although many of the outside walls and façades survived. In the 1960s the city magistrate planned to build a modern office building on the site. The then Minister of Economy in Hessen, Rudi Arndt, earned the nickname *Dynamit-Rudi* when he proposed to blow up Germany's most beautiful ruin 'with a little dynamite'. Arndt later said that this was not meant seriously.

A citizen's initiative campaigned for reconstruction funds and the building was reopened on August 28, 1981, to the sounds of Gustav Mahler's Eighth Symphony, *The Symphony of a Thousand*. The Grosser Saal (Large Hall), with its fine acoustic, seats 2,500 and the Mozart-Saal, 700. Smaller halls are used for conventions.

Sir Georg Solti, who many years earlier had a close association with the city of Frankfurt, both as a pianist and conductor, was approached by the Intendant of the newly renovated Alte Oper to arrange a bi-annual Mozart Festival. The plan was to have four orchestral concerts in the large Concert Hall and chamber music in the smaller recital hall.

The Junge Deutsche Philharmonie, also known as the Deutsche Akademie, receiving a generous grant for all its musical activities, had recently established itself in the City. It was given a restored warehouse, as a base, rehearsal hall and instrument store.

Their General Manager, Karsten Witt, was naturally confident his orchestra would be chosen as the resident orchestra for the Mozart Festival. Indeed, Sir Georg had already made an approach and auditions were underway, but he had an idea to create a new European Orchestra. With this in mind, he contacted me to ask if there might be a possibility for some of the COE musicians to be involved.

We had several meetings at his London house, in Elsworthy Road, and I tried to convince him he should instead consider, a 'ready-made', quality, European orchestra in the form of COE.

At first, he could not be persuaded, but I continued to impress upon him the Orchestra's merits. Eventually, he did agree, but stubbornly insisted it should be viewed as 'his new creation' and for the COE name not to be mentioned, but I told him that was unacceptable.

Prepared to walk away, I suggested he should perhaps after all re-reconsider using the Junge Deutsche Philharmonie players, who no doubt would be willing to adhere to his requests.

Although not entirely happy, Sir Georg relented and accepted to keep the COE name, provided we agreed a compromise, whereby it would be translated into German, as *Kammerorkester aus Europa* below which *Chamber Orchestra of Europe* would appear in English in very small type. We were extremely uncomfortable with this, because the name for the Orchestra had been arrived at, after considerable thought and discussion, and it had been decided that every effort should be made for it always to be publicised, in full, in English, although this was not always achievable, particularly in France, where, often, it appeared in a French translation.

The First Mozart Festival took place in summer 1983 and was a great success and led to regular engagements. Karsten Witt was extremely unhappy his musicians had been overlooked, a grudge I believe he carried with him into his next appointment as Intendant of the Konzerthaus, in Vienna, because he never invited the COE to give concerts there during his tenure, in spite of the Orchestra having a long and successful relationship with the city. Years later, when he had moved on to become Managing Director of Deutsche Grammophon, he mellowed slightly, having to acknowledge the successful recordings already made with the COE.

Karsten's successor at the Deutsche Akademie in Frankfurt, Andreas Moehlich Zebhauser, and General Manager, Annette Wolde, both great supporters of COE, together created the possibility for the Orchestra to share their new rehearsal space. In addition, they offered generous financial support for a series of annual concerts in the Alte Oper Concert Hall. Regular visits to Frankfurt formed part of European tours, often with prior rehearsals taking place in the facility set up for the Junge Deutsche Philharmonie.

Later, Andreas went on to manage the new concert hall in Baden-Baden and, frequently, invited the COE to perform and record there. Annette moved to the Koeln Philharmonie where she stayed until her retirement.

## Vienna

At the end of the concert which had taken place in Munich's Herkulesaal during the 1982 European tour, Claudio introduced me to Hans Landesmann, an influential Viennese businessman and entrepreneur. He had travelled to Munich specially to hear the Orchestra and was so impressed he invited me to have a drink with him afterwards. During the conversation, he explained he was about to take on the role of Intendant of the Konzerthaus and Vienna Festival and, once installed, would be interested to invite the COE.

As the evening progressed over a light supper and a few glasses of wine, he began to express his personal sorrow at having recently lost his son, who had apparently taken his own life. It had obviously profoundly affected both him and his American wife Elaine, who had since become somewhat of a recluse.

I felt sorry and slightly embarrassed that he should speak about something so personal to me, a complete stranger.

We met on several occasions, after that meeting, and I was invited to his summer house at Mondsee, near Salzburg. Elaine welcomed me but appeared withdrawn and I detected she was not altogether comfortable and maybe even slightly suspicious. Hans' Assistant at the Konzerthaus, Suzanne Baumgaertl, told me, sometime later, that he had mistresses and Elaine, with whom she was very friendly, obviously knew about them. Perhaps she mistakenly thought I might have been another!

The reason I was there was because Hans and I had agreed to drive together to Pesaro, to join Claudio and the COE who were working on *Il Viaggio a Rheims* and, while there, we were to begin planning the Orchestra's future visits to Vienna.

Our next encounter was in Venice, where Claudio and the COE were taking part in the Bi-ennale Festival, performing Luigi Nono's *Prometheus* in the Arsenale. We had the odd meal together and, one evening, Hans became a little too familiar and I had, delicately, to avoid what might have otherwise become an embarrassing situation.

The following year, the COE gave its first concerts in the Konzerthaus, which were a great success, and it was agreed the Orchestra would appear, annually, in a series of short residences, from where we would be able to repeat the same programmes in other cities in Austria, Hungary and Czechoslovakia.

An early project was a recording for Deutsche Grammophon of Haydn's Cello Concertos directed and performed by the soloist, Mischa Maisky. The sessions did not go well, because Mischa, who was very highly strung, damaged his thumb and found it difficult to play his instrument. There were tantrums and several excuses, which created a very unhappy atmosphere. Although the recording was completed, he was not content and at first did not want it to be released but eventually relented.

Following a major tour, which commenced in London's Barbican Hall on January 13, 1989, and continued in Cologne, Berlin, Vaduz with the final concert taking place on the 22nd in the Mozart-Saal of the Konzerthaus in Vienna, pianist Andras Schiff recorded for Decca all of JS Bach's seven keyboard concertos and *Brandenburg* Third and Fifth Concertos.

A recording of Mozart's C minor Mass was scheduled by CBS to take place in the theatre in Bratislava, using a Czech choir and international soloists.

Buses were organised to take the Orchestra from Vienna, which involved travelling over badly made roads and passing through various checkpoints on the way. Unfortunately, the sessions did not go well, because Claudio was unhappy with the Principal Soprano and the recording was never released. He later recorded a version with the Berlin Philharmonic Orchestra with different soloists.

For the next three years, we gave many successful concerts at the Vienna Konzerthaus and, during this period, I became good friends with Suzanne. She was a close friend of Leonard Bernstein, a regular visitor to Vienna. She told me stories about when, after a concert, they would spend many hours together in her apartment, sometimes into the early hours, drinking wine, while discussing world affairs and the writings of famous authors and poets.

Sometimes, she invited me to stay with her in her penthouse apartment. Over a delicious breakfast, we chatted for hours, comparing notes on our personal experiences of male chauvinism, which seemed to have been even more prevalent in Viennese life. She also formed close personal relationships with some artists, including Paul Gulda, son of pianist Friederich Gulda and later married the doctor son of composer Richard Strauss.

Eventually Hans left the Konzerthaus to take up the position of Intendant of the Salzburg Festival and was succeeded by Alexander Pereira, with whom we had previously had a brief association when he organised a COE concert in Frankfurt for the Bach Society. His approach was completely different from Hans' and he was sometimes difficult to deal with. However, he did become committed to the COE, almost possessive, to the extent he insisted upon our agreeing to exclusivity with the Konzerthaus and not to perform in any other Viennese concert hall, including the prestigious Musikverein.

However, Claudio, who had meanwhile been appointed Music and Artistic Director of the Vienna State Opera and contracted to conduct concerts with the Vienna Philharmonic in the Musikverein, had other ideas. As the Artistic Adviser of COE he considered it important for the Orchestra to perform in the Musikverein, thereby causing a conflict of interests. Thomas Angyan, the Musikverein's Intendant was very receptive to the idea.

Alexander felt betrayed by both Claudio and COE and no matter how much he protested he could not change Claudio's mind and the die was cast. Afterwards his attitude changed. Demonstrating his hurt feelings, he told me the relationship had soured and he could no longer guarantee future regular concerts in the Konzerthaus.

It had always been a tradition for The Vienna Philharmonic to give a concert in the Musikverein at the beginning of November to celebrate All Saints. However, for the concert in 1990, Claudio insisted the COE should be engaged for the project. A Schubert Mass, *Tantum Ergo* and Schumann's *Requiem for Mignon* with American soprano, Barbara Bonny, and the Vienna State Opera Chorus were performed and recorded 'live' by DGG. Needless to say, this did not go down well, nor help to improve Claudio's and the Orchestra's relations with the Vienna Philharmonic Orchestra and certainly not with Alexander at the Konzerthaus.

Some years later, Alexander was engaged to run the Opera House in Zurich. His successor was Karsten Witt, who later moved on to run Deutsche Grammophon and in turn was succeeded by his former assistant, Christoph Lieben.

Politics changed and the Konzerthaus underwent major refurbishment, the result of which was the tightening of available funds for promoting concerts.

The world had moved on and there was little appetite to invite COE, on account of it being too expensive. Following several attempts and an offer to perform for a considerably reduced fee, subsidised by the Orchestra, Lieben agreed to just a couple of concerts.

During the intervening years, the COE managed to maintain its relationship with the Musikverein, but Claudio had meanwhile moved on from COE to concentrate on his new baby, the Vienna-based Mahler Youth and Chamber Orchestras. The Chamber Orchestra became a major competitor, and due to the absence of available and acceptable conductors, the COE consequently became less attractive.

## Salzburg

The City of Salzburg featured often during my long career, the first and second visits in 1973 and 1975 with the London Symphony Orchestra, and frequently during my 25 years with the Chamber Orchestra of Europe.

Memorable COE concerts were given there, with conductors Claudio Abbado, Nikolaus Harnoncourt, Michael Tilson-Thomas, Yehudi Menuhin, Marc Minkowski and soloists, Jessye Norman, Anne-Sofie von Otter, Thomas Quasthof, Bryn Terfel, Friedrich Gulda and Alfred Brendl.

Belgian impresario, Gerard Mortier, took over as Intendant of the Salzburg Festival in 1991. He had formerly been in charge of opera at La Monnaie, in Brussels, and the Paris Opera. He was controversial, a self-confessed Machiavellian, personable, courteous but also steely and ruthless. Provocation was his element and nobody in the world of opera was better at delivering it than he was.

His tenure as Director at La Monnaie set off its share of controversy, but paled in comparison to the furore that surrounded him in Salzburg. He declared war on the well-heeled international opera circuit and proclaimed his determination to root out the 'mafia' holding the Festival to ransom. The seigneurial rights to Mozart's music, arrogated to themselves by the Vienna Philharmonic were challenged by Mortier's desire to develop a kaleidoscope of possibilities with the Chamber Orchestra of Europe, Camerata Academica and other ensembles, conducted by innovators such as Nikolaus Harnoncourt, Roger Norrington, John Eliot Gardiner and Simon Rattle.

He came to London for various meetings and asked to see me. I invited him to my office and aware of his reputation, prepared myself for a difficult encounter. He certainly lived up to his reputation of being personable and courteous and expressed his desire to rattle the Vienna Philharmonic's cage. One of his plans was to mount a new production of *The Marriage of Figaro* in 1995 with Bryn Terfel as Figaro, and for Nikolaus Harnoncourt to conduct the COE in the orchestra pit.

Mortier's approach in the event proved less successful than he might have hoped but the innate conservatism of the Vienna Philharmonic at least came under scrutiny. It certainly did not improve the already deteriorating relationship between the Vienna Philharmonic, Nikolaus and the COE. Interestingly, when the same production was revived two years later, Nikolaus did not conduct but was replaced by Edo de Waart.

However, he did conduct the Vienna Philharmonic for a new production of the Opera in 2005, strangely enough four years after Mortier's departure.

Charles brought my mother to Salzburg and they both joined me in a balcony box, for one of the performances. Although Mozart's music was as heavenly as ever, the set was shrouded in darkness for much of the time and, for some reason only known to the producer, Bryn Terfel had to sing an aria while writhing on the floor. It was the first time my mother had ever seen a 'live' opera and this one must have been a strange experience for her. She suddenly developed a fit of coughing and Charles had to escort her outside to find some water.

In December 1991, on the occasion of the 200th anniversary of Mozart's death, the COE was invited to perform two marathon concerts comprising his last three symphonies. The performances took place in the Salzburg Grosser Saal and were recorded live by Teldec. Re-take sessions were scheduled immediately after the final concert, by which time everyone was exhausted. A third much shorter concert took place the following morning in the smaller Kammermusiksaal.

There was a very moving live recording taken by Teldec of a performance of Beethoven's *Missa Solemnis* conducted by Nikolaus Harnoncourt in the Grosses Festspielhaus. The Orchestra Leader Marieke Blankestijn's very moving violin solo brought shivers down the spine and tears to the eye. Two complete Beethoven and Schubert Symphony Cycles were performed with Harnoncourt and Claudio, respectively, in the Mozarteum, and regular invitations were also received to take part in the Mozartwochen each January. The Orchestra was also invited to give special New Year's Eve and New Year's Day concerts in the Grosses Festspielhaus with Marc Minkowski.

## Graz

Nikolaus Harnoncourt had strong family connections with the town of Graz and was regularly invited to give concerts with his own orchestra, Concentus Musicus, as part of the annual Styriarte Festival. The programmes were also performed beforehand in the Feldkirch Festival. Following the successful concerts given in the Vienna Konzerthaus in 1985 with the Chamber Orchestra of Europe, Nikolaus introduced the

Orchestra to both Festivals.

For many years, the COE continued each summer to give a series of concerts and operas, which were also recorded live by Teldec, many of which received world-wide critical acclaim and won major prizes e.g. *Gramophone Record of the Year* for the Beethoven Symphony Cycle.

The annual visits also coincided with the Harnoncourt's wedding anniversary, and my own birthday. Special birthdays were celebrated with the whole Orchestra and the team from Teldec, who were in Graz to record the concerts.

A party for my 50th was organised for the day before because I had promised to fly back to the UK to celebrate with Charles and close friends. However, I arrived home to find a large basket of flowers from Teldec on the doorstep, which had been left there because no one was at home to answer the door.

Charles had recently been headhunted by the Kuwaiti Ministry of Information to be part of a team to set up and publish an international daily newspaper in the UK.

There had been no time for him to let me know that he had been urgently requested by the Minister to fly with him on his private jet to Kuwait to finalise the details.

Like ships in the night we must have crossed in the sky.

Saddam Huseein had just been forced to vacate Kuwait, setting fire to the oils wells as he was leaving. Still burning, Charles could see them from the plane as it was approaching the airport.

*Nikolaus Harnoncourt rehearsing with the COE in Graz 1988*

I entered the empty house wondering how I might celebrate alone. I remembered there was a bottle of gin in the drinks cupboard and luckily found some tonic water.

Happily my friends had other ideas and soon arrived with a large birthday cake and a bottle of champagne.

I made a promise to myself never to make the same mistake again and all future special birthdays would be celebrated in Graz with or without Charles. Having a guilty conscience, he now keeps a photograph on his desk of me cutting my birthday cake with only three glasses on the table.

# Claudio Abbado

During the time I worked with the LSO, Claudio was never easy to pin down. He always did his best to avoid any meetings with management, preferring, instead, to have conversations with the musicians. This was to continue, later, when I became General Manager of the COE, by which time, he had taken over from Andre Previn, as Principal Conductor of the LSO.

Claudio's new position required him to give more time to the Orchestra, which entailed overseas tours and more appearances in London. His UK Manager, Lies Askonas, found him a small, terraced house in Kensington which Gabriella, his second wife, a celebrated Italian interior designer, immediately set about converting and extending, to give each of them a space in which to work, including a music studio and a very large kitchen, with an area for entertaining.

Often, having requested a meeting, I would be invited to the house, which seemed like entering a Tardis, Gabriella having waved a magic wand over what, originally, had been a very small dwelling. I would then be expected to accompany him in his chauffeur driven car to an appointment, which might have been with his dentist. Those journeys were usually very short, so little was actually achieved. On the other hand, I welcomed the occasions when I was invited to lunch at the house and, if Gabriella happened to be at home, she would quickly rustle up spaghetti and salad. It was a question of making the most of such opportunities, to gain as much information and future commitment as possible.

One day, the LSO were rehearsing with Claudio Abbado in Henry Wood Hall and he suggested we have lunch together afterwards at a local Italian restaurant. After we had eaten, I offered to drive him back to his Kensington home, but was mortified to find the Hall's car park locked with my car still inside. It was getting late and took some time to locate the caretaker. He eventually appeared, and opened the gate, I was able to retrieve my car and deliver Claudio to his home.

When, in late 1976, I joined the European Community Youth Orchestra, where Claudio was Music Director, there was no opportunity to come into direct contact with him, as I did not stay for very long. It was not until 1981, when I became General Manager of the Chamber Orchestra of Europe, that I was to meet him again.

There is no question, to my mind, that Claudio played an important part in the establishment and life of COE. He introduced the Orchestra to an exciting and glamorous world. Without his input and dedication, I am convinced the Orchestra would never have succeeded to the extent it has and become so well-known, respected and in demand, internationally. During its important formative years, Claudio devoted much of his busy schedule to working with the Orchestra, providing so many opportunities to appear in major concert halls and festivals. He persuaded Rainer Brock, his Deutsche Grammophon Producer, to work with the Orchestra, which resulted in several recordings which received coveted international awards and prizes. He also used his influence to enable the Orchestra to perform regularly in Vienna, Berlin, Ferrara and Paris.

Some reports have it that he founded the COE, which is not strictly true. He did encourage its formation and stepped in to conduct the second half of the inaugural trial concert in Merchant Taylor's Hall on May 18, 1981, which helped to raise sufficient funds to get the project started. However, he bided his time, always keeping a watchful eye from a distance.

## First European Tour

It was not until October 1982 that he truly came on board and agreed to conduct the Orchestra on a major European tour. My memories of that tour are very special. The whole occasion caused much excitement amongst the musicians and, in my case, many tears to be shed during performances of Ligeti's *Ramifications* and Brahms' First Serenade; Schubert and Rossini encores brought the house down. The audiences and critics alike were particularly impressed, not only with the musicians' musical ability, but with their youthfulness, verve, enthusiasm, commitment and obvious enjoyment of making music together.

Particularly, I remember the concert in Budapest. I was so overcome and had tears streaming down my face when I went backstage to congratulate Claudio. Amused, he made fun of me and laughingly suggested I should use his bathroom to recover, before fans and other well-wishers arrived.

The final concert took place in the Maurice Ravel Auditorium, in Lyon. It was a Sunday and, when we arrived in the afternoon, there was no one on duty to help move the instruments or to set up the stage. The previous evening, there had been an opera performance and the orchestra pit had been left open. This was a disappointing end to what had been a most successful tour. When someone eventually did turn up, we asked for the pit to be covered, as it would have affected the sound. All that was produced was a black curtain which was carelessly placed over the opening. The hall itself was anyway not really suitable for an orchestral concert; it had thick carpet on the floor and the seats were covered in heavy velvet, all of which were sound absorbent, resulting in a very dry and dead acoustic. Nevertheless, Claudio remained good natured and invited everyone to dinner afterwards to sample Lyon's famous cuisine.

## Rossini in Versailles

In May 1985, Claudio and the COE were engaged by Italian entrepreneur and film producer, Andrea Andermann, to take part in a special documentary film. It was to be made in the guise of an imaginary nineteenth Century gala tribute to Rossini, based on his visits to Paris during later life. A co-production between Rada Film and Antenne 2, the producer was BBC's Humphrey Burton, and the setting the theatre chapel and gardens of the Palace of Versailles.

British actor, Paul Brooke, took the part of Rossini and read from his writings from that period; Claudio and the Orchestra musicians, dressed in wigs and period costume, played in the orchestra pit. The star line-up of singers, also wearing period costumes, included Francesco Araiza, Samuel Ramey and Ruggiero Raimondi. Two grand divas, soprano Montserat Caballe and mezzo soprano Marilyn Horne, both well-endowed, heavily made up and dressed in wigs and crinolines, filled the theatre's small stage space and were hardly able to touch hands as they sang a duet from *Semiramide.*

## Summer Festivals

In the summer of 1986, the Orchestra was invited to take part for the first time in the Salzburg Festival. Two concerts were given on August 7 and 8 with Yehudi Menuhin and Claudio. One of the soloists was American mezzo soprano Jessye Norman who sang four songs from Mahler's *Aus des Knaben Wunderhorn.*

The same year, Claudio and the COE gave their first BBC Promenade concert in London's Royal Albert Hall, with Hungarian pianist Andras Schiff as soloist, who later developed his own close relationship with the Orchestra.

Two concerts at the Edinburgh Festival followed, featuring the Orchestra's violin soloist Marieke Blankestijn and Russian violinist, Viktoria Mullova, who performed Vivaldi's *The Four Seasons* later recorded for Philips in the mountain resort of Vaduz. It was during this period, a close personal relationship began to blossom between Claudio and Viktoria, which later resulted in the birth of a son, whose parentage Claudio was to dispute for some time.

The Orchestra was invited, with him, to the Radio France Festival in Montpellier. Driving from the airport, I was amazed at the variety of stunning contemporary buildings. Montpellier started to get a reputation for bold new architecture in the late 1970s, when the Antigone neighbourhood was built on the site of former barracks near the old town. Devised to look like a model Renaissance City, it is a monumental mix of offices and apartments by the Catalan architect Ricardo Bofill.

As it was summer, the concerts were performed in a courtyard in the open air and because there was a gentle breeze, it became necessary to secure the music to the stands with pegs.

On the day of the second concert, the morning was free. Claudio and I were invited to lunch at the home of one of the Festival's wealthy patrons and afterwards to swim in a luxurious pool but as I did not have a swimsuit with me and anyway am not a very good swimmer, I declined. However, Claudio asked our glamorous hostess if she would kindly loan one of hers. Thankfully it was nothing like the one I borrowed from Frau Jochum, many years before; it was flesh-coloured and figure-hugging which made me feel self-conscious but, after taking a deep breath, I quickly composed myself and joined Claudio in the pool.

## Lost shirts in Spain

During a Spanish tour he sent his shirts to be laundered but unfortunately they did not arrive back in time for that evening's concert, so he had quickly to purchase another. The concert programme concluded with Mendelssohn's Third Symphony, *The Scottish*. Towards the end of the last movement, members of the Orchestra could just be heard softly singing along with words hastily composed by one of the musicians:

> *'Where are my shirts*
> *I sent them to the cleaners*
> *they took them away*
> *and put them in the garbage*
> *oh what a dismay*
> *My chest is on display'*

## USA and Japan

In addition to European concerts and recordings, major tours were undertaken to the US, the first shared with James Judd and Alexander Schneider.

The second, sponsored by BOC, took the Orchestra firstly to the West Coast and on to Japan to perform all Schubert symphonies and Beethoven piano concertos with Murray Perhaia.

## Fierrabras in Vienna

In May 1988, the COE took part in the Vienna Festival, with Claudio conducting performances of Schubert's little-known opera *Fierrabras* in the Theatre an der Wien. This was another of Maurizio Pollini's pet projects, which he had researched extensively. Accepting his inadequacies from previous attempts at conducting, he offered the first performance to his friend.

Schubert had never witnessed the work premiered, because of various conflicts. Indeed the work languished, for a long time, without a performance, let alone any great success. A concert version of several numbers was staged in Vienna seven years after the composer's death. Numerous other concert versions took place over the years in different countries. However, this was to be a complete staging of the opera, likely the first performance using all of Schubert's music.

The production caused controversy and discontent. It had always been expected the Vienna Philharmonic would undertake such a project and

*Schubert Symphonies recording with Claudio Abbado*

they were naturally not pleased a young upstart rival had been afforded the privilege. Ruth Berghaus' modern staging caused problems from both technical and performing points of view and the production did not go down well with the conservative public and press.

Since the opera had never been recorded, Claudio insisted Deutsche Gramophone should be present. However, they were not keen and gave the excuse they had no recording team available, as they were deployed elsewhere. My own belief was they did not envisage public demand or financial return. Surprisingly, the recording received seven awards.

Claudio was not to be put off and urged to me to resolve the problem. Time was running out and I was still pleading the case the day before the dress rehearsal, but finally managed to persuade DGG to re-route one of their recording teams to Vienna. They travelled overnight through Europe, arriving, much to everyone's relief, just in time to set up their equipment and record the general rehearsal. The situation was saved and Claudio had successfully got his own way, once more

# Berlin

Claudio's influence was of paramount importance when he approached his friend, Ulrich Eckhardt, at the time Director of the Berlin Festival, and persuaded him to put forward a proposal to the Berlin Senate for the COE to be given a residency.

In December 1989, the COE was in residence with Claudio. Martha Argerich was the soloist in a performance of Ravel's *Piano Concerto* and Barbara Sukova the narrator for a performance, in German, of Prokofiev's *Peter and the Wolf*, which DGG recorded and released in several different languages, using the voices of artists famous in each of the countries in which it was to be marketed, e.g., Charles Aznavour (France), Roberto Benigni (Italy) and Sting (UK and USA).

At the time of signing, the contract contained a clause that he agreed to commit to conduct at least once every season. At the time it did not appear to present any problem, as Claudio was still Music Director in Vienna. However, he surprised everyone by being elected by the Berlin Philharmonic Orchestra musicians as their Chief Conductor following the death of Herbert von Karajan. Lorin Maazel had been considered the main contender with Claudio only having an outside chance. This appointment made it difficult, if not almost impossible, for him to honour the commitment made to the Senate.

He tried to get around the issue by inviting both orchestras to take part in a complete Schubert Symphony cycle during the 1997 Berlin Festival. Neither orchestra was happy, particularly the COE who had recently performed in concert at the Salzburg Festival and recorded the complete cycle for DGG, which had been awarded a Gramophone Record of the Year, *Choc D'Or* and several other prestigious awards. They were allocated the early symphonies to be performed in the Kammermusiksaal and the BPO the later ones in the larger Philharmonie.

Claudio did manage to conduct on a few other occasions, but as time passed, with pressure from the Berlin Philharmonic, he found it increasingly more difficult and eventually we only met him in Ferrara and occasionally in Paris.

## 60th Birthday

In June 1993, concerts were organised in Ferrara, to coincide with his 60th birthday. During the same period Deutsche Grammophon scheduled recordings of Mozart Piano Concertos, K461 and 453, with soloist Maria Joao Pires, who, unfortunately, was not able to take part in the concert performances because she had commitments in Japan and could only arrive in time for the recording sessions. Luckily, Radu Lupu was available and agreed to be the soloist just for the concerts.

Alessandra and her Festival colleagues arranged a surprise birthday party in the grounds of the converted convent where the musicians of COE were staying.

It was a balmy summer's evening in Ferrara, the convent's gardens were decorated with fairy lights and the heady fragrant aroma of jasmine wafted through the air as people brushed past; wine was flowing freely and stomachs were satisfied with appetising Italian dishes.

Towards the end of the evening to the delight of everyone, a large birthday cake appeared followed by loud cheers and applause as Claudio made a wish and cut the first slice.

Afterwards, with a glass of cognac in one hand, he was seen puffing away on one of his Cuban cigars and thoroughly enjoying himself chatting with friends and family.

Radu also seemed genuinely pleased to have been invited and joined in the celebrations.

Joao, having missed all the fun, arrived the following day, and the serious business of making a recording took over.

*Claudio Abbado 60th birthday party  Ferrara, Italy 1993*

*Claudio Abbado with Radu Lupu Ferrara  Italy 1993*

# Claudio: Meetings and Conflicts

Meetings with Claudio continued to be a challenge. On one occasion, I had to fly to Milan to visit him in his apartment. By then, he had separated from Gabriella and Viktoria Mullova had moved in. While she practised in another room, he and I had lunch, together, in the kitchen and took time to make future plans.

A particularly annoying incident occurred when COE were performing an opera with him, in Ferrara, with a repeat performance in Parma. Having requested a meeting so many times, Alessandra, who had the unenviable task of organising his diary, finally managed to arrange an appointment at his hotel in Parma.

I travelled ahead of the Orchestra and duly arrived at the appointed time, only to be kept waiting in the hotel lobby. After a while, I saw a young female holding a score get into the lift, I guessed to his suite. Either he had conveniently forgotten our appointment or more than likely considered it more important to discuss music than dates and programmes. I showed my irritation, later, in his dressing room at the theatre, which he ignored and asked me to come to see him during the interval, which was a complete waste of time, as nothing was achieved.

Usually, full orchestral meetings took place during a tour and Claudio, as Artistic Adviser, was invited to attend a meeting in Vienna. He took the opportunity to express strong views about a certain issue and was met with opposition from some of the musicians. He found it hard to accept, not having the final word and was challenged by one particular musician, who told him, 'he had only one vote, like everyone else'. To loyal Claudio supporters this was an affront, rude and a gross insult. After he had left the meeting there followed a heated discussion, which continued outside the hall, where an apology was demanded from the offending musician.

He was always insistent as to which musicians should play for him, always preferring his favourites, many having worked with him in the European Community Youth Orchestra and not all of whom had become members of COE.

The musicians jealously guarded their right to decide who should play but more often than not he got his way causing bad feeling and sometimes resentment. Claudio's stubbornness, and insistence, no matter what it took, resulted in several conflicts, not only with the orchestral musicians, but with artists and other conductors. My own patience was tested many times and Claudio seemed always to enjoy irritating me.

## Luciano Pavarotti

A gala concert was arranged in the Ferrara Theatre, featuring Luciano Pavarotti, Claudio and the COE. A German television company was engaged to record only the Pavarotti contribution. He arrived, together with his entourage, consisting of personal assistants, cook and vast quantities of pasta and fruit. Before the concert, one assistant applied what looked like shoe-blacking to his hair and eyebrows!

There was obvious tension between conductor and soloist, possibly related to a previously difficult operatic collaboration, and Claudio demonstrated, once again, how stubborn he could be. Luciano was well known for singing romantic 'bel canto' arias and it had been many years since he had sung anything written by Mozart which required him to use a different technique and tessitura. However, Claudio insisted he should sing a Mozart aria and Luciano reluctantly agreed, but he was obviously not at all comfortable and struggled during the performance.

At the time, he was also having problems with his health, finding it difficult to walk unaided, needing to be assisted on to the stage. Once in position, with legs astride and supported by a high stool behind him, he stood motionless throughout the performance. It was frankly embarrassing and although filmed by the TV company, the programme was not actually released until many years after his death.

## Don Giovanni

In 1996, I was invited to Ferrara to discuss budgets for a new production of *Don Giovanni*. I had earlier submitted a costing for the Orchestra's participation, which the Management found too expensive, and requested a reduction, because they had so far not been able to raise sponsorship and might have had to cover all costs, themselves.

I told them it was impossible and politely suggested they should perhaps consider delaying the project, until such time as the necessary funds would be available.

This did not go down at all well and I was firmly informed it would be out of the question, because it was Claudio's wish and had to take place.

Discussions continued and after both sides had made concessions, terms were finally agreed and the performances took place the following January.

As the Principal Oboe and Principal Horn players had other commitments and could not be available, we engaged our top deputies as substitutes. The replacement French Horn player had originally been in the second position during the Orchestra's early days and, sadly for him, that was how Claudio remembered him, even though he had since become a very respected Principal Player, in his own right.

Realising Claudio would not be happy, I did my best to explain the reasons why the two Principals could not be present, but he was not prepared to be reasonable and responded angrily with, 'if I can find the time to be available, so should they'. Nevertheless, the performances went very well, but he gave the replacement a hard time.

Sir Georg Solti wished to capitalise on two earlier successes and invited the COE for another tour with concert performances and a recording for Decca of the same opera. Claudio, meanwhile, had persuaded DGG to record his version and was adamant the COE should not play for both projects.

Since both recording companies happened to be part of the same larger Phonogram Group, they agreed between them that the problem could easily be solved by organising release dates far enough apart so as not to clash. Sir Georg accepted this compromise but only with the understanding his recording would be released first! Claudio, true to form, remained stubbornly opposed and no amount of persuasion could change his mind.

Embarrassed, I called Sir Georg, and told him that, as the DGG recording contract was exclusive for five years, there was nothing more I could do. I expressed the Orchestra's disappointment, but he was angry with Claudio's intransigence and reluctantly withdrew the invitation. Instead he offered the project to the London Philharmonic Orchestra.

Not long afterwards, I was asked by the Aix en Provence Festival to submit a financial proposal for the Orchestra to take part in yet another production, which was to be directed by Peter Brook with the conducting shared between Claudio and Daniel Harding. The Festival's Management came to meet with me, in London. They were obviously not happy. Their original plan had been to perform the opera with young singers and orchestra with Daniel as the only conductor. In addition, Peter Brook had requested that everyone should spend at least five weeks in Aix, ahead of the performances, in order to let the production evolve naturally.

Daniel, who had earlier worked as Claudio's assistant, sought the latter's advice as to whether he should accept the engagement. As he had never worked with Peter Brook and saw an opportunity to do so, Claudio proposed that he should personally become involved and insisted the COE should be invited to play. This turned the whole project upside down and could, potentially, have completely blown the budget, which caused confusion and great frustration for everyone. The problem was, no one wanted to go against Claudio's wishes.

I explained to the Festival people there was simply no possibility the COE musicians could make themselves available for such a long period because when not working together they had other commitments in their respective countries, and even if it had been possible, the cost would have been prohibitive. Moreover, from a professional point of view, we were already committed to the Styriarte Festival and Nikolaus Harnoncourt for projects in Graz during the same period. As was becoming a habit, I tried reasoning with Claudio, who was not prepared to be understanding or sympathetic but, instead, became obstinate and outrageously, even suggested that Peter Readman should find the money and risk upsetting Nikolaus Harnoncourt!

The unfortunate incident put a strain on our relationship with him. Even though disappointed and very upset, he nevertheless went ahead with the project, sharing the conducting with Daniel, and chose instead musicians from the Mahler Youth Orchestra, a consequence of which was the birth of the Mahler Chamber Orchestra, which became one of COE's rivals. Relations with him deteriorated after that and he distanced himself, refusing or ignoring invitations for future projects. When I met him again in Berlin, some years later, it was at the end of a rehearsal with the Berlin Philharmonic. Putting his arm around my shoulders he invited me to join him in his dressing room, where he expressed his continuing hurt and disappointment.

During one of the COE's visits to Salzburg I came across the conductor Ricardo Chailly, in town. We chatted for a while and he told me he was planning to record Rossini Overtures and asked if the Orchestra could be available for the project. I thanked him, but had to explain it was not possible, because we had already recorded them with Claudio for DGG.

## The Final Curtain

With little or no contact, or the prospect of any further projects with him in the diary, we were alarmed to hear that he was seriously unwell and had undergone major surgery.

It was not until May 2002 the COE had an opportunity to work with him again for the very last time. A prestigious video recording of Schubert Song Arrangements was scheduled with DGG at the Cite de la Musique in Paris, with soloists Thomas Quasthof and Anne-Sofie von Otter, with whom we had previously performed the Arrangements at the Salzburg Festival.

Claudio was just recovering from his serious illness and it was a shock to see him a shadow of his former handsome self. Before the concert he invited me into his dressing room for a chat, during which he asked me to button his shirt and straighten his bow tie, just like old times.

Several former members of COE were invited to join the project to boost the size of the Orchestra for the larger works and it was a very sentimental and moving occasion. He appeared to enjoy being amongst old friends, smiled a lot and complimented the musicians, which encouraged everyone to hope that after such a long time it would cause a spark to ignite a desire to work together again.

He accepted our invitation to supper which had been organised for the Singers and Orchestra after the performance in a restaurant nearby. Peter made a short speech, expressing pleasure at seeing Claudio again and presented him with an engraved silver plate which had been commissioned in London in recognition of the special relationship. There was little response, he did not stay long and left without giving any future commitment or even saying goodbye.

I found the whole episode upsetting. Distraught, I left for my hotel in floods of tears with a strong feeling this might also be the end of the line for me. I fled the following day to my house and husband in Brittany and again shed buckets of tears to a concerned Charles, who wondered what on earth had happened.

The COE never worked with Claudio again. He instead concentrated on his commitment to young musicians, making time to work with his new orchestras, the Mahler Chamber Orchestra and later the Mozart Orchestra, based in Bologna, in which he invited some of his COE favourite musicians to take part, and where he was in close contact with his medical team and his daughter Alessandra, who remained constantly at his side.

He also became Music Director of the very successful Lucerne Festival Orchestra for which he chose his favourite musicians from the Berlin Philharmonic, Vienna Philharmonic and COE for the Principal positions. The Mahler Chamber Orchestra made up the rank and file. He also continued to invite some of his closest COE and LSO sailing friends to join him in Sardinia, where he had a house and a large boat.

Sadly, Claudio died in 2016 and will be much missed, but he has left a wonderful legacy and souvenirs of so many years of beautiful concerts, overseas tours, operas and recordings, not forgetting the jokes and parties with him.

Over the years, Claudio and I had become good friends and he always claimed he had personally recommended me for the position of General Manager of the COE, which was not strictly true. It had been Gina Cowan, at the time his manager at Harold Holts, who suggested the idea to her boss Martin Campbell White.

I often teased him about the fact he was eight years and two days older than me, both born under the sign of Cancer. He chided me for not learning to speak Italian, although Henrietta did give me a few lessons and, over the years, I picked up a number of phrases, unfortunately some I remembered from Italian Opera. When one time I was asked my name, I replied, 'Mi chiamano June', copying *Mimi* from Puccini's *La Boheme*!

After a COE London concert, which Claudio had conducted and celebrated pianist Rudolf Serkin was the soloist, Peter and Victoria Readman invited Claudio, Gabriella, myself, a few friends and supporters, to their home for a late supper party. During a conversation, an elderly lady expressed her admiration for Claudio, hailing him as a genius. Gabriella, who was within earshot, quickly interjected with, 'no way could he be a genius because he was born under the sign of Cancer and therefore only be good at what he does.'

Claudio was very generous, often inviting everyone in the Orchestra to join him at one of the best Italian restaurants in town, where he was known. He always chose the finest wines and usually ended the meal with a favourite digestif and a very large Cuban cigar.

One day, after a rehearsal, I went to see him in his dressing room and found him very excited. Sebastien, his son with second wife Gabriella, had, for sometime, expressed a desire to own a yellow London taxi and Claudio had managed to locate one. He wanted to surprise Sebastien on his birthday and had arranged for it be delivered that day to the London home he shared with his mother.

I am not convinced he ever grew up. Although always surrounded by sycophants, colleagues and admirers, he cut a lonely figure. He clearly preferred to be in the company of young musicians who appreciated his mischievous sense of humour and he theirs, always avoiding, if possible, anyone who represented Management. I also believe many of the female members of the Orchestra were, secretly, a little in love with him.

# Alexander Schneider

Alexander Schneider's life is like a novel, which he recounted in his memoirs *Sasha, A Musician's Life*. He was born Abram Sznejeder, in Vilnius. At the age of 16, he left Vilnius in 1924 and joined his brother Mischa Schneider in Frankfurt. In 1927, he became leader of an orchestra in Saabruecken and it was, at the point, he changed his name. He held subsequent Leader positions with German orchestras but, in 1932, he lost his job, as a result of the ongoing Nazi campaign against Jews, and soon had to leave Germany.

Sasha led a very colourful life. Before leaving Europe, as a young man, he would play the violin in cafes and restaurants, in order to make a living. He also played chamber music, together with his brother, and they later formed the famous Budapest Quartet, giving many concerts and making several very successful recordings. In 1934, the Nazis made threats and the Quartet left Berlin for Paris, the next day, never to return to Germany. When war broke out in 1939, they happened to be on tour in the United States and obtained permission to stay and from then on made it their base. In 1954, he married film actress Geraldine Page. They divorced in 1957.

He famously studied in Prades, in the south of France with Pablo Casals, who refused to give concerts in countries which had recognised the Spain of Franco. It was there, Sasha had the idea of founding the Prades Festival and persuaded Casals to participate in the 1950 Festival, to honour the 200th anniversary of Bach's death.

In the US, after leaving the Budapest Quartet, he became involved with various ensembles and projects. This allowed him to devote his time to the Marlboro Summer Festival, working together with eminent musicians, giving master classes and performing together with his students, one of whom was Douglas Boyd, who was so impressed with his teaching methods and music philosophy, that he suggested Sasha should be invited to London to work with the young COE musicians.

Through our City of London connections, we were invited to take part in the City of London Festival. The concerts were conducted by Sacha with Marieke Blankestijn, the youngest and one of our most talented violinists, as the soloist. The project was a great success both with the audience and most importantly, a great relationship was forged between Sasha and the Orchestra, in particular with members of the Wind Section, with whom he later made very successful recordings of Mozart's compositions for Wind Ensemble during an enjoyable weekend at Forde Abbey in Dorset.

He also made recordings for full orchestra and soloists which were issued on the COE own label. For the recording of Mozart's Clarinet

Concerto, Richard Hosford had one of his instruments specially modified by extending its length and adding keys so as to enable him to play lower notes as the composer intended. The recording with Sasha of Dvorak's Wind and String Serenades stands out as one of the best.

He conducted concerts in the Lichfield Festival, and undertook major tours with COE to Italy and the United States. The Italian tour was shared with celebrated cellist Mitslav Rostropovich as soloist, which did not always go well. There were musical disagreements, which resulted in Sasha insisting that Slava should direct himself.

He also shared a US tour with Claudio Abbado and James Judd. Following an afternoon concert in Hertford Connecticut, the Orchestra was due to fly to New York, but because of bad weather the flight was cancelled and we had instead to organise buses to transport the musicians.

Sasha, who was not involved in that section of the tour, was an accomplished cook and wine connoisseur, and had invited the whole Orchestra to supper that evening in his apartment in an old, converted warehouse. We arrived very late but he warmly welcomed everyone with a glass of very good wine and sensing how hungry everyone must have been after the long journey, immediately set about serving the delicious meal he had prepared earlier. Needless to say, tiredness was soon forgotten, it was a memorable occasion and everyone had a good time.

The COE was also invited to give a private concert at Blenheim Palace for one of our major sponsors BOC and I offered to drive Sasha to and from the venue. Unfortunately, during the return journey it was dark and raining so heavily I found it difficult to see the road. Spotting a petrol station, Sasha asked me to stop while he went inside. He returned holding a can of Pepsi, which to my horror he threw over my windscreen, a trick he must have used before because it immediately cleared the screen and I was able to continue driving and return him safely to his hotel.

He was never one to hold back his opinions, considering it his mission to give advice and at times even castigate. He was so convinced he was the holder of the truth and it was his duty to convey this to his friends, even if it was unpleasant to hear. He behaved this way with many people, some of whom got angry with him, but he was very much loved and respected as a musician and teacher.

Celebrated violinist, Yehudi Menuhin, conducted the COE during one of its visits to the Salzburg Summer Festival and after the concert was invited with the whole Orchestra to supper at one of the castles. Unfortunately, the Orchestra's musicians were not allowed to enter by the main entrance with the other important guests but were ushered in through the back door. One of the Jewish members of the Orchestra was overheard comparing this treatment to the horrible experiences suffered by many of his race during the Nazi occupation! When he heard about the incident, Sasha, a fellow Jew, was incensed at the idea of Yehudi ever having agreed to set foot in the country!

In later life, he lived alone in his converted New York warehouse loft. It was sparsely furnished but did have a very well-equipped kitchen and a collection of fine wines. He had so enjoyed the pleasures of life that he could not bear the trials of growing old, no longer being able to play the violin and gradually losing his sight, having difficulty climbing the stairs and moving about in his house.

He also owned a villa in Paradou in Provence, to where he would escape as often as possible. He sent many loving post cards to me from there. He had been in the habit of proposing marriage not only to me, but also to several female members of COE! No-one took him seriously, and I suspect, neither did he.

Until his death in 1993, aged 84, he remained Artistic Director of the Schneider Concerts at the New School (New York City), under whose auspices, together with his manager Frank Salomen, he founded in 1993 the New York String Orchestra.

# Nikolaus Harnoncourt

Nikolaus Harnoncourt was born Johann Nikolaus Graf (Count) de la Fontaine d'Harnoncourt-Unverzagt on December 6, 1929, Saint Nikolaus day. His mother was a great-grand-daughter of the Habsburg Archduke Johann, making him a descendant of various Holy Roman Emperors and other European royals.

He played cello in the Vienna Philharmonic Orchestra and together with his celebrated violinist wife, Alice, formed their own orchestra, Concentus Musicus, dedicated to playing early classical works in an authentic style with period instruments. String players did not use vibrato, trumpets and horns had no valves and the timpani had goat skin heads instead of plastic.

Nikolaus became well-known as a pioneer of the Early Music Movement which was to be emulated later by others and had a large following amongst academics and students, some of whom happened to be members of the COE, who were so impressed they suggested he should be invited to work with them.

In 1986, Alexander Pereira, at that time Intendant of the Konzerthaus in Vienna, invited him to conduct two concerts with the COE with violinist Gidon Kremer as soloist. Beethoven's Sixth and Eighth Symphonies, both of which the COE had performed many times before, were the first to be rehearsed in a musty recording studio in the bowels of the Wiener Konzerthaus.

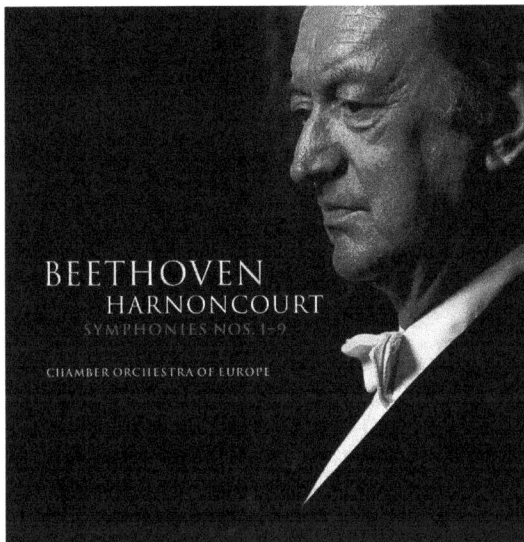

Beethoven Symphonies Recordings with Nikolaus Harnoncourt

For so many years influenced by Claudio Abbado, this was indeed a whole new experience which necessitated a drastic change in the style of playing. The results were often instantaneous, the musicians quickly grasping the ideas and techniques of a rhetorical approach to music making. He always managed to get a desired effect or sound by encouraging the musicians to use their imaginations, describing images or scenes with amusing anecdotes or reciting English poems which his nanny had taught him. Our Principal Timpanist, Geoffrey Prentice, who at the time was a vegetarian, was not at all comfortable and offered not to play, because he was required to switch from his plastic head instruments, to those with animal skins. It took a lot of persuading before he finally, but reluctantly, agreed.

Hans Landesmann, a Viennese businessman, Salzburg Intendant and Alexander's predecessor, invited Claudio to accompany him to the second concert which concluded with Beethoven's monumental Fifth Symphony. Playing the piece for the first time, the musicians were possessed by the music and the new musical language. After the final chord there was only silence followed by a loud groan from a member of the audience and then a spattering of applause which slowly grew. Hans and Claudio were overheard expressing their dislike of Nikolaus' style and did not go backstage afterwards to congratulate him.

As for members of COE, they were entranced and eager for more. For both Orchestra musicians and Nikolaus Harnoncourt there was mutual admiration and respect, and thus began a long, fruitful and successful relationship, which led to residencies for COE in the Austrian towns of Feldkirch and Graz. The annual invitations gave opportunities for Nikolaus to expand his repertoire, having previously concentrated on early music with his own orchestra.

There were very few personal meetings with him. We met mostly at social events and receptions after concerts. Champagne was always served in his dressing room after a concert, when an elated and sweaty Nikolaus would hold court, entertaining everyone present with a musical history lesson.

All planning meetings for future projects were conducted with Alice. Sometimes we would meet over coffee at her hotel or rented apartment. We also sat together during rehearsals, trying to whisper so as not to disturb Nikolaus and the musicians. She enjoyed any scandal and stories about the musicians, which were probably shared with her husband, later. When we were overheard, he would turn to glare at us both, or interrupt our conversation to ask for Alice's opinion on a musical point. As a very accomplished violinist, she had responsibility for inserting all string bowings and Nikolaus' markings into the orchestral parts.

Nikolaus had meanwhile moved allegiance to the German recording company Teldec, later bought by Warner Classics, who encouraged him to schedule a Beethoven Symphony Cycle. Each year different symphonies were rehearsed and performed, first in Feldkirch and afterwards Graz, where the concerts were recorded 'live' with re-takes the following day. A video documentary about the making of the symphonies, featuring interviews with the musicians and myself, was commissioned and later transmitted by BBC 4. The recordings were a great success and received numerous prestigious awards, including *Gramophone Record of the Year* and *Choc D'Or.*

Personally, I prefer the live recording of a brilliant and exciting COE concert performance of the Third Symphony *Eroica*, with the Swedish conductor Herbert Blomstedt. Since he was a Seventh Day Adventist and observed the Biblical Sabbath, I had to avoid scheduling any rehearsal or concert between the hours of Friday and Saturday sundowns.

Recordings of all the Beethoven Overtures followed, some of which took place in the newly built concert hall in Athens. Later performances and live recordings of Beethoven's Five Piano Concertos took place in Graz with Pierre Laurent Aimard.

Prestigious tours were also undertaken with Nikolaus throughout Europe, with performances in major concert halls. Other Symphonic cycles by Schumann and Mendelssohn were planned in Graz, as well as complete opera productions and recordings of Beethoven's *Fidelio,* Schumann's *Genoveva*, Offenbach's *Grande Duchesse de Gerolstein* and Gershwin's *Porgy & Bess*, which Nikolaus said he had grown to love, when he was a boy. He was also encouraged to move on to more romantic repertoire, performing works by Dvorak and Brahms.

Having achieved considerable success and international recognition, Teldec were ambitious for him to be working with the world's major symphony orchestras, such as the Berlin Philharmonic. He already had an association with the Concertgebouw in Amsterdam, which he often guest conducted. With this in mind they convinced him that Brahms symphonies required much larger orchestral forces. I did my utmost to keep the recordings for COE, exceptionally offering to increase the size of the string sections, but the die was cast. The project took place with the Berlin Philharmonic which led to further engagements, giving Harnoncourt the desired exposure which helped to promote his international image and consequently boost the coffers of the recording company. We did, however, manage to keep the Dvorak *Slavonic Dances* recordings, which went on to achieve critical acclaim and were voted *Gramophone Magazine Record of the Year* in 1992.

*1992 Gramophone Record of the Year Award*

## Beethoven in New York

Nikolaus hated travelling long distances, which was of concern to Teldec who wished to promote their recordings overseas, particularly in the US. While in charge of Carnegie Hall in New York, Franz-Xaver Ohnesorg introduced the idea of COE performing a Beethoven Symphony Cycle with Nikolaus but, unfortunately, due to a major disagreement with the Board, he was fired before the project materialised.

Happily, the new management team agreed to go ahead with the project and I successfully negotiated a contract for two Cycles, but the fees offered were very low. I agreed instead to a percentage of the audience income which, even with full houses, was unlikely to cover the enormous costs. Teldec were persuaded it was in their interest to contribute financially, in addition to undertaking publicity and promotion, and BOC had interests in the US, and were happy to act as sponsor, generously making up the remaining anticipated deficit.

Nikolaus was miserable in the US, not at all comfortable with the hustle, bustle and noise of the city that never sleeps. He suffered from jet-lag and his routine was upset by the time change. It was up to Alice to keep him happy and to make sure that he did not take off on the next plane back to Austria. She also needed access to a supermarket, to buy food and at least to keep life as normal as possible, by preparing lunch in their room. To add to his woes, there was building work going on at his hotel, which he found disturbing and we hastily moved him to a quieter part of town.

There was a partial transformation once he was in the theatre and able to concentrate on making music.

While the Orchestra were rehearsing, Charles and I decided to go for a walk. The record stores were full of publicity for the Beethoven Cycle and promotion for Teldec/Harnoncourt recordings with life-size cardboard cut-outs of Nikolaus. We had fun searching through the CD racks placing COE recordings at the front. We also took the opportunity to visit a *Sounds by Singer* showroom and fell in love with German manufactured Audio Physic speakers. As soon as we arrived back in the UK we contacted the company in Frankfurt to order a pair. They gave us a great deal of pleasure for a few years before, twice, being replaced with higher and more expensive models, which had to be placed in critical positions necessitating re-arranging the other furniture in the room.

For each concert, the Orchestra was allocated complimentary seats in a balcony box and we were sometimes joined by special guests, one of whom was conductor Sir Andrew Davis, who was in town to conduct the New York Philharmonic Orchestra. He was very enthusiastic and eager to listen to Nikolaus' interpretations of the symphonies.

Peter and Victoria attended every performance and were joined one evening by married friends who lived in New York. The wife, who, like Charles, was Lebanese, had apparently been a former girlfriend of Peter but she and Victoria seemed to get along very well. The project was a great success; all concerts were sold out and well received by the critics; importantly, we also managed to keep within budget.

Although pleased with the results, Nikolaus vowed never to travel long distances again, a promise he did not however manage to keep, as some years later he was persuaded, no doubt with difficulty, to tour Japan with the Berlin Philharmonic Orchestra. When I heard this news I smiled to myself, remembering the occasion when COE performed before an audience of sleeping university students. I tried to imagine how Nikolaus might have reacted faced with such a situation!

## Salzburg

Nikolaus did not much enjoy living in the modern world, detesting noise from mobile telephones, aeroplanes and airports. On one occasion, he even stopped the Orchestra playing, when he heard the sound of a mobile telephone, turned around to scowl at the audience, then began again from the beginning.

In the summer of 1988, we were invited to give an open-air concert with him in the Salzburg Town Square (Domplatz). This took place the day after a performance in Attergauer, and the day before the official opening of the Festival. Celebrated Austrian pianist Friedrich Gulda, was the soloist in a Mozart piano concerto and was joined for an encore by the jazz pianist Chick Correa. I remember spotting the reclusive conductor Carlos Kleiber in the audience, who had come from his home in Munich especially to hear the concert.

To the delight of everyone both pianists met up afterwards with Joe Zinwalder and his group for a late-night jamming session in the square.

During another of the COE's visits to Salzburg, I was privileged to be invited to the Harnoncourt home for lunch. Hiring an automatic BMW, I drove on a bright summer's day through the beautiful Austrian countryside to their house, which was situated in a small village about 60 kilometres away. The large rambling family home, recently decorated for the first time for more than 25 years, was comfortable but simply furnished, most items inherited or bought second-hand and become worn over time.

Alice confided in me that, when they were first married, they rented a small apartment in Vienna and, not earning very much money, lived very frugally. She confessed to having owned only two skirts and two sweaters. Nikolaus never liked shopping for clothes; whenever he needed underwear or a new dress shirt for a concert, it would be Alice who purchased it for him. He proudly wore a suit and a pair of brown leather shoes inherited from his father many years before.

To save money, Alice always prepared lunch at home, hotel room, or wherever they happened to be staying when on tour. Fame and fortune did not change them. Alice might spoil herself occasionally by buying a new dress and maybe a pair of shoes and Nikolaus did have a suit especially made for the occasion when he conducted a New Year's Day concert with the Vienna Philharmonic Orchestra which was transmitted for television around the world.

Alice had prepared lunch on this occasion, which the three of us ate together in the enormous kitchen. After the meal I was given evidence of exactly how their money had been invested and shown a valuable collection of oil paintings and antique harpsichords from around the world, some of which Nikolaus had restored himself. I was also taken to see what used to be his workshop where, as a young man, he carved wooden marionettes, some destined for performances at the Marionetten Theatre.

With the success of the Beethoven Symphonies in August 1994, the Orchestra was invited by the Salzburg Festival to perform two Cycles with Nikolaus in the Grosser Saal of the Mozarteum. Every concert was sold out, reminiscent of my very first visit to the Festival, in 1973, with the London Symphony Orchestra. However, I suspect for political reasons, the concerts did not take place in the Grosses Festspielhaus but in the much smaller venue.

The temperature outside was more than 30 degrees and because Nikolaus hated air conditioning it was turned off. The heat generated by so many bodies inside the hall rose to an even higher level, making it extremely uncomfortable, especially for the musicians, who were worried about how it might affect their instruments. Fortunately, instead of the usual formal evening attire they were encouraged to wear lighter summer clothes. Nikolaus appeared in a billowing smock, looking more like a country yokel than an eminent conductor! Reviewed in the Austrian Press, the performances were described as *'superlative, impeccable, unparalleled'*.

As my mother was an admirer of Nikolaus, I invited her to all the concerts and she showed her enthusiasm by applauding, cheering and stamping her feet along with the rest of the audience. After the first concert, I went as usual backstage to Nikolaus' dressing room in order to congratulate him. We exchanged kisses on both cheeks and he handed me a glass of champagne. We had begun to speak about the performance when suddenly my mother, who had followed me and not wishing to be left out, exclaimed 'what about me?'. Not recognising her, Nikolaus just stared in disbelief. Feeling extremely embarrassed I made a hasty introduction, he quickly recovered and graciously proffered a cheek. She had brought with her a poster with his photograph, earlier obtained from Teledec, and placed it in front of him to sign, along with an autograph in the evening's programme. It was eventually framed, hung on the wall in her bedroom and received a goodnight kiss just before she turned out the light.

Later she was thrilled to be given a boxed set of the Beethoven Symphonies which she listened to on her Sony Walkman while working around the house.

## Nikolaus the Leader

Following a period at the Styriarte Festival in Austria, we were invited to take part in a Music Festival in the northern German town of Bremen. The instruments were transported by truck overnight and members of the Orchestra travelled by chartered plane on the day of the concert. I had a meeting scheduled in Bremen and arranged to take a commercial flight a day earlier. Nikolaus also wished to travel a day earlier but Alice, who would normally have accompanied him, had necessarily to take a later flight. She was concerned he would be travelling alone and was relieved when I offered to look after him.

Our flight to Bremen was not direct and we had to change planes at

Frankfurt. The transit time was extremely tight and became more so as our flight from Graz arrived a little late and we had to hurry through the vast terminal building in order to locate the shuttle bus to the terminal for the Bremen flight.

We found ourselves negotiating a warren of corridors and eventually began to feel lost. Sighting a lone official sitting at the end of a long empty corridor, Nikolaus remarked how it reminded him of a scene from a Kafka novel. At this point he was beginning to question my leadership ability and decided to take charge, which he justified by telling the story of when as a young man he was on a trip to Australia and had got lost, but found the way back to his hotel by following the sun's direction! Without the benefit of the sun to guide us we finally made it to the shuttle, arriving just as the flight was about to close, for which, of course, he took the credit!

On several occasions after that, especially during a dinner party, he took great delight in re-telling the story to a captive audience, sometimes exaggerating it to his advantage.

## Interpretations

During the long association with Nikolaus, the COE was able to perform and record with many international soloists. He had eminent admirers, among them conductors Simon Rattle, John Eliot Gardiner and Roger Norrington, all of whom were prepared to travel long distances to attend his concerts and his influence could subsequently often be heard in their own performances.

However, there were a few who did not agree with his musical interpretations or subscribe to the original instrument movement. In particular, one was the pianist Murray Perahia who Nikolaus invited as soloist to Graz. As was his usual habit, Nikolaus sent Murray a score of the concerto, with his own markings and ideas as to how it should be performed. Murray did not react well to this and was tempted to cancel. Fortunately, he had second thoughts, but was not at all happy and during the rehearsals there was tension and disagreement between them. When some, time later, he worked again with the Orchestra as a conductor and soloist, he spoke with some disdain about the experience.

The COE often performed both in concert and recording with Gidon Kremer and undertook several tours with him. He was also a favourite of Nikolaus and joined in the Beethoven cycle to perform and record the Violin Concerto and Romances. For the first and third movement cadenzas in the concerto he controversially preferred to use Avo Paert's arrangement of Beethoven's original version written for piano.

This was accompanied by timpani and a specially tuned piano, which were located in an ante room. A television monitor  linked to a camera focussed on the conductor in the hall, was installed in order to synchronise with the rest of the Orchestra.

Russian Valery Afanassiev was the pianist and the intention was to give the impression of the composer being present!

## The Schubert Debacle

The COE made many successful recordings with Claudio Abbado for DGG, one of which was a complete cycle of the Schubert Symphonies, recorded in different European venues over a period of two or three years.

Cycles were also scheduled with Nikolaus in Feldkirch and Graz, which both he and his recording company, Teldec, wanted to record, but it was not possible, because a five-year exclusive contract had been signed with DGG. This irritated and made Harnoncourt very unhappy and, instead, the recordings were made with the Concertgebouw Orchestra in Amsterdam. However, 'live ' radio recordings of the Graz concerts, taken by Austrian broadcaster ORF, were re-mastered and issued on CD in 2020.

An unfortunate situation occurred during Hans Landesmann's tenure as Intendant of the Salzburg Festival. He discussed with Nikolaus Harnoncourt the possibility of his conducting a complete cycle of Schubert symphonies with the COE, but later changed his mind and, instead, offered the project to Claudio. This caused a very serious problem for COE; maintaining good relations with both conductors was extremely important.

I tried to reason with Hans, but as Claudio had already agreed, it was a fait accompli. He told me not to worry and gave assurances he would personally handle the matter with Nikolaus, who, unfortunately, took the news very badly. He was naturally disappointed and angry, but rather than complain directly to Hans, he blamed me, believing I had in some way been complicit. It blighted what had been a very good relationship.

Whether Hans had lied or been economical with the truth we shall never know. It would also not have been surprising if Claudio had proposed the project himself and Hans had found it hard to refuse someone with whom he had formed a close relationship, in Vienna, and he was never a great fan of Nikolaus.

On several occasions after that, I was cold-shouldered by both Alice and Nikolaus and meetings became very formal. It was during one such meeting in London, the subject was raised. They both made it clear again they considered I had been duplicitous and dishonest! I tried to defend myself and to convince them Hans had been solely to blame, but once more this fell on to deaf ears, because, in their view, he was honourable and much respected in Austrian Society.

It was only much later when, having experienced a serious unrelated problem with Hans, Nikolaus finally realised and acknowledged the truth. I received an apology and slowly the atmosphere warmed and, I am pleased to say, we again became friends.

## Health Issues

In November/December 2000, Nikolaus was due to conduct the Orchestra on a major European tour. The plan was to rehearse in London and give the first concert in the Royal Festival Hall. However, just before the tour I received a telephone call from Alice to say Nikolaus was unwell and wished to cancel. This caused alarm because his involvement had been crucial to the success of my negotiations with the various concert promoters.

Nikolaus was sometimes suspected of being a hypochondriac and, during my conversation with Alice, I concluded it was one of those occasions. So I thought it worthwhile taking a strong approach with her to try and persuade Nikolaus to come to London, at least to rehearse, conduct the first couple of concerts and then decide whether or not he would feel well enough to continue the tour. In the event, Alice was successful but he stubbornly insisted he could not possibly continue after Paris, the second concert.

It dawned on me, that I should immediately try to find another eminent conductor who might be free and willing to take over. Not an easy task at such short notice. Luckily, Paavo Berglund came to the rescue and was available, not only to step in, but also willing to keep the same repertoire.

The next obstacle to be overcome was to persuade the promoters to accept the change and not cancel.

Baden-Baden and Cologne, in particular, refused and Vienna were not happy. Had they all decided to cancel, this would not only have left a huge hole in the tour schedule but would have resulted in considerable financial loss?

When Nikolaus was made aware of their reactions, he became incensed and immediately set about writing personal letters to each promoter. He castigated them for their unreasonable and unprofessional behaviour, emphasising his personal respect for his colleague, Paavo, and shamed them into agreeing to his replacement. His intervention saved the tour, no-one cancelled and, thankfully, it went ahead without mishap and was a success.

Gradually, the number of annual projects with Nikolaus decreased, mainly due to his failing health, dislike of travel and no longer wishing to tour. The popular visits to Graz continued for a few years, but gradually he gave less time. The annual Festival had been built around him and had attracted audiences, but without him the politics changed, there was less funding available and the Festival's management was forced to re-structure. Affordable projects were shorter in length and shared with other less expensive artists.

Nikolaus and Alice were both invited to become Honorary Members of the Orchestra.

# Paavo Berglund

Paavo first worked with the COE in 1985. We invited him to conduct the Orchestra for a tour of Spain, with concerts in Madrid, Bilbao, Barcelona, Valencia and Roquetas de Mar in Almeria. The programme included works by Haydn, Bartok and Beethoven. It was an occasion for the young musicians to get acquainted with this elf-like, left-handed, dry, unsmiling Finn, who usually dressed all in grey or black. Free times were spent by the pool when Paavo, still dressed the same, joined in.

The concert in Almeria was held during an afternoon in a beautiful little stone washed church with bright sunlight shining through brilliantly coloured stained glass windows. The doors either side were left open to allow a breeze and the audience encouraged to come and go, never staying very long to listen. Curiously, a man entered through one door with his dog, crossed in front of the stage and left through the other.

The tour ended with two concerts at the Evian Festival and the American soprano Barbara Hendrix performed Samuel Barber's *Knoxville summer 1915*. A particular favourite encore of Paavo's, the melancholy *Valse Triste,* was often played at the end of his concerts.

Beneath the austere exterior lay a warm and generous nature and he possessed a mischievous sense of humour. A very special relationship developed over the years, which led to regular engagements and tours with some very interesting concerts and recordings.

*Sibelius Symphonies recording with Paavo Berglund*

## Sibelius Symphonies

Paavo had previously recorded all the Sibelius symphonies with Finnish and Bournemouth Symphony Orchestras. Performing another cycle with COE brought a new dynamic, using the regular smaller string strength of the Orchestra for Symphonies Three, Four, Five and Seven, and augmenting them for One and Two, although not to full symphony orchestra size. The COE musicians, unused to this kind of repertoire, admirably rose to the challenge.

The recordings took place in various European concert halls, the last in Holland, in December 1990 at the end of a tour. Unfortunately, many of the musicians had become unwell with a nasty virus, but, as it was imperative for the cycle to be completed, they bravely vacated their sick beds, coughing and spluttering during the recording session, which more than tested the expertise of Tony Faulkner the recording engineer! Press comment: *'glorious, inspirational, wholly magisterial'*. With the success of the recordings, invitations were received to give performances at the 1998 Edinburgh and Helsinki Festivals. Performing all the symphonies over four days gave everyone a chance to visit the house of the composer. The comfortable home, situated in the countryside on the outskirts of Helsinki, had been left almost exactly as Sibelius and family had lived and worked.

After the final concert Paavo and his wife Kirsty kindly invited the whole Orchestra to their home for supper, which was a very happy occasion. Although he did not partake, he generously offered the musicians some very fine wines from his cellar.

## Brahms Symphonies

Paavo was persuaded to include Brahms' Third Symphony in one of his programmes, which was performed with the COE in Paris. Again, he was working with a smaller string strength than he was used to but was very happy with the result, as were the audience and Orchestra alike. My unsuccessful attempts at trying to persuade Nikolaus Harnoncourt and Teldec to record all four symphonies gave me the incentive to suggest to Paavo that he should perform and record them 'live' with the COE in the new concert hall in Baden-Baden.

The Finnish Recording Company Ondine, agreed to undertake the recordings on a royalty only basis and secured sponsorship to help with costs. Our old friends the Teldec recording team were engaged for the project which took place in May 2000 and was immediately followed by a tour with one concert in Frankfurt and a further three in Spain.

The Spanish tour was organised by an agent with whom it would be the first and certainly the only tour. During contract negations he had appeared genuine and gave assurances of having received firm sponsorship to cover all costs. As usual I requested a cash advance for the musicians' subsistence, which we duly received on arrival. However, despite numerous requests and subsequent threats to sue, no fees materialised afterwards, only a feeble excuse that funds had become tight and a promise to pay sometime in the future, which never happened. The result was a heavy overall financial loss and the only occasion when I had to admit failure. Although small comfort, I was later informed by the Manager of the Toulouse Orchestra that he had a similar experience with the same agent.

## Health Issues

It was rumoured that  Paavo was an alcoholic and often went on the wagon. and this was to become evident during COE tours. Usually at a dinner or an Orchestra reception, he would refuse a glass of wine and ask instead for water. His wife Kirsty, a lovely lady, who was wheelchair bound, would accompany him as often as possible and it became clear her presence helped Paavo to remain sober.

We first experienced a real problem with his drinking during a tour when Kirsty was not present and only able to meet up with us in Paris. We were performing concerts in various German cities and the manager of one hotel angrily informed me that Paavo had trashed his room and would not be welcome to return.

While waiting at the airport for our flight to Seville, where a concert was to take place the same evening in the Teatro de la Meastranza, we became worried when there was no sign of Paavo. I telephoned the hotel and was informed he had left only a few minutes before and was obviously going to be late. He eventually arrived looking confused and slightly dishevelled. It was obvious he had been drinking and needed help to find his airline ticket, which was discovered in his overcoat pocket. Two of the musicians escorted him to the plane and he slept throughout the flight.

After checking in to our hotel, I managed to get him into bed, concerned he might not be fit enough to conduct that evening. William Conway, our Principal Cellist, who was also making a second career as a conductor, agreed to be on standby and spent the rest of the day studying the score of Brahms' Fourth Symphony. Amazingly Paavo somehow made it to the concert, but had to conduct sitting on a chair with everyone holding their breath, willing him to get to the end of the performance.

The following morning, we flew to a sunny and very warm Mallorca for a concert in the Auditorium de Palma. When we arrived at the hall for a rehearsal, we discovered the promoter had advertised the concert for the wrong day. Frantic telephone calls were made to schools, hospitals and other institutions to rustle up an audience but, in the event, very few came. Nevertheless the concert went ahead and I found myself seated practically alone in the auditorium, doing my best to give support by clapping as loudly as possible. A tired Orchestra flew the next day to Barcelona and the tour finally ended in Bilbao, with Paavo somehow managing to stay the course. When Nikolaus Harnoncourt cancelled in November 2000, fortunately Paavo had been available and agreed to replace him.

In October 2001, concerts were again scheduled with him in Cologne, Berlin and Paris and Christian Tetzlaf was engaged as the soloist for performances of Sibelius' Violin Concerto. The programme also included Mendelssohn's Fifth and Sibelius' Seventh Symphonies.

However, Paavo became unwell in Cologne and was unable to continue the tour. At such short notice, I was unable to find a suitable replacement and, instead, proposed to Christian that he should consider directing the concerto from the violin and for the Leader of the Orchestra to take charge of the rest of the programme, from the first violin desk.

Understandably, Christian was at first reluctant, particularly as the concerto was notoriously difficult to play. I also had to persuade Berlin and Paris to accept the compromise.

Happily, it worked very well and both musicians received a standing ovation. In the second half of the concert, a more relaxed Christian was happy to give the Leader support, by joining the violin section for the symphony.

Our sponsor BOC, had business interests in Lithuania and in October 2003 invited the COE to give concerts with Paavo in the Vilnius Concert Hall. The visit aroused much excitement and interest among many of the local musicians, who attended the rehearsals and performances and had an opportunity to meet and chat to the COE musicians. Although a new member of the European Union, and the City centre had been given a face-lift, behind the facade there was much evidence of poverty and deprivation. The Vilnius concert, began what was Paavo's last tour with the COE. The programmes included compositions by Tchaikovsky, Mendelssohn and Dvorak, with additional performances in Frankfurt, Cologne and Barcelona.

Again, he travelled alone and appeared lost. He invited me to accompany him at mealtimes, sometimes in his hotel room, but one evening he kept me waiting in the hotel lobby. Concerned, I asked the hotel manager to go to his room to check on him. When Paavo eventually emerged, he was much the worse for wear.

We arrived in Barcelona the evening before the concert day. Conscious of a looming problem, I had taken the precaution of investigating other conductor availabilities and put together a short list, with emergency telephone numbers. After checking into the hotel, Paavo went straight to his room, ordered room service and was not seen again during the evening. The following morning, suddenly, I was woken by the telephone ringing and, when I answered, a shaky voice asked me to come to his room. I dressed, quickly, and went to reception to ask for someone to accompany me to open Paavo's door. When we entered, we found the room in total disarray, clothes strewn everywhere, the television set had been knocked over and Paavo was lying on the floor, with a nasty injury to his head.

We called for an ambulance and, when the paramedics arrived, they searched the room and Paavo's belongings, discovering his concert tails and jacket screwed up and several empty vodka bottles in his suitcase It was not difficult to speculate on what had happened. He had obviously drunk too much, slipped, scattering furniture and the television as he fell, and hit his head on the floor.

I accompanied him to the hospital and, after examination, he was told he would have to remain under observation, with no possibility of being able to conduct that evening's concert. While waiting at the hospital for news, I consulted my standby list of conductors and checked availabilities with agents and the willingness of someone, not only to fly at a moment's notice, but keep to the same programme. Luckily, Janos Fuerst was available and able to book a last-minute flight from Switzerland. A car was sent to pick him up at the airport and drive straight to the hall to rehearse with the Orchestra.

The promoter, without knowing the real reason for Paavo's indisposition, agreed for the concert to begin one hour later than scheduled. Spanish audiences are not usually known for their patience and understanding but, strangely, on this occasion accepted the late start and change of conductor. The concert went very well and the Orchestra received a standing ovation.

As Barcelona was the final concert of the tour, the Orchestra were to disband the following day and everyone return to his or her respective country. Paavo had meanwhile been allowed to return to the hotel. Prior to my departure, I arranged for him to stay on for a few days, before he flew home to Finland. I called Kirsty to inform her of what had happened, but she appeared not to be unduly surprised. I could not stay on, but Eddie, our stage manager, offered to look after Paavo and to get him safely on to the plane.

My last meeting with Paavo took place in his room. He presented a very sorry sight, his faced badly bruised. He apologised for all the trouble he had caused and promised never to drink again. I suggested that for the sake of his health, and career, he should make that promise not to me but to himself and try to keep it. I later discovered that he did not fly directly back to Helsinki but booked himself into a rehabilitation unit in Germany.

It was sometime before he conducted the COE again, and I was pleased to learn that he was invited to do so before he died in 2012 at the age of 83. There was always a genuine fondness and mutual respect between the musicians and Paavo, which endured until his death.

# Lorin Maazel

Lorin Maazel came to London to conduct the LSO's final concert of the season at the Royal Festival Hall on July 3, 1975. He had insisted on an all- orchestral programme, featuring two major symphonies by Tchaikovsky and Shostakovich and no soloist.

Although he was internationally famous, he had not conducted very often in London and seemed surprised and disappointed to discover the hall was not sold out, having arrogantly expected his reputation alone to have been sufficient to attract an audience.

We met again, much later, when the Chamber Orchestra of Europe was invited by Andrea Andermann, an independent promoter and film maker based in Rome, to give concerts with him in Italy. The first took place in 1985 in the Santa Cecilia Concert Hall in Rome. The programme included a performance of Vivaldi's *Four Seasons* with Lorin as the soloist.

He had been a child prodigy in the US, performing violin concertos with major orchestras in prestigious concert halls. This had obviously gone to his head and helped to develop his very large ego. He was intelligent, very well read and clearly did not tolerate fools easily, lapsing into boredom in the company of those who did not possess the same level of intellect. It also soon became clear that he had a photographic memory because when I gave him a list of the musicians taking part, he scanned the paper, put it into his pocket then proceeded to name each individual and his or her instrument.

The first morning, the musicians were assembled on stage, waiting for Lorin to arrive to take the rehearsal. For some time there was no sign of him so I suggested to the Leader, Gerard Korsten, also a budding conductor, that he should begin, directing from the violin. The rehearsal was well underway when Lorin, with his coat draped around his shoulders, finally appeared in the hall. Spotting him I went to welcome and guide him to the stage but he held me back. He listened and watched the Orchestra for a while before turning towards me and commenting sarcastically, 'they obviously do not need me'. I was not sure whether or not this was meant as a compliment! Nevertheless, he slowly took out his baton from its case, walked onto the stage, said good morning, and with no apology for being late or thanks to Gerard, continued the rehearsal.

After the break, he appeared with his violin to rehearse the Vivaldi, which he took at a painfully slow tempo. He had not played the instrument in public for some considerable time and was out of practice. Embarrassingly this became evident during the actual concert and several members of the audience, including myself, wore shocked looks on their faces. However, the evening was fortunately saved by the excellent renditions of the orchestral works expertly played by the young COE musicians.

There were several other Italian tours with Lorin. In 1986 Andrea invited the Orchestra to take part in a spectacular mid-summer concert in Florence, to be televised simultaneously all over the world. On a hot June evening it was performed in the open air, the animated Italian audience was seated on specially constructed raked scaffolding, and loudspeakers were positioned all around. As darkness fell the lights were turned low, the audience decibels decreased, and a spotlight was focussed on a smiling Lorin, wearing a white suit and holding a baton with flashing fairy lights, as he made his way onto the podium. He was obviously enjoying himself. The long programme, which went on late into the evening, contained several works including some of Lorin's own compositions written specially for the occasion. His large ego was very much on display that evening!

In the spring of 1987, a tour of the US East Coast was organised by New York Agent Douglas Sheldon of Columbia Artists Management (CAMI). A young German violinist, Frank Peter Zimmerman, little known at the time and a favourite of Lorin's, was engaged as the soloist.

The tour began in Florida and once again Lorin did not appear at the first rehearsal but instead sent a message to the effect that he had a family engagement and had confidence in Gerard to take over. However, during the actual performance, it was obvious Gerard had rehearsed Beethoven's *Pastoral* Symphony at a different tempo to that preferred by Lorin. Determined to exert his authority, Lorin deliberately slowed the Orchestra down mid performance, and luckily proved how closely the musicians had been following him.

The tour continued but there was a general air of discontent. Only after the final concert, and during a reception, he surprised everyone by congratulating the Orchestra and apologising for his unacceptable behaviour!

Lorin's reputation for being rude to orchestral musicians was well-known. He was once overheard swearing during a London performance. Socially and privately, however, he was charming, very interesting, able to converse on practically any subject, and possessed a sense of humour.

During another Italian tour, we had some free time in between concerts and he and I were invited by Andrea Andermann to visit a Truli village in Bari and went on to have a very enjoyable lunch together.

He was an amusing and perfect host. He was once directing Verdi's opera *Nabucco* at La Scala in Milan and invited me to attend a performance and afterwards to join him and his new young German actress wife, Anna, for supper at their apartment. I had received a card announcing their marriage, inside which had been two large, decorated hearts, each containing a smiling photograph of one of them. I find it a pity the orchestral musicians rarely had an opportunity to see this side of his character.

*Visiting the Trulis with Lorin Maazel in Bari Puglia during an ilalian tour*

# Sir Georg Solti

As the reputation of COE grew it came to the notice of Sir Georg Solti. He first approached me to discuss whether it would be possible for members of the Orchestra to take part in a new Mozart Festival in Frankfurt for which he had been invited to become Music Director (see Residences). The first festival took place in 1983.

In March 1985, he agreed to conduct two concerts in Nottingham and Croydon. The programme included Haydn's Symphony No. 104 and Schubert's' Symphony No. 5 with as soloist the Spanish pianist, Alicia De Larrocha, who played a different Mozart piano concerto in each concert (*K491* and *K537*) both recorded for Decca over three days in London at Henry Wood Hall. Initially I had great difficulty in trying to persuade him to reduce his fee for the concerts and he only agreed when I informed him Claudio had offered to do so, provided no-one else received more.

There was little opportunity to work with him during the next few years since both he and the Orchestra had very full diaries. However, one day I received a telephone call from Charles Kaye, Sir Georg's Personal Assistant to ask if the Orchestra could be available in January 1991 to undertake a major European tour of semi-staged concert performances and a recording for Decca of *The Marriage of Figaro*. Swedish mezzo soprano, Anne-Sofie von Otter, although almost seven months pregnant at the time, sang the *trouser* role of Cherubino.

We were thrilled to accept the invitation and the project was so successful it encouraged Sir Georg to plan another tour in April 1994. On that occasion the opera was *Cosi fan Tutte*. American soprano, Renee Fleming came in as a last-minute substitute in the role of Fiordiligi which was her European debut and helped to launch her international career. The Times headliine on the recording was '*Cosi fan Tutte: eclipsing all other recent versions*'.

Sir Georg was very pleased and, without the conflict with Claudio Abbado, more projects with him would have materialised. Unfortunately, the Orchestra never worked with him again, although a few musicians were invited to play in a symphony orchestra which was put together specially each year to raise money for charity with hand-picked members of major international orchestras with whom Sir Georg regularly worked.

# Sir Colin Davis

Always an admirer of Colin, as a conductor, and believing, if he had the chance to work with the COE it would go well, I suggested to the Orchestra committee that he should be invited to conduct a charity concert in the Queen Elizabeth Hall (QEH) in March 1985 to help raise funds for *Help a Child*, whose patron was the Duchess of Gloucester, who attended and we met together back stage, afterwards. Stephen Bishop Kovacevich, a personal favourite of Colin's, was the soloist in Beethoven's Piano Concerto No.4, which they had previously recorded together for Philips.

Unfortunately, the first rehearsal went badly particularly insofar as the German musicians were concerned as they resented what they perceived as Colin's 'schoolmasterly' approach. After the rehearsal, I received complaints and immediately informed him of the criticism. The atmosphere did improve and the final musical results were excellent, but the doubts and mixed feelings remained.

He had already been engaged to conduct another concert in the QEH in May the same year. The COE Principal Clarinettist Richard Hosford was to be the soloist in Mozart's Clarinet Concerto, and became excited when told that Colin was to conduct as he also played the clarinet and was particularly admired for his interpretation of Mozart's music.

The concert went very well but I still sensed unease amongst the musicians and a wish not to re-invite him. The chemistry had not worked, which I very much regretted.

During my final season, the COE celebrated its 25th anniversary. Special concerts conducted by Douglas Boyd, were organised in London's Queen Elizabeth Hall and the Stefaniansaal in Graz during the Styriarte Festival.

The London programme included Berlioz's *Sinfonie Fantastique* and was recorded and broadcast by the BBC for Radio Three, quite an undertaking for Douglas, whose conducting career was in its infancy. He regularly attended physiotherapy sessions with Colin's wife, Shamsie, at their home in North London, and while there took the opportunity to seek Colin's help and advice, knowing how respected and famous he was for his acclaimed interpretation of Berlioz's music in both concert and recordings.

The *Sinfonie* required larger forces than was usual for a chamber orchestra, and several past members of the Orchestra were invited to make up the numbers. During the rehearsal, the BBC recording crew became ecstatic and marvelled at the standard and commitment. Press reviews, afterwards, described the concert as '*one of the highlights of the London season*'.

Colin and Shamsie both attended the performance in the QEH and I sat next to them.

Afterwards he expressed his pleasure and satisfaction with Douglas' interpretation and the Orchestra's performance. He also said how sad he was at not having had another opportunity to conduct the Orchestra himself.

*With the Duchess of Gloucester backstage at the Queen Elizabeth Hall*

# Sir Roger Norrington

Roger possessed a good tenor voice and sang in choirs, so it was natural that his early career should find him specialising in that genre. He studied violin and conducting at the Royal College of Music, whilst continuing his love of singing.

He became Director of Kent Opera, formed his own orchestra which gave him exposure as a conductor focussing principally on choral repertoire and allowing him to specialise in performances of the classical repertoire using original instruments and no vibrato, interpreting works as far as possible as the composer intended.

I later learned he was an admirer of Nikolaus Harnoncourt, who had already established himself as the pre-eminent exponent in this field. He even attended one of our concerts in Birmingham to listen and observe the Maestro at work.

Roger happened to be a neighbour of Wilson's brother who, over lunch one day, asked me whether he would ever be invited to conduct the COE. Purely based on his reputation at the time, together with his lack of experience conducting international orchestras, I dismissed the idea.

It was in fact some time before he gained international recognition and it was not until March 1990, we felt the time was right to invite him. The first concerts took place in the Kammermusiksaal of the Berlin Philharmonie, with performances of Haydn's *Creation* and *Harmoniemusik*, followed by a Haydn Mass in London's Barbican Hall.

His approach to rehearsals was rather unconventional. Without his shoes he sat on an office swivel chair, with the musicians positioned all around him.

He also had a wry sense of humour and sometimes his use of English was somewhat lost on the continental members of the Orchestra; others did not appreciate it and were not amused!

Unfortunately, during the 1990s, Roger valiantly battled with a severe form of cancer, which necessitated surgery, followed by intense alternative treatment.

He travelled regularly to the US to see a specialist who prescribed a very strict diet which required the daily consumption of grated carrots and taking of many vitamin pills. The prognosis had not been good but miraculously over time, Roger managed to fight the illness and was finally given the all clear, although it resulted in the loss of hearing in one ear.

During all this time he continued to work. The COE invited him to conduct concerts in Germany and Flanders and at the time Roger, not knowing whether or not he would pull through, requested we should programme Mozart's *Requiem*.

The performance and circumstance, aroused much emotion but, unlike the composer, Roger did survive and went on to conduct the COE and other international orchestras for many years afterwards.

Charles was invited to a business conference in Casablanca and asked me to accompany him, promising that afterwards we would spend a long romantic weekend in Marrakech, where we stayed in a magnificent hotel. We engaged a personal guide to show us interesting sights of the city, including snake charmers and visits to the souk.

As we were being guided around an archaeological site, we noticed coming towards us from the opposite direction, Roger and his wife, Kay. They happened to be staying in the same hotel, where we also came across TV presenter Joan Bakewell who Roger knew.

We spent a most enjoyable weekend socialising with Kay and Roger, who was still on his course of treatment, daily popping pills and grating carrots. We flew back to Casablanca together to catch a flight to the UK surprisingly finding ourselves travelling on the same plane as the future King of Morocco, a regular visitor to Marrakech.

I became good friends with Roger and Kay and more successful concerts and recordings followed, which finally allayed any earlier scepticism.

*Enjoying lunch with Kay and Roger Norrington in Marrakesch*

# Michael Tilson-Thomas

The American conductor/pianist, a former protégé and admirer of Leonard Bernstein, succeeded Claudio as Principal Conductor of the London Symphony Orchestra before finally heading back to the US to become Music Director of the San Francisco Orchestra and Founder and Artistic Director of the New World Symphony, an American orchestral academy based in Miami Beach, Florida.

Taking advantage of his time in Europe I invited him to work with COE. The first occasion was for a short tour in Italy in 1987, which went well and led to further engagements.

In the summer of 1990 Michael was engaged to conduct two concerts during the Salzburg Festival.

The first took place in the Grosses Festspielhaus with soprano Maria Ewing singing Berlioz's *Les Nuits d'Ete.*

The second was in the Felsenreitschule, the riding school featured in the final scene with the Von Trapp family in the film *Sound of Music.* Two of the Orchestra's Principal Wind players were the soloists in performances of Richard Strauss' Oboe Concerto and Mozart's Concerto for Bassoon.

Performances of Kurt Weil's *Seven Deadly Sins* were given with Michael in the Berlin Philharmonie Kammermusiksaal in 1991 and repeated in Potsdam's Hans Otto Theatre. Just before the general rehearsal, he and I took a walk around the Theatre's gardens.

*Hans Otto Theatre*

Sharing a pre concert joke with Michael Tilson Thomas in the Hans Otto Theatre Garden Potsdam

Michael, showing off his black silk stockings, Potsdam

While we were chatting and sharing jokes, he surprised me by asking if, during the rehearsal, I would to go to a nearby haberdashery and purchase for him a pair of black silk stockings.

I thought this a strange request and it set my imagination wondering for what reason. Having purchased said stockings, I gave them to him, at the end of the rehearsal, where he unpacked and held them up in front of the Orchestra! I never did discover what he did with them afterwards.

We met again in San Francisco when COE was on a tour of USA West Coast. He paid the Orchestra a huge compliment by telling me that the time spent working with COE had inspired him to found the New World Symphony.

# Sir Andras Schiff

From the early days, Hungarian born Austro-British pianist, Andras Schiff, has played a very important role in the musical life of the COE. He emigrated from Hungary in 1979 and, after vowing never to return, took Austrian citizenship. He is known for his public criticism of political movements in Austria.

In 1985, He made his first appearance, with the COE, at the Lichfield Festival, in a series of concerts together with his violinist wife Yuko Shiokawa, oboist Heinz Holliger, and eminent piano and harpsichord player George Malcolm. The following year, he was invited, by Claudio Abbado, to be the soloist in a performance of Mozart's Piano Concerto, K271, in a BBC Promenade concert at the Royal Albert Hall. Later, he chose the COE as his preferred orchestra for concerts and recording for Decca of all seven JS Bach's keyboard concertos and Third and Fifth *Brandenburg* Concertos at Vienna's Konzerthaus.

Choosing programmes with him was always a difficult process. The Orchestra committee and I would make suggestions, which Andras, more often than not, rejected. Instead, he proposed alternatives usually comprising at least four lengthy items, including two major pieces for piano, and as a result programmes became very long and interval timings had to be carefully planned.

Over the years, many extensive European tours have been undertaken with him conducting orchestral works and directing concertos from the piano.

In 2004, a tour began with four days of rehearsals in Zurich, concerts in Lucerne and Baden-Baden, then a plane journey to Princeton New Jersey, in North America, for further rehearsals and a concert of works by Mendelssohn and Bach as a run-in before New York's Lincoln Centre and Carnegie Hall. The next stop was Chicago's Symphony Hall, and the tour finally ended in San Francisco's Davies Symphony Hall. Andras' performances of both Mendelssohn piano concertos will always remain in my memory as the finest I have ever heard.

The Wigmore Hall engaged him as Soloist and Director for a special Schubert Festival, lasting several weeks, with performances of all the composer's piano solo and chamber music, for which he invited individual members of COE to join him.

The German City of Bremen regularly invited the COE to give concerts, as part of their annual Festival and decided to honour Andras, also a frequent visitor, with a special commemorative dinner. He requested I should be invited as a guest and we spent a very enjoyable evening, together with his wife Yuko and the Festival's Director, Thomas Albert.

Andras was also very generous and invited the musicians to dinner on several occasions after a concert.

His close association with COE continued after my departure and I understand he has been added to the special list of Honorary Members of the Orchestra. In 2014, he was created a Knight of the British Empire, for his services to music.

# Sir Bernard Haitink

The Orchestra was invited to perform at the prestigious Lucerne Festival with Andras Schiff. He was a good friend of the conductor, Bernard Haitink, who had a house there, and invited him to the concert with his wife, Patsy (a former a fellow student of the COE's Principal Timpanist, Geoffrey Prentice), and a string player with the Royal Opera House, Covent Garden, where she had met Bernard, when he was Music Director.

Bernard had previously only worked once with the COE, a few years earlier, when he deputised for Maris Janssons, who had cancelled due to illness.

Although re-invited many times, nothing had materialised, mainly due to his busy schedule and the fact most COE projects involved touring and performing between four and six concerts in one week, each in a different city.

He was used to conducting international orchestras with a permanent base, a large government subsidy and regular seasons, giving the luxury of being able to afford to invite major conductors for only one or two concerts.

Patsy spotted me in the hall and beckoned me to sit with them. During the performance I kept glancing in Bernard's direction. He was obviously in another world, with eyes closed, his head moving in time with the music, and this inspired an interesting thought.

Several times the Lucerne Festival Intendant had urged me to try and persuade Nikolaus Harnoncourt to conduct a Beethoven Symphony Cycle with the COE, but he had always declined the invitation, because the dates coincided with the precious time he set aside for an annual walking holiday, in the Engerdine, with his wife Alice.

Seizing the moment, during the interval, I was encouraged to ask Bernard if he would be interested to conduct a Beethoven Cycle with COE, not mentioning, of course, that Nikolaus had been asked. He appeared to like the idea, he was not getting any younger and obviously did not enjoy travelling so much.

The fact that he owned a house in Lucerne and the whole project could take place, virtually, on his doorstep, also gave me confidence. I immediately went in search of the Festival Director, Michael Haefliger, to put the idea to him and his response was extremely positive. The two men met backstage after the concert and, encouraged by Andras, Patsy and me, Bernard agreed.

The Haitinks also had a house in West London, where I was invited for a meeting to discuss future plans. Bernard, casually dressed and wearing his slippers, warmly greeted me and seemed very happy and relaxed, as we sat chatting together in his comfortable drawing room.

The Beethoven Cycle, which was planned to take place after my departure, together with a full two-year diary and a surplus at the bank, became one of my legacies.

The success of the Beethoven project led to further symphonic cycles with Bernard in Lucerne, including those composed by Brahms, Schumann and Schubert, and repeated in the Concertgebouw in Amsterdam. There were also appearances at the BBC Promenade Concerts in the Royal Albert Hall.

He was made an Honorary Member of COE and I was very pleased the relationship with the Orchestra lasted until his 90th birthday in 2019.

# Martha Argerich

*'Likes to play the piano*
*but does not like being a pianist'*

During my long career, I had the privilege of working with many of the world's greatest musicians, but only a few have a special place in my heart and for whom I have the highest regard. Top of the list is Martha Argerich; wild, unpredictable! She and I were born the same year in the same month of June just three weeks, but worlds, apart.

Our first encounter was during the 1970s when the LSO were on tour in Spain, with their Guest Principal Conductor, Claudio Abbado. Martha had arrived early in the afternoon of the concert day to try out two of the theatre's pianos before deciding on which she would perform Tchaikovsky's First Concerto.

Unfortunately, neither pleased her and she insisted on another being found immediately. Urgent calls were made to a Steinway specialist dealer who fortunately had a good instrument in his showroom and promised to deliver it straight away with an expert to tune it.

Martha was still backstage working with the piano tuner when the Orchestra musicians began to arrive for the rehearsal which made everyone concerned it might not start on time. In those days she was fascinated by superstitions, the dark arts and occult which she would bring into conversation over supper.

It was some years after I had moved on from the LSO before we were to meet again. It was December 1987 in Vienna, when she played Beethoven's Second Piano Concerto, on that occasion with Claudio conducting the Chamber Orchestra of Europe.

In July 1989, she was invited by Nikolaus Harnoncourt to be the soloist in a performance of the same concerto during the Graz Festival in Austria. I found it fascinating to watch her working with Nikolaus, for the first time; the two personalities could not have been more different. His interpretation of how Beethoven should be performed must have seemed alien, but she appeared unperturbed, having already established a good rapport with musicians in the Orchestra. She was, again, soloist with COE and Claudio in December of the same year, for a performance of Ravel's Piano Concerto at London's Barbican Hall and caught up with them three days later in Berlin's Kammermusiksaal for yet another performance of Beethoven's Second Piano Concerto.

Martha and Nikolaus met again in April 1991. Beethoven's Ninth Symphony was scheduled at the Barbican Hall and she was to perform his First Piano Concerto. She travelled, on the Eurostar, from her home in Belgium to Waterloo station, where I met her, and we took a taxi, together, to the Savoy Hotel. On the way, she told me she had recently returned from Santa Monica, in the US, where she had been receiving specialist treatment for a malignant melanoma, which had taken hold on her leg, and had just received the news that she was in remission, otherwise she would have cancelled. A reception was held after the concert and Martha was relaxed, clearly in good spirits, no doubt due to the good news from the US.

In 1995, there was a recurrence of the cancer which had metastasised to her lungs and lymph nodes. Again, after treatment she went into remission and since then I understand has remained cancer free, although I believe she continued to smoke cigarettes.

The next occasion was in July 1992, in Graz, for two performances of Robert Schumann's Piano Concerto in A minor, Opus 54, when the conductor was once again Nikolaus Harnoncourt. Teldec were also very keen to take the opportunity to record the work with her.

She had a reputation for sometimes being difficult, even cancelling at short notice, so everyone was on tenterhooks, wondering whether or not she would turn up; I took the precaution of calling her, a few days before, just to check. She seemed surprised by my call, indignantly responding, 'I have been engaged, so of course I will come'.

Wolfgang Mohr, Artistic Manager at Teldec and I met her, at the airport, and we drove together, to her hotel. On the way, he tried his best to persuade her to give permission to record the performance 'live', with a possible re-take session the following day. Martha was not interested and refused, because she had previously recorded the work for another company. We suggested she should sleep on it.

Just before the following morning's rehearsal, Wolfgang tried coaxing her once more, and she finally agreed to the microphones being present during the general rehearsal and performance, on condition she would make the final decision as to whether or not the recording could be released. After taking time to listen to the tapes, she gave her approval and the concerto, coupled with Schumann's Violin Concerto with Gidon Kremer, was released. However, it was not the final version, as she recorded the concerto, yet again, with another conductor and orchestra and a different recording company.

Myung Whun Chung asked me to visit him in Rome, to discuss dates and programmes for a future tour. He was there to conduct the RAI, an Italian radio symphony orchestra, and Martha was the soloist.

During our meeting, Chung invited me to that evening's concert and, afterwards, to join him and Martha for supper at a local restaurant. It was good to see her again, after so long, and she was in very good form, eager to catch up with the latest gossip and exchange jokes, mostly about other artists. Unaware of the time, we stayed chatting until quite late.

A frequent and popular visitor to Japan, Martha appeared there with several orchestras, including the NHK Symphony Orchestra based in Tokyo, and had built a large following.

She joined the COE and conductor Emmanuel Krivine for a tour in November 1997, when she performed Beethoven's First Piano Concerto.

Conductor and soloist worked together with COE on two further occasions.

In March 1999, Martha performed Chopin's First Piano Concerto in London's Barbican Hall and was the soloist for a performance of the Schumann concerto which took place during another tour of Japan in October 2000. Her friend and neighbour, cellist Mischa Maisky, also played a concerto by Robert Schumann.

She was a very social animal and not being able to retire to bed after a concert, would often be seen enjoying the company of musicians, well into the early hours, with the result she found it difficult to wake early the following day and any rehearsals with her would necessarily have to be scheduled as late as possible.

That was the last occasion I saw her personally, although I have always remained one of her biggest fans and often listen to her fine recordings of my favourite piano concertos.

It is gratifying that she continues to give such pleasure both in concert and recordings after a career which has so far spanned more than 60 years.

# Don Alfonso Aijón

## 'Don Quixote'

I collaborated with many concert promoters, artists' agents and impresarios. I got along with very well with most, but there is someone who, for me, stands head and shoulders above the rest.

Fondly called Don Quixote by his friends, Alfonso Aijón was born in 1931, in Santander. He left Spain when Franco took over the country and went into self-imposed exile, wandering the world, experiencing a life from beach combing in South America to digging graves in Eastern Europe. With no possessions and very little money, he could not afford accommodation and would sometimes spend the night on a bench in the grounds of a five-star hotel, vowing at the time that one day he would have enough money to stay there.

He returned to Spain in 1966 and, in 1970, with financial help from his wife's family, launched 'Ibermusica' an artist's agency in Madrid.

He dedicated himself to discovering unknown artists, all of whom were destined to become internationally famous, Maria-Joao Pires, Andres Schiff, Krystian Zimmermann, Gidon Kremer and Yuri Bashmet. He met Claudio Abbado in 1956, when he was a pianist in his father's orchestra in Italy, and Zubin Mehta in 1964 in Romania.

All those artists were to remain loyal to him throughout their careers. He also became close friends with Ricardo Chailly, Daniel Barenboim and Simon Rattle.

Unfortunately, due to low audience attendances, the agency experienced its first bankruptcy after 10 years and his father-in-law again came to the rescue and kept the company afloat until Alfonso separated from his wife.

At this point, Alfonso decided not to continue, solely, to represent artists and turned, instead, to promoting orchestras since, in 1985 there was little symphonic music in Madrid, let alone the rest of Spain. Apparently, he was allergic to singers!

Alfonso's love for and dedication to music of the highest quality spurred him on and he was determined never to ask for any subsidy. His symphony orchestra cycles in Madrid became well known and most of the world-famous symphony orchestras took part.

Those occasions were extremely expensive and, even with sponsorship, would often lose money. Alfonso once confessed that he even had to mortgage his house to help pay the bills, but considered it important and worthwhile.

With eventual success, Alfonso kept the promise he had made to himself, many years before, that he would one day only stay in the best hotels and have a chauffeur to drive him. His only other pleasure, apart from music was, each summer at the end of a busy season, to walk in the Himalayas, climbing as high as 5,500 meters eating rice, lentils, local vegetables and maybe chicken, if it came from a village nearby. This, he said, would help to clear his thoughts and refresh his mind and body in preparation for the next season.

Wealth and possessions never interested him. When in 2015, with the global financial crisis and dwindling audiences for his symphonic cycles, and several patrons having died, he again experienced severe losses and many of his closest friends rallied round, some offering to perform without payment and even to put on special concerts to raise funds in their own countries. Daniel Barenboim urged him to retire and was quoted to have said,'Alfonso your mistake is to have made the exceptional normal'.

I first met him when he invited the London Symphony Orchestra to the Granada Festival and we stayed in touch for many years afterwards becoming good friends, particularly when, purely on my recommendation, he took a risk with the Chamber Orchestra by offering a tour of major Spanish concert halls, including an appearance in his own series in Madrid.

This dapper bearded man, small in stature, looking as though he might have stepped out of a Goya painting, strong-willed and focussed on his mission, was extremely generous to all his artists. He would make sure that everyone stayed in the very best hotels and tours would be organised in the most professional and efficient ways possible.

There would also be lunches and after concert dinners, arranged at his cost in the finest restaurants. It was on one of those occasions, when, after a late concert in Madrid, the restaurant was only serving oysters, something I had never before tasted, nor had ever wished to. Watching my fellow guests relish them with delight and feeling very hungry, I plucked up courage and decided to try one and was surprised to find it really was not so bad after all. However, years afterwards, I was served some at a friend's house in France, became violently ill and vowed never to eat oysters again!

Alfonso had three principles which he kept throughout his life. The most important, never to get angry at anything; eat little meat and more vegetables; walk as much as possible.

In 1983 he received an OBE for services to British Music, and in 2020 was made an Honorary Member of the London Symphony Orchestra.

At the time of writing, he was still going strong, having only recently handed over the reins of 'Ibermusica' to Llorenc Caballero, former Artistic Director of the Cadaques Orchestra in Bilbao.

# European Women of Achievement Awards

The annual awards were organised by the European Union of Women, (EWOA) a non-political organisation set up to highlight women with outstanding achievement in their chosen field, which had a significant European dimension. They were meant to provide an opportunity to recognise and applaud women who were helping to reshape Europe for the better.

In 2001, I was approached by Margaret Olwyn-Saunders an active member of the organisation, who suggested I should consider putting my name forward as a candidate. At first, I was reluctant, since I had always considered my role to be part of a team effort, enabling talented artists and musicians successfully to reach the pinnacle of their profession.

Margaret finally persuaded me and offered to act as my sponsor. She also urged me to practise her own mantra, 'if you do not blow your own trumpet, no-one else will'. I was invited to attend interviews with eminent members of the music and media professions and finally put on a short list of six in the category of Arts and Media.

IBM sponsored the event, which was attended by several European dignitaries, past recipients, International Press and TV. All the finalists were invited to attend a luncheon at the Grosvenor Hotel, in London. Charles came with me to give support, while my mother stayed at home awaiting news.

Prior to the lunch taking place, the contestants were assembled in another room and each presented with a certificate by the organisation's president Gillian Clarke, wife of the politician Kenneth Clarke.

Afterwards, we were taken to the upper landing and then, in the glare of a spotlight and cameras, descended one behind the other, down the long staircase into the hall and guided to our designated tables. At this stage, none of the candidates had any idea who had won, although the way Margaret was fussing around me, with a knowing look, made me suspect she already knew the results.

Possessing very little appetite, I nervously attempted to eat lunch and had to endure listening to several speeches before the actual award ceremony commenced.

The procedure went very much like the BAFTA and Academy awards, whereby profiles of the six finalists in each category were put up on a screen followed by an announcement of the winner. The competition was strong and I was certainly not confident, in fact surprised when my name was announced. Who would ever have thought it could happen to a working-class girl from London's East End! A spotlight was shone onto me as I made my way to the podium to receive a Winner's Award, which was a mounted engraved silver scroll. I must, however, be honest and admit I had earlier rehearsed in my head what I might say.

The rehearsing paid off, I did not feel nervous and gave a respectable acceptance speech, including a tribute to Joy Bryer, founder of ECYO, and a previous recipient of the award who was also a guest. I also made reference to the fact that many of COE musicians had graduated from the Youth Orchestra and one of the reasons why we had not approached the EU for funding, apart from wishing to be financially independent, was because we did not want to step on her toes.

Although honoured to receive such an award, it is no sign of modesty when I say I felt humbled, as I watched, in awe, as the recipients in other sectors, such as humanities, medicine, professional, entrepreneur and business, were called to the podium. In those categories, the competition had been particularly strong so the calibre of the women (and what they had achieved) extremely high.

Special Achievement Awards were also given, that year, to the yachtswoman Helen McArthur and to Annabel Croft, former Wimbledon Tennis player turned successful Businesswoman. A few years later, a recipient in my own category was the TV presenter, Angela Rippon.

All winners were invited to a dinner, with eminent politicians and other dignitaries, in the House of Lords Dining Room. I was seated next to Kenneth Clarke, whose wife, Gillian, had presented me with my certificate, and we chatted during the meal. He was very charming, our conversation covered several topics and continued after the meal, through clouds of smoke coming from a large cigar Ken was enjoying, with a glass of cognac.

A few months later, IBM organised a mentoring session at the Warwick Classic Car Centre for several of their brightest junior female managers. The EWOA award winners were invited to attend with their partners and each allocated a small group. Running an arts organisation is somewhat different from that of an IT company, but for a couple of hours we managed to find common ground and I was able to pass on useful advice based on my managerial and business experience.

It was a very enjoyable day, which concluded with a tour around the exhibition and an opportunity to test the new Jaguar Land Rovers, through difficult and muddy terrain, which, although scary, was great fun.

In subsequent years, I was invited, as a guest, to the annual awards which, in the meantime, had been extended beyond Europe to Asia and the Middle East, from where it was interesting to note how many women were beginning to be recognised in their respective chosen fields, sometimes having taken considerable personal risks.

*Receiving European Woman of Achievement Award certificate from Gillian Clarke London 2001*

*Receiving EWAA Winner's Trophy from Director of Granada Television*

# Winds of Change

From the late 90s, various changes to Concert Hall Management and a generally difficult financial climate, took their toll on the COE's activities. For the first 15 years we had run the COE on straight forward business lines and were able to break even. Only since 1998 had it become necessary to dip into our reserves in order to preserve financial stability. When schedules began to look less fruitful, Peter and I agreed certain projects should be subsidised by the COE e.g. recordings and private concerts for the Friends to raise funds.

Audiences were in decline, sponsorship became difficult and almost disappeared. New Intendants wishing to effect changes, in some instances, were faced with the additional problem of radio and other national orchestras folding, due to their reliance on public funding, which had been drastically cut.

As a consequence, our appearances in London became fewer. Following the fall of the Berlin Wall, and the subsequent Unification of Germany, our financial support from the Lottery/Senate was reduced significantly and we were no longer able to appear there as often, certainly not in residence. Established series in Frankfurt and Cologne were in jeopardy, through lack of funds and selective audiences. One constant in the schedule, surprisingly, was Ferrara, with whom we had an agreement until 1998/99. The annual Graz Festival continued for so long as Nikolaus Harnoncourt was at the helm.

Problems which the Recording Industry was experiencing began to filter through, with most companies drastically cutting back on production to concentrate on marketing product which had been stockpiled in warehouses, or to making money from sure successes such as the Three Tenors, Goreczki and Gregorian chants.

Commitments were reduced to exclusive artists, and showed little, if no, interest in recording those who were not on their books, such as orchestras, unless they had particularly strong ties with an 'in house' artist. They were also reluctant to pay fees up-front and preferred instead to negotiate royalty deals with potential income forecast years into the future. This was naturally not so attractive financially for the musicians but most of them accepted so the Orchestra could benefit from promotion and publicity.

The COE had no official base and received no public financial support, relying entirely on concert and recording income, sponsorship and private donations through its charitable status. New avenues were urgently sought to fill gaps in the diary and in some years financial sacrifices had to be made by the self-employed musicians.

We started to experience unrest, due mainly to the musicians feeling very insecure about their future. In my view, this had been exacerbated by both Peter and I declaring our intent not to be around beyond 2004/5 and the need to find a new way forward with a new Chairman, Board and General Manager. I believe the problem really began when Peter announced, that I was thinking of leaving, to do other things. From that day I was already gone, and the musicians took it upon themselves to set about finding my successor.

Peter had contemplated and discussed with me the possibility of disbanding the Orchestra. His favourite saying was 'it is like re-arranging the deckchairs on the Titanic'. He went so far as to invite his long-time banker friend and COE supporter, Michael Hoare to join the Board of Trustees to help achieve this. Martin Campbell-White had, in the meantime, been asked to resign due to a conflict of interests.

Thankfully, however, thing began to settle down and the situation gradually improved. From the beginning, Peter had interested David and Susie Sainsbury in supporting various projects and to giving generous donations from their private Foundation.

He also became an adviser to the David Sainsbury Trust and secured a sizeable underwriting to annually top up the reserve pot. We always maintained a healthy surplus each year and for some time had no need to call upon the full amount, only whenever it became necessary to support certain projects.

When our lease at Southampton Place expired, Peter and the COE Management were offered luxurious office accommodation and given technical and computer support in Sir David's own personal office building. I was given the office previously occupied by his wife.

# Moving On

After twenty years with the COE, I was ready for a new personal challenge, believing I had fulfilled my role and it was time for someone else to come with fresh ideas to take the Orchestra further. I seemed to be treading water, endeavouring to keep the Orchestra going, and trying hard to maintain the very high standards and level we had achieved together.

When five years later, I finally informed Peter of my intention to step down, he found it difficult to accept. He never liked change or the idea of working with anyone new.

I had already thought about who might replace me, and had in mind, my long serving right hand Simon Fletcher. At first Peter and the Orchestra Committee had reservations but after some gentle persuasion, they finally agreed to give him a chance.

Time has proven it to have been the right decision.

As I write, many years later, the COE is thriving under Simon's stewardship, in spite of the many difficulties and lack of income experienced during the Covid epidemic. A few founder members, some having reached the age of 60, continue to give their commitment and play in the Orchestra.

Unknown to Peter, I was twice head-hunted by an American agency, apparently recommended by my old sparring partner in Vienna, Alexander Pereira. The St. Paul Chamber Orchestra in Minneapolis was looking for a new General Manager which, although attractive, I did not pursue, because I considered there was little point in moving from the best Chamber Orchestra in the world to another.

The second opportunity, more prestigious, and potentially very lucrative, was to be in charge of the Los Angeles Philharmonic Orchestra (LA Phil) and management of the Hollywood Bowl. I was invited to attend several interviews, firstly with the recruiting company, who came to see me during a COE tour in Italy and, later, with the President and members of the Board of the LA Phil, in Paris.

The LA Phil were in the middle of a European Tour and the meeting was arranged at Brasserie Le Flo.

Charles came with me and we were both pleasantly surprised to find that the President also happened to be of Lebanese descent which helped, immediately, to warm the atmosphere. It was proposed I should also arrange to meet the Music Director, Elsa Pekka Salonen, in Salzburg.

After the meal, we moved to the Chatelet for the concert, which was conducted by Pierre Boulez. During the performance, I was struck by the advanced age of so many of the musicians. Observing them play made me realise just how much I missed the verve and enthusiasm of the young COE musicians.

The attraction of a very comfortable life in the US, with its financial perks, was not enough to persuade me to uproot us, even though, all along, Charles had encouraged me to do so. Later, thinking it through, I had to admit to myself that I was probably not the right person anyway and suggested it might be better for the LA Phil to engage an experienced American who would be familiar with the US scene, particularly when dealing with blue-rinse supporters and sponsors and, importantly, handling negotiations with the notorious US Musicians Union.

The LA Phil Board obviously came to the same conclusion and succeeded in enticing the very capable and experienced Deborah Borda away from the New York Philharmonic Orchestra. She and I happened to meet in Salzburg some years later, when we both were invited to attend a Salzburg Seminar for the CEOs of major international orchestras and institutions, which had been organised by Ernest Fleischmann.

## Salzburg Seminar

The alumni were allocated accommodation in the same building and there was a good deal of camaraderie, some having known one another a long time.

During the three day Seminar, each was invited to speak about his or her own experiences, which was then followed by general discussion. After an evening meal together, many of us made for the wine cellar in the main building, where over a drink or two the networking continued.

One evening, we were joined by the Russian conductor, Valery Gergiev, who had a free evening in between Festival performances. As Music Director of the Mariinsky Theatre and a close friend and supporter of President Putin, he had received international recognition and was in great demand to conduct the worlds leading orchestras.

I spotted him smoking a very large Cuban cigar, with a glass of Vodka in his hand, laughing and enjoying the company of the group of managers surrounding him, each hoping to lure him into a private conversation and persuade him to work his or her orchestra.

Eventually managing to get close, I took the opportunity to remind him that the previous year, due to ill health, he had had to cancel the two COE concerts he had agreed to conduct in Ferrara. I expressed how disappointed the musicians were, particularly as they had been looking forward to performing Tchaikovsky's *String Serenade* with him and how pleased they would be if he committed to conduct them on a future occasion.

He apologised, and said although he very much admired the Orchestra and would like to be able to work with them, unfortunately his diary for the next few years was already very full and he no longer had any free time.

Clive Gillinson, who I had known previously as a cellist with the London Symphony Orchestra, had since taken over the position of Managing Director, and was obviously more successful. Later that evening I saw him in deep conversation with the Maestro.

In 2004 Valery Gergiev conducted the LSO in performances of all seven symphonies by Sergei Profiev and the engagement led to his appointment in 2005 as the Orchestra's fifteenth principal conductor, succeeding Sir Colin Davis from January 2007.

# Last Season

Stephen Wright had resigned as Managing Director of the Artists Agency IMG, to become free-lance and concentrate on media projects.

One day, he called to let me know that he was in the process of putting together a commercial film of Mozart's opera *The Magic Flute*, which was to be produced by Kenneth Branagh in a new translation by Stephen Fry and conducted by American James Conlon.

The plan was to feature young, little known, talented singers in the principal roles. Liverpool Football Pools millionaire, Philip Moore, who was passionate about opera, had agreed to sponsor the project. Stephen was already familiar with and admired the COE and had the intention to recommend to Philip Moore it should be chosen to record the soundtrack.

He warned me, however, we would be in competition with other major chamber orchestras and probably more expensive.

As the recordings were to take place in London, the COE would have been classed as 'non-listed' and probably eligible to be paid at the higher 'general rate'. Therefore, prior to submitting a financial proposal, I took the precaution of consulting the Musicians' Union.

In the event, I was able to negotiate a very good deal and the recording took place at EMI's Abbey Road Studios. Realising they had entered the world of the Beatles pop group, the musicians took time out to take photographs on the famous zebra crossing.

Both Kenneth Branagh and Stephen Fry attended every session; the Beatles Producer, George Martin, made a surprise appearance and expressed his admiration for the quality of the music making. There was no doubting the high standard of the orchestral playing, but many, including myself, had reservations about the singers.

Stephen Fry's refreshing libretto had been brought up to date to compliment Kenneth's concept of the action, set in a modern war zone, with the *Queen of the Night* and other characters arriving on armoured tanks.

The sessions went well and the film was eventually shown at the Venice Film Festival, but sadly not well received by the critics. It never made the general circuit, as a consequence of which the very expensive project made a financial loss.

Originally the plan had been to issue the soundtrack on CD, but it was recognised the young inexperienced singers could not compete with the many successful professional versions already on the market, so was never realised.

Peter and I decided to invite Stephen Wright to lunch, in order to thank him.

During the meal, I happened to mention my decision to leave and Peter made it plain he was not at all happy and was nervous about the future. Seizing upon an opportunity, Stephen said he might possibly be interested in becoming involved artistically.

Although he did not say so, at the time, once back in the office Peter made it very clear he was in fact very strongly against the idea and had no wish to take it any further.

This opinion was later confirmed when a proposal arrived from Stephen with excessive financial demands for just two days a week, which, from my point of view, were grossly disproportionate to what I was receiving as a full-time General Manager, sometimes working seven days a week.

We both agreed it was unacceptable.

It took a great deal of effort, on my part, before Peter agreed to a further meeting, in order to put the matter to rest. However, a complete 'volte face' occurred when Stephen let slip he had been to Cambridge University and knew people in common with Peter.

I was speechless, completely ignored, and might just as well not have been in the room while the two men embarked upon an animated conversation, reminiscing about their university days. I was astonished at Peter's change of heart and from that moment on Stephen seemed to take control of the situation.

Adding insult to injury, to make his life even easier, Stephen recommended the additional support of artists' agency Harrison Parrott, to assist with finding new projects and to be paid a commission.

His plan was for them both to work alongside the new General Manager.

Visions of a fast-vanishing, hard-earned, healthy bank balance flashed before my eyes.

Again gender discrimination was in play and the old boy network prevailed. For 25 years I had never made excessive demands, always keeping in mind the Orchestra's financial situation and, importantly, deliberately keeping them in proportion to the fees of the musicians.

As I was self-employed, it was also necessary for me personally to provide for my retirement, thereby saving the COE money.

Furthermore, I would be handing over to Stephen a well-oiled, established and financially sound machine with prestigious projects already in place for the following two years, giving him a firm basis from which to operate.

To his credit, he did in fact acknowledge these facts and expressed admiration for what I had achieved.

# Farewell

On the occasion of the Orchestra's tenth anniversary, in April 1991, Peter and I were each presented with a tree. In my case it was a seven year old pear, which Enno Senft very kindly delivered to my home and we had an emotional planting ceremony in the garden.

Three years later I moved house, which meant that the tree also had to be up-rooted, so another planting ceremony took place in the new garden. Each year, I watched the tree grow – I even talked to it!

Even though sometimes cheated by the birds and squirrels, the amount of blossom and subsequent fruits became an indicator of the state of the Orchestra's health.

Unfortunately, when Charles and I moved to France, we were unable to take the tree with us, but, judging from the Orchestra's success, I like to believe it has survived and continues to blossom.

The Orchestra's annual visits to the Styriarte Festival in Graz always coincided with my birthday and, finally, I chose my 65th to take my leave.

The musicians arranged a surprise party for me in the Hotel Weitzer, the evening before and, between them, had raised sufficient money to buy a beautiful pearl necklace and earrings as a parting gift.

The hotel, where we stayed regularly, produced a huge birthday cake to celebrate both my birthday and the COE's 25th anniversary, and a small group of musicians from the Orchestra serenaded us in the background. Colleagues from London also travelled to Graz for the occasion. It was an extremely emotional moment for me, and I was very glad to have Charles there for support.

The following day was my actual birthday and, in the evening, there was to be a special anniversary concert conducted by Douglas Boyd. Unfortunately, that morning I woke up with a sore throat, could hardly speak and, by the time of the concert, had completely lost my voice.

The soloists taking part were from the Orchestra, with a beautiful rendition of Ralph Vaughn Williams' *Lark Ascending* played by Marieke which, just as on so many occasions, moved me to tears. The situation was made even worse when, at the end of the concert, the Festival Intendant, Mathis Huber, gave a very moving speech highlighting the long and successful relationship with COE and mentioned it was also my birthday and retirement. He made a gesture for me to stand to acknowledge the ovation from the audience and presented me with a large bouquet.

After the concert a civic reception for COE was held in the adjacent hall, at which Peter made a speech and presented me with an inscribed silver dish on behalf of COE, similar to the one presented to Claudio.

*My 65th birthday Serenade Graz 2006*

*COE 25th Anniversary and my 65th Birthday cake Weitzer Hotel Graz 2006*

Victoria gave me a porcelain pill box, on which was painted the COE's red bird with the dates of my 25 years' service.

The Festival Chorus performed a surprise farewell song, in my honour, to which, unfortunately, I could only nod and smile in acknowledgement and appreciation, due to my having lost my voice, which did not return for a couple of days.

Following my departure, with a higher expenditure budget in prospect, it became obvious additional funding needed to be found. During my time as General Manager, Peter and I had agreed it was important to stay independent and in control of our own affairs so, deliberately, we had avoided making a formal approach to the EU, despite getting pressure from some of the European members of the Orchestra to investigate the possibility.

However, it was later to receive the support of my successor, Simon Fletcher. To his credit, after a great deal of paperwork and number crunching, he managed to obtain a substantial annual grant from the EU. Ironically, the success of his application had been assisted by having an 'insider' contact at the Commission who also happened to be an associate of Stephen Wright!

Hungarian conductor, Ivan Fischer, who worked with COE on a number of occasions, was very interested to learn how it was structured and managed. He later paid the Orchestra a huge compliment by forming his own Hungarian Festival Orchestra along similar lines.

When, in 2007, the Orchestra was appointed as a Cultural Ambassador for the EU, he was invited to conduct a concert performance to celebrate the 50th anniversary of the signing of the Treaty of Rome.

# Peter and Victoria

It is fair to say, without the involvement of Peter Readman, encouraged by his wife, Victoria, the Chamber Orchestra of Europe would probably never have got off the ground.

Peter was a successful businessman, an amateur horn player and a member of a choir which, every Christmas time, sang carols to the Queen but had no previous experience of orchestra management.

Victoria spoke fluent Italian, played piano, had been a junior ice skating champion, a model for a cosmetic company, ran an art gallery and, after raising a family, became a justice of the peace.

When I first joined the Orchestra, I had found it a struggle to establish myself as the General Manager but, over time, managed to develop a good working relationship with Peter.

However, he never seemed to accept that a woman was generally in charge. When introducing his friends and business associates, he rarely used my title, often referring to me as, 'someone in the office', or 'the person who runs the Orchestra.' On the other hand, in those occasions when I knew conductors, artists and promoters who had no idea who Peter was, I would be sure to make them aware of his importance as Chairman.

Nevertheless, with Peter's enthusiasm and business acumen, combined with my own experience and professionalism, we somehow complimented one another. He had useful contacts who gave generous donations and, briefed by me, was able to make impressive presentations to potential sponsors.

We often travelled together to meetings, with very successful results but Peter, annoyingly, often left everything until the last minute and sometimes arrived late. There was an occasion, when the flight had already closed, and was about to depart just as he turned up at the airport, but somehow managed to persuade the official to let him board the aircraft.

Many hours were spent discussing all aspects of the Orchestra's life and future plans, often continuing after everyone else had left the office. He sought my advice on a number of issues and, on the whole, listened and respected my point of view, but there were times, perhaps having sought someone else's opinion, when he seemed to change like the wind.

He often played the politician by sitting on the fence.

Not once, during the 25 years I was with COE, did Peter enquire after my health, family or general situation, but would talk a great deal about his own. He related stories about when he served as an officer in the Duke of Kent's regiment and, one time, was attached to the SAS and confronted by terrorists in the Middle East. For that reason he always placed his desk facing the door!

For anyone to take time off for feeling unwell, which, thankfully, rarely happened to me, would be an inconvenience. Victoria, on the other hand, was intuitive and empathetic, always ready to help and give advice particularly to musicians with young families.

Peter, obviously, felt more comfortable having women around him. At home, he was one male amongst four females. Christabel, their first child, was born on January 22, 1984, which coincided with a COE concert scheduled, that evening, at London's Queen Elizabeth Hall with pianist Maurizio Pollini as the soloist.

Victoria was already in hospital in the final stages of labour, which left Peter in a quandary as to whether to attend the concert or be at his wife's side!

It took a while for him to decide but, nobly, he did his duty and missed the concert.

He often boasted, afterwards, that, if he had not been there, to assist at the birth, his daughter might never have survived, at which Victoria always smiled wryly and raised a knowing eyebrow!

They had two other daughters, Emma and Katie but, sadly, lost a fourth child, Poppy, to cot death syndrome. Their tragic loss and grief were especially felt by everyone, when they bravely attended a COE concert in St. John's Square, shortly afterwards.

Every year, Charles and I received a Christmas card containing a recent photograph of the whole family and, over the years, were able to follow the development of the girls, as they grew to become beautiful and intelligent like their mother, each with a successful career, and a credit to both parents.

The Readmans were very generous. Every Christmas time, members of Peter's own staff at Abercromby and those of the COE administration, together with partners, were invited, either to their Kensington home or to a restaurant, for a sumptuous meal. Everyone used to joke that he was like the Lord of the Manor, inviting his serfs to celebrate a good harvest!

Appreciating how much Nikolaus Harnoncourt hated strange hotels, whenever he was working with the Orchestra in London, he was invited, together with his wife Alice, to stay in their home.

Peter organised his busy schedule to coincide with the Orchestra's and often attended concerts on tour, with Victoria. They both enjoyed chatting to the musicians, backstage, afterwards and, if no reception had been organised by a promoter, would invite artists and myself to supper.

He always thought of the COE as his other family and the musicians viewed him as their benefactor. Although, personally, he did not contribute financially, he encouraged others to do so. Instead, he gave his time and commitment and made sure the Orchestra's administrative staff had comfortable office accommodation, usually in the same building as his own. In that way, he could keep in close daily contact with everything that was going on.

Peter endeavoured to make himself available to chair Orchestra Meetings and announce any end of year bonus or increase in fees to the musicians. We used to call him *Father Christmas*.

In 2006, when I received a European Woman of Achievement Award, I was saddened and disappointed there was no acknowledgment, let alone congratulations, from either Peter or Victoria. Conversely, I received many compliments and good wishes from my colleagues around the world. For my part, I had been more than happy to add my signature to the letter recommending he should be considered for an honour!

Charles and I were invited to a special Friends concert which was organised after I had left the Orchestra.

At the end, Peter made his customary speech. Amongst his friends and associates, he and Victoria had always been given full credit for the Orchestra's existence and kudos for its success and, therefore, were more than likely anticipating Peter's usual mention of his wife's support and contribution.

However, on this occasions they were probably surprised, no more than I, by his finally acknowledging, in public, the important role I had played for 25 years and his reliance upon my guidance and experience.

Afterwards, several of his friends and business associates eagerly shook my hand and offered congratulations, some even professed they had, of course, always known!

I also received the following email from Joe Lesser, Peter's long time business associate in New York.

'*I understand you are taking a well-deserved rest from the orchestra. You have done a wonderful job in building the orchestra to a point where it is considered one of the top musical groups in the world. While Peter takes the credit, we all know that you are the motivating force. They and I will miss you.*

*However, this will give you an opportunity to visit New York and America without having to drag the orchestra and Peter with you. When you arrive we can personally show our gratitude for a job well done. Please visit soon.*'

For six months I continued my association with COE as a paid consultant, assisting Simon and Peter. With the arrival of Stephen Wright, I ceased my involvement, still feeling sore about the terms of his appointment, which I expressed in a letter to Peter.

We rarely met after that and, usually, only at a COE concert. Although always courteous, he appeared uncomfortable and not eager to enter into any meaningful conversation. Victoria, on the other hand, was always her usual polite and gracious self, entering into small talk about life in general.

I am very proud of all our achievements, made possible, I believe, only through the unwavering commitment and combined effort of every member of the Management team and Orchestra.

Artists' Agent, Jasper Parrott, someone with whom I had battled on numerous occasions when I managed the LSO, once suggested, patronisingly, to me that the COE could never succeed.

He had, in fact, once made an unsuccessful bid to take over the Management of the New Philharmonia Orchestra, which was turned down on the grounds of a conflict of interest.

Many years later when we met again at a concert in which one of his artists, pianist Helene Grimaud, was taking part as soloist, he was to eat his words and confess he had, after all, been wrong! Although, what he had been right about, was the wonders of the fax machine, to which he had introduced me!

*The COE Management Team in the Southampton Place offices Holborn London*

Salzburg Seminar Alumni August 2002 with Deborah Borda next to me fifth from the right

Signed photo presented to me by the COE musicians on my retirement 2006

# 10  Life after COE

## Brittany

We bought our first French house in 1989, as a second home. It was a rundown farmhouse, with outbuildings, in a tiny rural hamlet in the Morbihan region of Brittany. Left vacant for a number of years, it was desperately in need of love and attention and became a wonderful escape from our busy lives and somewhere to invite our friends.

After eleven years, we decided to sell and look for another property, further south. Mistakenly believing it would take some time, we decided to take up an offer to stay with Charles's nephew who lived in Biarritz, to begin our search. However, while en route, we received a call from the estate agent to inform us that someone was very interested in buying our house and suggested we should return immediately.

One balmy evening, we were sitting outside, enjoying a glass of wine and listening to Rachmaninov's Second Symphony playing in the background, feeling sad we no longer owned a French property.

The next day we poured through the properties for sale pages, in a Bretagne paper, and came across a house approximately a hundred kilometres further west, close to the town of Gourin. We immediately rang the owner and arranged an appointment to see it.

Our first viewing took place during late spring, when everything was in full bloom. Although the house appeared rather small and in need of a great deal of improvement, what finally tempted us to buy was the magnificent garden of just under two acres, which surrounded the property. It had been the previous owner's pride and joy and he had planted several species of conifer, oak and chestnut trees, as well as an assortment of magnolias, camellias and rhododendrons. Not being experienced gardeners, it was going to be a challenge for us and a daunting task just to keep it all in good shape, let alone to get the moles under control. Thankfully, my mother came to our rescue and offered to buy a ride-on mower for my birthday.

As seems to have become a habit, we had chosen to live in the middle of nowhere, this time on an even higher hill. However, we considered ourselves very lucky to have such a beautiful a panoramic view across the lush surrounding countryside.

We spent seven years converting and extending the house and garden and, in 2007, the year after my retirement from the COE, decided to sell our UK property and move permanently to France.

Gourin, like so many other small French rural towns, has a large church in the middle of its square and a chateau on the outskirts. Once a thriving community, a difficult financial climate had forced many shops and businesses to close and with the consequential lack of employment, many of the inhabitants, particularly those amongst the younger generation, had moved to larger cities to find work.

However, a few restaurants did remain open, one of which was the local pizzeria. We got to know the owner very well and, one evening, she introduced us to Silvano, a successful Swiss banker from Berne. Passionate about horses, he had chosen to take early retirement and, together with his partner, purchase a vacant small holding in the area, which had sufficient land to create stables and a dressage training ring.

We were invited to pay a visit and, when we arrived, found Silvano training one of the two magnificent white Arabian stallions he had brought with him from Switzerland.

When the session ended, he beckoned us to follow him to the stables where, on each of the doors, the name of the horse was engraved on a brass plaque. Then we proceeded to an adjacent area dedicated to grooming the horses. No expense had been spared. In addition to large showers, romantic multi-coloured halogen lamps, similar to a disco and an elaborately constructed overhead solarium had been installed.

While the horse was being showered, rubbed down and dried under the solarium, a recording of an opera was played over a loudspeaker. According to Silvano, the horses loved the music and it helped them to relax.

The house, itself, was full of antique furniture, lamps, paintings and objets d'art. Over afternoon tea, I was keen to learn more about Silvano's musical tastes. From the vast collection of recordings, it became evident that opera was his first love and discovering my own involvement in classical music, he explained that he came from a musical family. His deceased father had been a Conductor with a Swiss orchestra and his mother had played First Violin. We were later encouraged to meet his mother, when she came to visit and spent a most pleasant and interesting afternoon with her.

The Château of the Traon Joliff, or Tronjoly as it is known today, was built in the eighteenth century. The building's elegance is enhanced by the beautiful park which surrounds it. Tronjoly Park is also the starting point for hiking trails that lead to the Black Mountains.

In 1984, after the death of the last owner, the estate was purchased by the Gourin Municipality and given a new lease of life.

A green outside theatre was created for large outside gatherings such as the Crêpe Festival or the traditional music and dance championship. The interior of the Chateau was converted to provide a museum and gallery for various arts and crafts exhibitions, during the summer. It was somewhere we often loved to visit, if only to stroll around the grounds or occasionally attend a chamber concert in the Chateau, usually performed by a group of visiting musicians.

Our closest friends and neighbours were Jean-Pierre and Karen, who had met through an online dating agency and relocated to Brittany from Burgundy.

Originally a professional photographer and former member of the Paparazzi, Jean-Pierre had turned his interest and expertise to taking photographs of Breton wildlife.

He would often spend many hours at the coast, capturing on film the interesting activity taking place during the changing tides and light. Several of his dramatic photographs were exhibited and successfully sold at the Chateau.

His partner, Karen, with whom I attended a weekly Yoga class, was an artist with a vivid, sometimes scary, imagination. She painted with oils and was invited to exhibit some of her more disturbing works at the Chateau.

Living in rural France gave few opportunities to listen to good quality classical music. Apart from the occasional chamber concert performed in the local chateau or church, we would travel to Paris, Bordeaux or Toulouse to hear professional musicians in a good concert venue. The COE sometimes performed in those cities and we organised trips to coincide with their concerts and to meet up with old friends.

The Bretons have their own music, played on traditional instruments, usually the French bagpipe called a *Cornemuse*, a conical double-reed instrument (a cross between an oboe and trumpet) called a *Bombade* and a Breton clarinet called a *Treujeun-gaol* (Breton cabbage-stalk). As with the rest of France the accordion and French harp are also very popular.

We attended street parades and annual Celtic village festivals, when the Bagad bands played, much to the delight of locals and tourists. We joined in the fun with our Breton friends, holding hands and dancing around in a circle. The Bretons love to gather around the performers and their instruments, singing and dancing into the night, often while enjoying a cool local cider.

Jazz was also very popular and we were spoiled for choice as to the number of opportunities to attend concerts and the many festivals, both locally and in other French towns.

There was one particular traditional group made up of French and English musicians, called *Good Time Jazz*, who used to play regularly in a bar at Chateauneuf du Faou, in Finistere just over the border from where we lived.

Several of the players were professional and others just very good and they blended well together. Their leader, clarinettist Trevor Stent, originally a schoolteacher from Liverpool and well known there as a member of a traditional jazz band, lived locally, and each year organised a summer festival on the banks of the River Aulne, to which he invited well-known soloists and groups from other countries to take part. Some were given accommodation in a nearby hotel and others in the homes of local residents.

We got to know the band musicians very well and, one year, offered to sponsor the Festival, through a donation from a French company, which developed an environmentally efficient waste management process, with which Charles had become involved.

Often good summer weather permitted audiences to sit on the riverbanks and listen to the music. Unfortunately, that particular year, typically for Brittany, the weather was not favourable. Indoor facilities, in addition to large marquees, had to be provided into which the audiences were squeezed, some dressed in anoraks, their wet umbrellas dripping pools of water onto the floor.

However, with a good supply of hamburgers, hot dogs and French fries, together with local cider to keep stomachs satisfied, with the rain forgotten, everyone seemed captivated by the syncopated rhythms and quality of the music. Several couples even found a vacant spot to try out their jive routines.

Although we thoroughly enjoyed our life in Brittany, it remained our ambition to move south. We put the house on the market but unfortunately, it took two years before someone fell in love with it, possibly because it was in a rural area of Brittany. In the meantime, we had changed our minds and decided to return to the UK!

# Foray into Pantomime

We purchased a large modern five bedroom house in Leighton, a pretty village outside Welshpool in mid-Wales, a few minutes away from Powys castle, which had an active and lively community.

Traditionally every year, a neighbouring village, Forden, put on a pantomime. However, the Leighton committee considered it was time to mount one of its own which would be performed in the newly renovated village hall. *Cinderella* was chosen and the villagers were encouraged to take part in the production, to stage-manage, paint scenery, or generally help out.

Allan Smith, a former school headmaster and successful author, agreed to produce and I was asked to put together the musical content. This was a new challenge for me since I would be working with a completely new genre. For advice, I turned to my COE Tour Manager, Christopher Smith-Gillard who, in his spare time, for many years had written and directed pantomimes.

An initial approach was made to a local pianist, who played the organ in church, and she agreed to play for the rehearsals and subsequent performances.

However, when I gave her the selected piano music she decided to withdraw because she found it too challenging and felt out of her depth. Changing tack, I resorted to downloading material from the internet and using extracts from some COE recordings.

Since we were to perform before a family audience and children from the local school were to take part, popular material in the form of backing tracks, to which the performers could sing and dance, were included. Teaching some of what I thought were well-known songs to the principals, proved an uphill struggle, but we got there in the end.

I also invited Cinderella and Prince Charming to my home for coaching sessions, and choreographed a dance for them, which they practised, to a waltz by Shostakovich, in my large kitchen.

Very kindly, Chris put together and recorded the overture, and was invited as a special guest to the opening night. All the recorded material was put into a special file on my old laptop which, for rehearsals and performances, was linked to the hi-fi sound system belonging to one of the residents. Sitting at a desk in the hall and following the script, it was my responsibility to press the right button at the appropriate time in between action and dialogue.

Amazingly the whole exercise, which for me had been nerve-racking, turned out to be a great success, with full houses for three performances. From comments made afterwards, I gained the impression everyone had a good time and particularly loved the music.

The collaboration blossomed into a close friendship with Allan and his partner, Geoff. For him it had not been an easy task getting headstrong amateurs into shape. He said it had been far easier working with a group of school children and vowed never again!

Although he received repeated requests to be involved again the following year, he kept to his word. I also made up my mind only ever to work with Allan, which let me off the hook.

# France Beckons Once Again

For three years, we stayed in Leighton, but France beckoned once more. We sold the house, put everything into store and spent six months in a friend's gite in the Dordogne, while we searched for a new house. We viewed several properties, but nothing appealed, which led us into thinking we had perhaps made another mistake and decided again to return to the UK, this time to Shropshire, where we purchased a beautiful Grade 2 Listed Barn just outside the village of Cockshutt, close to Ellesmere.

We made many friends and there was a very active community but, after only nine months, we found ourselves missing France once more. The barn sold very quickly, to a cash buyer, so we needed to find an alternative, quickly.

We decided to search for a property in the Lot et Garonne region. After visiting several houses, none of which we liked, time was running out and we needed to get back to the UK to finalise our sale. There was one more house to see, the day before we were to leave.

Possibly because we were feeling desperate, we thought it was the right one. Originally a group of farm buildings, it had been renovated by its German and Polish owners, who were eager to move. It was in a pretty location, set in two hectares of garden, with a large lily pond, orchard and forest.

Without taking time to research the whole area, being anxious not to let an opportunity slip by, we rang the owner to ask if we could view the property again. In the same afternoon, we decided to buy it, agreed a price and became the potential owners of our third French property.

A few months later, with the barn sold, we moved back to France.

Many mistakes were made.

We had not thought it necessary to hire a surveyor as it had seemed perfect, nor had we thoroughly investigated the town of Fumel, which was located not far from a cement factory which had recently closed down and left many residents unemployed. It began to dawn on us that something was very wrong. We discovered serious defects in the house, which the previous owner had failed to point out, and became convinced it had bad vibes.

We did, however, meet some interesting people, artists and musicians. In fact, I became re-acquainted with Warwick Hill, an ex-violinist, who I had not seen for many years. I knew him from the time he was a Principal player with the London Symphony Orchestra. He lived with his wife not far from us and Charles and I were invited to his home for a delicious supper and we spent the whole evening reminiscing about old times.

However, we no longer felt comfortable and decided to sell the house, as quickly as possible, and take time before deciding our next move . We reduced the price, considerably, and included absolutely everything, even my Roland digital baby grand piano. Fortunately, we quickly found a cash buyer who was also happy to purchase the house and its entire contents, with the exception of my piano, which I managed to sell privately.

We left at the beginning of November, ending the final chapter of our chequered twenty-six year love affair with France.

Brittany will forever hold a special place in our hearts. We miss its wild and beautiful rugged coast, jutting out into the Atlantic Ocean, its verdant countryside, even the rain. Most of all, there were the happy moments shared with friends, at home, in a local restaurant eating freshly caught seafood and drinking cider, while listening to traditional songs with everyone joining in the chorus, or regularly attending Traditional Jazz sessions, tapping our feet in time to the music.

# COE at 35

In May 2016, Charles and I were guests at a private concert in St. John's Smith Square, to celebrate the Orchestra's 35th anniversary and were invited to join the COE staff at the Gayfare Street office for a pre-concert glass of champagne.

We took with us some Lebanese delicacies, which were quickly devoured and enjoyed by everyone. It felt very strange to see my old office again, after such a long period, now occupied by so many new members of staff.

My successor, Simon Fletcher, had increased the number and assembled a very glamorous bevy of managers, all of whom were obviously used to an active office social life. That evening, the Orchestra proved its continuing excellence and world-class status with a lively virtuosic performance of Mozart's Overture to *The Marriage of Figaro* and Symphony No. 29 without conductor. The two Leaders of the Orchestra, Marieke Blankestijn and Lorenza Borani gave an accomplished and brilliant performance of JS Bach's Concerto for Two Violins.

During the concert, I found myself thinking about the very first concert given at Merchant Taylors Hall, in May 1981 when Claudio Abbado was handed the baton by James Judd. On this occasion, it was Vladimir Yurowski, with whom the COE had recently struck up a warm relationship. He had been persuaded to attend as a guest, and had left opera rehearsals at Glyndebourne to be present. Producing just a pencil instead of a baton, he surprised and delighted the audience by conducting Rossini's Overture to *La Cenerentola* as an encore but, no matter how well played, I could not help but make comparisons. For me the familiar sparkle was not present.

As was customary at the end of every Friends concert, Peter made a speech recounting the Orchestra's history and latest successes, and thanking artists and sponsors. What shook us both, was his stated pride in the Orchestra's association with the European Union, having previously been opposed. Perhaps it was hardly surprising, as there was a member of the EU Parliament in the audience and Peter was acting the politician, leaning towards whichever way the wind was blowing, something he was always good at!

Admittedly, Peter and I had taken a trip to Brussels to meet with the EU Commission to investigate how COE might act as an ambassador. Containing the word Europe in its title, we suggested, would help to promote what was the relatively new European project, by displaying banners and handing out publicity at each venue in the various countries where the Orchestra were to perform. The idea appeared to be well received and, just before we left the Commission office, we were each handed a mounted key fob containing a newly minted Euro.

Mike Hoare, a close friend of Peter's and a current Trustee of COE commented to me, before the concert, how surprised he was that COE still existed, since he had been invited to come on board specifically to help wind it up! However, Peter's very strong emotional attachment to the original founding members had encouraged him to continue, possibly against his better judgement.

History has shown that, under Simon Fletcher's management and his ability to negotiate a good deal with the EU, the COE has remained one of the world's leading Chamber Orchestras, with a busy schedule. Unfortunately, funds from the EU eventually dried up. In order to keep the Orchestra financially sound, it again became necessary for Peter to seek private patronage.

After the concert, we were invited to supper in the crypt. Several musicians, many of whom had played in the Orchestra for many years, were friendly and welcoming. Former professional colleagues also greeted me, warmly; but I sensed a distancing from Peter and Victoria. Our parting in 2006 had not been on the friendliest of terms and the frosty atmosphere reflected this.

Clearly now considered to be part of the COE's past, we were seated at the extremity of a long VIP table, next to Jonathan Davies and his wife Veronica, who had also fallen out of favour with Peter, and others who had contributed to or assisted COE, through its 35 years' existence. Peter, Victoria, Simon and his wife, Lisa, sat on another table together with a frail looking Bernard Haitink, his wife Patsy and other important guests.

# Return to Cyprus

In September 2012, Charles and I decided to take a holiday in Cyprus, which had in the meantime joined the European Union, the currency changed to the Euro and inflation had soared. There was also evidence of the country having suffered severely from the 2008 financial crises. The economy was in bad shape, with many building sites left unfinished and abandoned.

We learned from Cypriot friends of how many had lost a great deal of money and the country was continuing to experience austerity. Compared to the UK, eating out was relatively cheap, as was shopping in supermarkets.

After retiring from the Orchestra, in 2006, and moving house several times between the UK and France, a decision had to be made as to where we might spend our twilight years. We had fallen in love with Cyprus and it was as close as we could come to Lebanon, without actually living there.

We returned, in 2015, to search for a property to rent for the next year or two, before deciding whether or not to stay permanently and purchase a new home. This decision was probably the wisest we may have ever made.

There are many similarities between Cyprus and Lebanon, the climate, terrain, mountains, sea, even the food, although, in my opinion, Lebanese cuisine, which includes the use of a variety of herbs and spices, has a great deal more to offer. They provide the taste explosion that makes the food so popular internationally

In 2018, we moved   permanently to Cyprus, but decided not to buy, opting instead to rent a beautiful villa, with a large pool, next to a seventeen century Venetian bridge and just twenty minutes from the sea. We are fortunate to be surrounded by mountains, vineyards, olive, almond and orange groves and fresh orange juice is on the daily breakfast menu. We co-exist with snakes, lizards and a variety of different species of birds, many of which are migratory, and have been adopted by a stray kitten which just happened to appear one day.

Although a little remote, it is very peaceful, except during the hunting season, when, despite numerous signs indicating a conservation area and that hunting is prohibited, certain periods and days of the year are allowed during which macho men, dressed in their fatigues, arrive in the area, armed with shotguns and occasionally accompanied by hunting-dogs. They appear to shoot at anything which moves and the loud bangs resonate around the mountains, no doubt scaring any wildlife which might still exist. Walks on those days need to be taken with caution! Although things are slowly changing, Cyprus continues to be a predominantly patriarchal society.

At the easternmost part of Europe, Cyprus is the third largest island in the Mediterranean with 10,000 years of history and civilisation. It constitutes a bridge between people of different religions, cultures and ways of life. The whole island is a virtual open-air museum with many sites listed as *UNESCO World Heritage.*

Living in the Paphos region gives us many opportunities to experience and enjoy its many wonders but, unfortunately, unless prepared to travel abroad, we miss and no longer have the luxury of being able to attend live performances of classical music and opera at the highest level.

However, there does exist a thriving musical community, supported by both Cypriots and the large number of resident ex-pats. Two of Cyprus' most important archaeological sites, which are located in the Paphos region, host annual Festivals.

*The International Pharos Chamber Music Festival,* acknowledged as Cyprus' most important annual classical music event, has a reputation for the quality of its concerts, as well as its enchanting atmosphere and setting.

Late May, early June Concerts take place in the Gothic Hall of The Royal Manor House at Kouklia, one of the finest surviving monuments

*Pharos Festival Chamber Music Concert in the Manor House Kouklia Paphos*

of Frankish architecture situated at the site of *Palaipafos* (Old Pafos in Greek), the original capital of Cyprus. Many well-known international chamber musicians are invited to take part and I was surprised and pleased to be re-acquainted with Diemut Poppen, a former Principal Viola of the Chamber Orchestra of Europe and friend of Claudio Abbado.

*Paphos Castle*, originally built as a Byzantine fort to protect the harbour, was rebuilt by the Lusignans in the 13th Century after being destroyed in the earthquake of 1222; was dismantled by Venetians in 1570 and later restored and strengthened by Ottomans to serve as a fortress. It was even used as a warehouse for salt during the British occupation of the Island.

More recently, it served as a backdrop to the annual Paphos cultural festival, which takes place at the beginning of September. Grand operas are staged by visiting international companies which are accompanied by the Cyprus Symphony Orchestra. The well-attended Festival is supported by the ex-pat community and attracts many overseas visitors. The Cypriot members of the audience appear to be not so interested in the music but more to be seen wearing the latest fashions, and to wander about taking photographs, perhaps using the occasion to meet up and chat with friends and then, unaware of the time, noisily search in the dark for their seats after the Performance has already begun. Some may be seen leaving before the end!

In 2017, Paphos was nominated 'European Cultural City' and a great effort went into improving the infrastructure, roads and buildings. There were ambitious plans for cultural events, although some believe not enough thought and expertise went into planning how the whole of Cyprus might benefit and capitalise in the future. Charles and I were thrilled to be able to attend a rare open-air concert with the Berlin Philharmonic Orchestra, on the first day of May as part of the celebrations. The conductor was Maris Janssons and the programme included Dvorak's Symphony No.8. The musicians and instruments had literally flown in the evening before and were to return to Berlin that afternoon.

The concert took place at midday, when it was very hot, with little or no shade from the sun for the audience, but the musicians at least performed on a specially constructed covered podium. We got some relief from the plastic fans provided by the organisers, but a few members of the audience, annoyingly, used them too vigorously. During the interval, I was very pleased to have an opportunity to meet up with the Principal Bassoonist and a member of the double bass section, both of whom played, from time to time, as deputies with the Chamber Orchestra of Europe.

Several open-air events took place in the ancient Odeon, most commencing late in the evening, when the air was a little cooler. The perfect acoustic of the amphitheatre made amplification unnecessary. Vladimir Ashkenazy and his pianist son gave a recital there in June. Unfortunately, a press photographer got too close to the performers, which annoyed Vladimir. He stopped playing the piano and angrily ordered the offender to leave. I took the opportunity to meet up with Vovo and his wife, after the concert, and we chatted about the occasions he performed with both the London Symphony Orchestra and the Chamber Orchestra of Europe. On another evening, we attended a beautiful performance given there by the Moscow Theatre Ballet.

*The Cyprus Symphony Orchestra* is the only professional symphony orchestra in Cyprus. There are a few international principals, the concertmaster is Austrian, but many of the musicians are Cypriot. The Orchestra gives approximately 80 to 90 concerts each season, performing 30 programmes in Nicosia, Limassol, Paphos and Larnaca. It has a strong commitment to local communities with outreach programmes, family and educational concerts, encouraging Cypriot composers to create works which will be performed by the Orchestra.

We first heard the Orchestra perform in 2017, in a theatre in Limassol. At the time the new theatre in Paphos was still under construction and a bus had been organised to take a group of Paphos music lovers. The Orchestra musicians were about to say farewell to their Music Director and to appoint Jens Georg Bachmann, from August that year.

*Sanctuary of Aphrodite Kouklia Paphos*

Although calling itself a Symphony Orchestra, in fact the number of string players was less than the Chamber Orchestra of Europe and the result was a thinner sound which was also not assisted by the very dry acoustic. I found the whole performance disappointing, but perhaps, I was making unfair comparisons.

When, months later, we attended concerts in the new Markideion Hall in Paphos, it was evident that a vast improvement had taken place under the leadership of Jens Georg. The young German clearly had the respect of his musicians and was a good communicator with audiences. He chose varied and appealing programmes and introduced to the public some lesser-known works, including compositions specially written for the Orchestra by Cypriot composers.

In 2020, for the 250th anniversary of Ludwig van Beethoven's birth, Jens Georg had scheduled programmes to include all his Symphonies and Piano Concertos, to be performed by the famous Cypriot pianist, Cyprien Katsaris.

We had been so looking forward to hearing them and to comparing the symphonic cycle with the COE's own award winning version recorded with Nikolaus Harnoncourt but, unfortunately, due to the Covid-19 pandemic, most of the project necessarily had to be cancelled or put on hold. In the meantime, I was sorry to learn, no doubt for political reasons, the musicians of the Orchestra had voted not to renew Jens Georg's contract.

*Technopolis 20* is possibly the most diverse arts and cultural centre in Paphos, covering anything from book presentations, musical events, films, lectures and discussion on a variety of subjects, to art exhibitions, all in a beautiful neo-classical space. The large private manor house, built in 1920, has been sympathetically adapted and kept many of its original features and is perfectly located in the city centre. The two young couples who run it are very helpful and knowledgeable about the arts scene in general. During the winter all events are held inside the house, while summer jazz performances which take place in the beautiful garden, are a special treat. Charles and I regularly attend events, mainly jazz, blues and chamber concerts, in which visiting artists from all over Cyprus and abroad take part, and we have enjoyed many summer evenings in the garden.

*Paphos Music Lovers* (PML) was set up by musician and entertainer Andrew Oliver, who has lived on the island for many years. Together with an army of volunteers, he promoted and presented classical, jazz and world music concerts in the Paphos area.

Little known international and Cypriot artists and groups were encouraged to participate and unusual venues chosen, which included municipal halls, hotels, restaurants and tavernas.

I met Andrew just after we had moved to Cyprus, when he organised a bus to Limassol for members of the PML to attend a Cyprus Symphony Orchestra concert. He already knew who I was, because he had been introduced to the Chamber Orchestra of Europe by Christopher Smith -Gillard, the COE Tour Manager, and attended a few concerts. They had both been students at Colchester Music College and remained friends ever since. Andrew tried to persuade me to join the Committee, but I opted, instead, to become a member of the PML, offering advice and suggestions, if asked, and giving support, by attending as many concerts as possible, However, I did introduce him to a major potential sponsor who agreed to give a substantial financial contribution on an annual basis.

Having since resigned as the President of PML, Andrew has turned his attention to promoting concerts in tavernas and restaurants which are situated in mountain villages.

High up on the other side of the valley where we live, are the *Yurts of Cyprus*, to which people may escape for a short break and experience living simply in a beautiful natural setting. Pavel, the owner, has built a small stone amphitheatre and at the beginning and end of summer, organises outside concerts, usually jazz, reggae or rock, and invites well-known groups to take part. Audiences are invited either to stay in one of the three Yurts, bring their own tents in which to camp, or even stay overnight in their cars in an adjacent field. We have no need to attend, as the music reverberates around the valley and we are able to listen while enjoying a glass of wine on our balcony and if the music is not to our taste, arrange to go out for the evening. We have joined Paphos Third Age, and are enjoying life on this beautiful and historic island. Unfortunately, apart from a few phrases, the Greek language has so far defeated us!

# 11 Unfulfilled Ambition

I have no regrets for the professional path I took but in the background there has always been lurking a musical ambition, never satisfied.

In my teens, while still at school, I took a Saturday job and, with my small wage, used to stop at a record shop on the way home to buy the latest recording by artists such as Rosemary Clooney, Doris Day, Peggy Lee, Nat King Cole and others, later moving into the realms of middle of the road and jazz singers like Frank Sinatra, Tony Bennett, Ella Fitzgerald, Sarah Vaughan, Julie London and Dinah Shore, who I attempted to copy.

Listening to recordings with big bands and jazz quartets, playing standards to which I could sing along, expanded my repertoire. I would play the records over and over again, and practise alone for hours.

After I left school and started work as a secretary, apart from buying new clothes, any spare cash would be spent on recordings from 45 EPS to larger LPs.

It was not until I met David that I was at last encouraged to sing again in public. We often went with friends to a jazz club, where the resident quartet, who were very good, were regularly joined by visiting professional singers. One day we were introduced to the owner, who was, himself, a very good jazz pianist, and David happened to mention how much I loved to sing.

Before I knew it I was being given an opportunity, the following Sunday.

I chose a song which I knew well and believed would suit my voice but, unfortunately, once on stage, and unaccustomed to performing before a knowledgeable and attentive audience, nerves suddenly took hold and I forgot the words.

Out of the corner of my eye I spotted raised eyebrows from the musicians who were accompanying me, which made me even more nervous. My legs began to feel weak, tears came into my eyes and my cheeks began to burn. Somehow, I managed to get to the end of the song but knew I had not made a good impression. Embarrassed, I left the stage and sheepishly walked back to our table. Sympathetic comments made afterwards fell onto deaf ears and I was eager to leave.

With hindsight, I had to accept the song I had chosen was a mistake. It was a hard lesson to learn and I really wished I could have been given a second chance.

Another possible missed opportunity might have been having the courage to ask Andre Previn to hear me sing when we had some free time during a tour in the US with the LSO. I had in my collection his recordings with Doris Day and Dinah Shore and knew the repertoire by heart. I would also have loved to perform with a big swing orchestra.

Even though friends have since encouraged me, with the exception of COE parties, I have refused to sing again in public, although secretly longed to do so.

Sadly, now that I am very much older, I can only dream of what might have been! These days my singing is confined to the house and the car, the only audience, my long-suffering husband.

# 12  Epilogue

Kate died in 2004, just a few weeks before her 86th birthday. The funeral service was held in the Chapel of the City of London Cemetery, attended by friends and relatives, some of whom had not been seen for several years, including David, my ex-husband who had been invited since he had been very fond of my mother.

As the coffin began to descend slowly out of sight, the small chapel was suddenly filled with the angelic sound of Kiri te Kanawa's beautiful voice singing Pie Jesu from Faure's *Requiem*, reducing everyone to tears, reminiscent of my wedding in 1967, particularly for those in the congregation who had been there. The recording of Mozart's Piano Concerto K467, performed by Maria Joao Pires with Claudio Abbado and the Chamber Orchestra of Europe, had been one of Kate's favourites, and it therefore seemed appropriate to play the second movement at the end of the service.

The body was cremated along with the large file of blue airmail letters which George had sent during the War and it was difficult deciding what to do with the ashes. It had been almost 50 years since George had died and we were told the local Council had the right to redevelop any plots which had not been looked after. Believing there to be little possibility of his grave existing, my husband Charles and I decided instead to search for that of my grandmother, who had died some years later. It proved to be an impossible task, the City of London Cemetery was vast, and we had no map. Holding an umbrella and tightly clutching the urn containing Kate's ashes, we walked up and down in the rain, for what seemed like hours, passing row upon row of graves, unable to locate it.

Determined not to give up, we decided to take a chance and headed in the direction of the railway line where, much to our surprise, we discovered several very old graves still there. Many headstones had sunken into the ground, others were either broken, had disappeared altogether, or were so weather-beaten it was impossible to read the inscriptions. Carefully treading amongst them I came across one which had a faded photograph. Peering more closely I realised it was that of the young child I had seen at my father's interment and there next to it, just visible above the overgrown weeds and grass, was the headstone of the grave I thought I would never find. Excitedly, I called to Charles to join me. Using our hands and a small trowel, together we cleared the area around the headstone, revealing a small spindly rose bush which had somehow survived over the years and I recalled the day my mother had planted it. We then exposed the metal vase which thankfully was still intact, and used its detachable base to collect water from a nearby tap to wash the headstone. Before replacing it we dug a hole and, saying a little prayer, poured in Kate's ashes. Our mission successfully accomplished, we tearfully said our good-byes, content in the knowledge that George and Kate had at last been reunited.

Circumstances never gave Kate an opportunity to fulfil her own potential, so I was happy to have been able to invite her many times to join me on my own musical journey.

One occasion remains vividly in my memory. She came to a Chamber Orchestra of Europe concert, which was conducted by Claudio Abbado at London's Barbican concert Hall. The programme began with a Rossini overture which she instantly recognised and loudly expressed her delight, oblivious of the annoyed glances from members of the audience seated nearby. After the concert, one of the Orchestra sponsors organised a reception backstage and I left my mother in the company of Christopher Smith-Gillard while I went to congratulate the artists in their dressing rooms. When I went in search of her, I found my mother seated on a chair, holding court with several young musicians and obviously enjoying being the centre of attraction.

As I get older and look into the mirror, I see her face; my hands are her hands; I am my mother's daughter! Music was in her blood and I feel fortunate it was passed on to me.

# Acknowledgements

To my husband Charles, all my love and thanks for his encouragement and support and with whom I have shared many adventures in Lebanon, France and Cyprus; not forgetting my first husband David Hall, without whose initiative I would not have embarked on a 42-year career in classical music.

I was privileged to meet many celebrities, conductors, singers, instrumental soloists, impresarios and politicians, some of whom are featured in this book. It has taken over sixteen years to complete and I have endeavoured to stay as true as possible to actual events. Fortunately, I was able to refer to my copies of The Chamber Orchestra of Europe work schedules, covering the formative 25 years I was General Manager, but forced to rely on memory and research for events with took place during earlier years with the London Opera Centre, The Royal Opera House Covent Garden, the London Symphony Orchestra and others. First efforts were hand-written on foolscap paper and put into a drawer, until several years later when by chance I was persuaded to join the Paphos Writers' Group in Cyprus.

I should particularly like to thank three members of the Group, John Goodwin, Robert F. Barker and Richard Powell, each an experienced published author, without whose advice and encouragement I might never have completed my story. Thanks also to Kay Barrett for meticulously labouring through the early text and for the confidence shown by my editor and publisher, Gaile Griffin Peers of U P Publications.

# Index

NB: Most people are listed by their first name

# Index

**Timeline Events**

Printed in the USA
CPSIA information can be obtained
at www.ICGtesting.com
LVHW050103250124
769813LV00079B/2421

9 781912 777785